Harvard Judaic Monographs, 1

David Kimhi
The Man and the Commentaries

Frank Ephraim Talmage

Harvard University Press
Cambridge, Massachusetts, and London, England
1975

In Memory of My Father

Preface

In presenting this book to the public, a word must be said about the nature of the material studied. R. W. Chambers, reflecting in his *Thomas More* on the comparison between Thomas More and Socrates, noted: "But one vital difference there is, which makes the compiling of a life of More the less impossible task. More, unlike Socrates, was a writer, and though some important things have been lost, there still remains to us a great mass of his works. An elaborate life of More could be put together, even though we had nothing to guide us save the words he has written." But this is not all, Chambers continued, for "so much remains that a life of More could be written, if we had no writings of his own, but merely the recollections of his friends." With respect to David Kimhi we are certainly deprived of the latter type of information, material reported by friends and family. For while two or three of kith and kin can be identified, they have left us no eyes (except for the episode of 1232) through which to see Kimhi. Nor are we much richer in the former class of materials—writings of the subject himself. For while Kimhi has richly endowed us with a literary legacy, there is just so much of a man's personality that may be reconstructed from his grammatical treatises. As for the biblical commentaries, we must remember that there Kimhi did not believe himself to be speaking but rather that, through him, the Bible spoke with ever greater clarity. We therefore do not have (again with the exception of the letters of 1232) anything that stands even remote comparison with the epigrams of More, the *Confessions* of Augustine, the letters of Abelard and Heloise. Perhaps it was more than ignorance that led the scholars of the Renaissance to speak of "Rabbi Kimchi Michlol" or "Rabbi Kimchi Compendium"—confounding the author with the opus. Yet Kimhi was not a book. He probably would not have understood the Grammarian of Browning who "decided not to Live but Know." And it is through the pages of the commentaries and excursuses of the Kimhi who Knew that the Kimhi who Lived may be seen to reveal himself. The medieval exegete was not a mere antiquarian approaching his text with a cool and dry detachment: though Scripture spoke of the past, it was viewed with the eyes of the present. The exegete could not help but impose—even if he resisted—his own world of ideas upon that of the sacred text. To be sure, great caution must be exercised in the use of these materials lest one be found guilty of esogesis of Kimhi's exegesis, of discovering that which was not there to begin with. However, I am well aware that owing to the scarcity of parchment in the Middle Ages, scribes could ill afford to leave very much room between the lines. I have therefore tried not to read there.

I wish to express my gratitude to two persons in particular: Professor H. H. Ben-Sasson, who prodded me over countless cups of Canadian coffee, English tea, and Israeli orangeade as this study was taking form, and Professor Isadore Twersky, who, as ever, helped bring order into chaos and gave much of his time and patience to see this work through publication.

Special thanks are due Harvard's Department of Near Eastern Languages and Civilizations and the National Foundation for Jewish Culture, which provided a subvention for publication of this work

Gratitude is expressed to the Canada Council, which generously supported research conducted in Europe and Jerusalem, and to the following for permission to cite or refer to passages of manuscripts in their possession: the curators of the Bodelian Library, Oxford; the British Library Board; Biblioteca Angelica, Rome; Biblioteca de San Lorenzo, El Escorial; Staats-und Universitätsbibliothek, Hamburg; Municipal Library, Narbonne; Biblioteca Palatina, Parma; Biblioteca Universitaria, Valladolid; Biblioteca Apostolica Vaticana.

Toronto, Canada   Frank Talmage
December 1974
Hanukkah 5735

Contents

David Kimhi
The Man and the Commentaries

I   Narbona: Villa Juzayga

Rabins David et Moise Kimchi . . .
se distinguerent dans les êcholes
juifves de Narbonne, alors les plus
fameuses du Monde.[1]

Narbonne

The invasion of Muslim Spain by the African Almohades in
1148 brought a temporary end to the toleration of the Jews in
Andalusia.[2] Yet through their expulsion, a signal service was rendered to Jewry abroad. The latter were to gain some of their most
distinguished leaders and leaders-to-be. Maimon ben Joseph, who
had been a judge in Cordoba, and his young son Moses made for
Africa. Judah Ibn Tibbon, a physician of Granada, departed for
Lunel with his son Samuel. There they became the deans of trans-
lators from Arabic to Hebrew. The Toledan philologist and scien-
tist Abraham Ibn Ezra never settled in one spot but traveled
constantly throughout Europe.[3] Joseph and Moses Kimhi, the
father and elder brother of David, ended their flight at Narbonne.
We would not be far amiss in assuming that this place of asylum
was chosen with considerable forethought.

By mid-twelfth century, the Jewish community of Narbonne
had attained eminence[4] after many centuries of associations,
both real and imagined, between Narbonne and Israel. According
to local tradition, ancient Narbonne had commercial contacts
with David, king of Israel. From these contacts, there "could come
the great power which the Jews had in Narbonne by virtue of the
great wealth they possessed."[5] Another Jewish monarch, Queen
Esther of Persia, was said to have been guarded by four officers
from Languedoc: Biztha from Beziers, Abagtha from Agde, Carkas
from Carcassonne, and Harbona from Narbona. But "of these
Gaulish knights favored by King Ahasuerus, we may conjecture
that the one from Narbonne was the first and dearest . . . for it
was Harbona whom the King ordered to *hang Haman.*"[6] Gradually the legends become somewhat less fabulous. Telescoping
and expanding certain historical events, both Latin and Hebrew
chronicles dilate on the alliance of the Jewish community of
Narbonne with "Charlemagne."[7] In return for their support
against the Saracens, the Jews were to have petitioned "Charle-

magne" for the right to live in Narbonne under a king from the
House of David. This was granted: One third of the city was to
be given to the count, one third to the archbishop, and one third
to the Jews under a Davidic ruler. Here legend and reality begin
to converge. In the eleventh and twelfth centuries, Narbonnese
Jewry enjoyed such distinguished political and spiritual leadership
under their Patriarchs (nesi'im) and rabbinic scholars that they
could invite contemporary comparison with the classic Jewish
community of Babylonia under the Exilarchs and Geonim.[8] Passing through Narbonne at about the time of David Kimhi's birth,[9]
the world traveler Benjamin of Tudela speaks of

> Narbonne, an ancient center of Torah, from which learning
> spread to all countries. There are great sages in it and at their
> head is Rabbi Kalonymus, son of the great R. Todros, entitled
> Nasi by virtue of his Davidic descent. He has estates and lands
> [granted him] by the governor of the city of which no one
> can forcibly deprive him. At the leadership [of the communi-
> ty] is R. Abraham, head of the Yeshivah, R. Machir, and
> R. Judah, along with many learned scholars. At the present
> time, there are three hundred Jews there.[10]

In the eighteenth century, the Minim chronicler Louis Picquet
could still boast of "Rabin Theodore" and "Rabin Kalonymus"
and of the biblical codices said to have been commissioned by
them.[11]

Of the Narbonne of the Kalonymides and the Kimhis little
remains above ground. If the eye is allowed to scrape the surface
of a few architectural palimpsests, some twelfth-century landmarks
emerge: the archbishop's palace; the Cathedral of St. Just; the
proto-Basilica of St. Paul Serge; the ancient Roman bridge, which
originally traversed the Aude, before it changed its course, and
now divides the unpretentious Robine canal below from the
stream of shoppers above. The portal of an old synagogue was
still visible in 1774.[12] Now no remembrance of Narbona Judaica
meets the eye.

The alleged tripartite division of the city was stillborn: Pepin
the Younger had apportioned it equally between the count and
the archbishop.[13] Originally, the principal Jewish quarter was the
villa juzayga (Latin d and c having given way to Provençal z and g)
in the suburbium east of the city flanked by the roads to Gruissan

and Ricardelle.[14] Eventually, in accord with the divided juris-
diction of the city, two Jewries were established: The viscomital
Jewry stood within the confines of the Cité while the archiepisco-
pal Jewry was situated in the suburb of Belvezé on the left bank
of the Aude.[15]

By the standards of the twelfth century, Narbonne would have
been considered quite metropolitan. Too much so perhaps for
David Kimhi, who shared the distaste for urban living expressed
by his contemporary Richard of Devizes.[16] "Rural areas," Kimhi
felt, "are more salubrious than walled cities . . . since [they are]
airier."[17] In that age, however, as now, ecology did not deter-
mine one's world.

The world of the Kimhis was one of books and scribes. When
Kimhi *père* wished to establish the unity of the Creator, he drew
on a parable of Bahya based on a scribe and his manuscript:

> Do you not see that it is apparent from all of creation that
> there is only one Governor, be He exalted and extolled! I
> shall explain this with a parable: When we see a book in a
> uniform hand, we say that one scribe wrote it. Even though
> it is possible that more than one scribe wrote it, we need not
> believe this unless there are witnesses to the effect that two
> or more scribes, whose hands are uniform, wrote it.[18]

In essaying to demonstrate the validity of inductive reasoning,
Joseph's theme is once again writing and the writer.[19] Where
Provençal Jewry generally expresses a preference for the live
teacher over the written word,[20] Joseph places text and teacher
on a par.[21] David takes up the theme in earnest. Scribal realia
appear in his commentaries.[22] His quest for books will lead him on
long journeys; concern for the craft of the copyist will cause him
to compose the *Scribe's Pen.*[23] He pays the writing of books the
highest tribute a Jew could pay any enterprise and declares it
equal to the performance of all the commandments together:

> There are two kinds of [religious] acts which profit a man
> in this world and the next. One is the fulfilment of the com-
> mandments and moral duties . . . The other is the writing
> down of the sciences and the explanation of the Torah and
> commandments, inscribing them in a book so that they may
> long endure. If the early sages had not written their words

in a book, all sciences would have been lost and the Torah and commandments would have been abolished.[24]

Books provide a kind of immortality: "In seventy years there is no time for one to learn all the sciences unless he finds the fundamentals written by his predecessors from generation to generation."[25] "The sages and scholars of Torah who write down their words and explanations leave a blessing behind them . . . They surely have not died."[26]

An overcrowded city had its compensations: it was a center of Torah. In general, Provençal Jewry had been "immersed head and shoulders in traditional learning—Biblical exegesis, midrash, Talmudic study, pietistic thought, liturgical poetry—and devoted themselves . . . to its development."[27] Narbonne itself, as Benjamin of Tudela records, was the home of the distinguished Abraham ben Isaac (d. 1178), author of the halakhic code, the 'Eshkol.[28] Narbonne might soon cede its preeminence in halakhah to Lunel.[29] Yet it still remained an important center of talmudic studies throughout the Kimhis' lifetime.[30] In any event, to a biblical scholar like R. Joseph, Narbonne would certainly appear congenial: "The achievements of the sages of Provence in midrash and exegesis were considerable. They created new midrashim and edited the old. They were the true bearers of the tradition of the [ancient] scholars of the midrash which they cultivated and nurtured. For generations midrashic literature in Europe drew from the wells of Provençal midrash."[31]

Since the time of Moses the Preacher (early eleventh century), Narbonne had been the center of midrash and exegesis in Provence. R. Moses left an exegetical work, the Yesod, which was well known to Rashi and the northern French exegetes.[32] Among his many midrashic compilations, that on Genesis was to become the subject of much controversy in debates between Jews and Christians.[33] R. Moses specialized in midrash, as his title, darshan or preacher, implies. But homiletics was not Narbonne's only approach to Scripture. Exegesis through le'azim or Provençal word translations was common. Many of these translations found their way to eleventh- and twelfth-century northern French exegetes such as Rashi[34] and Samuel ben Meir.[35] Other Zarefati[36] commentators, Menahem bar Helbo and Joseph Kara, are said to have been natives of Narbonne.[37]

Joseph and Moses Kimhi

The marketplace of Narbonne would be ripe for Joseph Kimhi's wares. He would have no need to travel farther. Once there, R. Joseph seems to have acclimatized quickly. Accustomed to a predominantly Muslim Arabophone culture, he nevertheless debated Christians with zest and in their own tongue.[38] Settled in Languedoc, he could be the model of many a Provençal Jewish intellectual: a polyhistor but not a dilettante; an expert in one science or two but at home in many. One envisions Joseph Kimhi as traveling light: his grammars in one hand, the rule of reason in the other. As household baggage, he imported from Spain the dual curriculum—the Torah and science—to a land where "they did not occupy themselves with other sciences because their Torah was their [sole] profession and because books about other sciences were not available in their regions."[39] Kimhi would set about filling the gaps. He would write Hebrew grammars to acquaint the Hebrew reading Provençal with Spanish philology.[40] Saturated with contemporary neo-platonism, he would further popularize the popular. He undertook to translate Bahya Ibn Paquda's *Duties of the Heart* and Solomon Ibn Gabirol's *Choice of Pearls,* although these translations were to be eclipsed by those of Judah Ibn Tibbon.[41] Above all he would explicate Scripture—new commentaries on Job, Proverbs, the Prophets, the Torah.[42] Narbonne, the home of Moses the *Darshan,* would now confront a new master. Midrash was put aside for the moment; the grammar lesson came first.

Although some in the twelfth century did not look kindly upon an overconcentration on philology,[43] R. Joseph felt secure in his calling. If philology is not the capstone of knowledge, it is certainly the threshold. Least prestigious, it is also least dispensable.[44] If in the eyes of some he is one-sided, he knew that

> one may have achieved a knowledge of astronomy or medicine, and so forth, being profound in one and not in others. Thus the expert in medicine can do in one moment what a hundred stargazers cannot do because of their ignorance of drugs. Similarly, one expert in astronomy can draw a conclusion concerning the constellations which a hundred physicians could not do because of their ignorance and incompetence with respect to the constellations. It has been said that

the science of medicine is not complete and perfect without
a knowledge of and acquaintance with the constellations [for
the effect of the drugs is related to the particular astronom-
ical configuration] . . . It is so with the various crafts. What
a smith can achieve [by virtue of his expertise in his craft] in
an instant, one hundred carpenters could not achieve. Similarly, in each craft, one is an expert in his own and ignorant of
the others unless he has learned it.[45]

Each craft, each science, however humble, needs its specialists.
And Joseph Kimhi's specialization was to be philology. Yet if
some were to say that R. Joseph traveled too long on one road,
his road too led to heaven. Without grammatical knowledge,
perfection in study and prayer was inconceivable.[46]

Throughout his writings, grammatical and exegetical, the note
of *ratio* reverberates like a *basso continuo*. Although not always
stated explicitly, it is unmistakably there. Reason guides him in
all directions. It is the sword with which he vanquishes the Christians. It is the proofstone of his own faith. For him, for any religious man, science and metaphysics are *sine quibus non*. God does
not lend Himself to direct observation: one cannot undertake a
journey to verify His existence as one can journey to Constantinople.[47]

The root of the knowledge of the Creator is not vision, for
[none] . . . are able to witness the Creator. We acknowledge
His unity and know His existence through His works . . . from
a world built without deficiency and founded with wisdom
and knowledge that one Creator created it; that God brought
it into existence by His grace.[48]

Words not from a book of philosophy but from a book of philology! Before R. Joseph lectures the *darshanim* of Narbonne on
syntax, he remembers to invoke *ratio*. *That* is the key with which
to open the Scriptures. *Wisdom and instruction* (Proverbs 1:2):
one without the other is like "a tent without cords."[49]

The history of Jewish biblical exegesis in Provence and Catalonia
is yet to be written.[50] Perhaps it is not premature to say that when
it is, the rivers and their tributaries will be found to flow back to
one source: Joseph Kimhi. He it was who pointed the way for his
pupil Menahem ben Simeon in Posquières. Menahem referred to
"my master, my teacher,"[51] as did David Kimhi to "my master,

my father." Menahem carried his master's teachings further than
did the master himself. For him, the science of grammar revealed
all that one could know or needed to know about the text.[52]

Moses Kimhi was Joseph's student *par excellence*. In his turn,
Moses would set the course for his brother David. David quotes
his father often—second only to the Targum, the Aramaic translation of the Bible. As we shall see, for David these were the only
two really worth quoting. Yet if all we had of Joseph's biblical
exegesis were what his son cites in his name, we should not have
a fair impression. In these citations, R. Joseph tends at times to a
cleverness bordering on the precious. With exegetical legerdemain,
he solves the problem of Jephthah's oath by reinterpreting one
particle. Joseph renders: *"Then whatever comes forth from the
doors of my house to meet me . . . shall be the Lord's or* (!) *I will
offer it up for a burnt offering* (Judges 11:31). *He shall be the
Lord's* if not suitable for a sacrifice or *I will offer it up for a burnt
offering* if it is suitable for a sacrifice."[53] This was the sort of
thing that the son was fond of citing. Perhaps he, sober David,
found this side of his father so fascinating precisely because it was
so rare in him.[54] Yet in fact, a perusal of the Job or Proverbs
commentaries reveals a highly rational and lucid exegete, producing
much that is similar to the work of David, with perhaps greater
verbal economy.

Joseph Kimhi died when David was barely ten years old. In later
life, David observed that "the nature of the mother is impressed
on the child more than that of the father. The Kings of Israel are
called by their mothers' names to indicate that the conduct of the
son is generally like that of his mother," insofar as it is not shaped
by one's individual nature.[55] However his "conduct" may have
been like his mother's, in terms of his destiny, methods, hopes,
and ideals, David was to follow the dictum of the rabbis: "Let no
one abandon his profession or that of his father."[56]

If Joseph was gone, David would be provided with a surrogate.
"My master, my father," would be replaced by "my brother, my
teacher."[57] Of Moses we know even less than we do of Joseph
or David.[58] The latter cites him less frequently than does their
contemporary, Menahem ben Simeon.[59] In general Moses is a
shadowy figure in Jewish tradition. Although appreciated by
Christian scholars of the Renaissance, his commentaries were

ascribed to another barely a hundred years after his death.[60] Yet the unusual honorific "my brother, my teacher," eloquently testifies to his importance for David. As with David of old, "the younger brother would listen to the elder."[61]

Moses would continue and reinforce the tradition set by Joseph: the study of grammar and exegesis. Of his grammars, one, *The Course of the Paths of Knowledge*,[62] was glossed by Elijah Levita and translated into Latin by Sebastian Münster. Under the title *Liber Viarum Linguae Sacrae*,[63] it was reprinted many times and became one of the most popular of the grammars used by the sixteenth-century Christian Hebraists. "Why that should be," exclaimed the Kimhis' biographer Abraham Geiger, "I do not know."[64] Perhaps Moses' insistence on keeping directly to the point in as few words as possible was not to the taste of the nineteenth century. Geiger did not think very much of Moses' commentaries either. Yet these were ascribed to Abraham Ibn Ezra for over five hundred years without suspicion. No mean compliment! Moses concentrated on the same books which had preoccupied his father: Proverbs[65] and Job.[66] Yet, like Menahem ben Simeon, Moses held predominantly to philological and syntactic analysis. Unlike Joseph, he was not inclined to embellish his explanations with a poetic quatrain[67] or a philosophic parable.[68] In his commentaries on Ezra and Nehemiah[69] we find an interest in the historical books, generally neglected by twelfth-century Jewish exegetes, which David was to share in his own complementary commentary on Chronicles. Here too, though, Moses' interests are almost exclusively grammatical. He made no attempt to fit these books into the larger problems of biblical historiography as did David.[70]

If Moses tried his hand at philosophical writing, we have no record of it. There is a reference to an ethical work, the *Joy of the Soul (Ta'anug ha-Nefesh)*,[71] but nothing more. Even in his commentaries on the wisdom books, he refrained from philosophizing and, in good Kimhian tradition, let the text speak for itself. It would stand to reason, though, that he shared his father's views on the natural kinship of philology and philosophy. *Sekhel (ratio)* and *da'at (sapientia)*, thematic catchwords of the rationalists, find their way into the titles of his grammars. As guide and pedagogue to his brother David, Moses would nurture the growth of a Spanish rationalist on the soil of Narbonne.

David Kimhi's Education

In the refurbished El Tránsito synagogue of Toledo, a marble
plaque boasts of the eminent Jewish residents of medieval Spain.
That country now claims David Kimhi as one of its own: Yet the
eighteenth-century chronicler Fr. Picquet would have considered
this "repatriation" overpresumptuous. Proclaiming the glories
of Narbonne, he vehemently denies David Kimhi's Spanish birth
and unequivocally declares him to be a native of Narbonne.[72]
Fr. Picquet was right. David was born in Narbonne in or about
1160.[73] Yet for the rest of his seventy-five odd years, he would
sign his name David ben Joseph Kimhi the Spaniard.

David Kimhi was a "Spaniard" not only in his adherence to
the Iberian intellectual traditions of his father and brother.

In the twelfth century, Narbonne was far less removed from the
Iberian Peninsula, both politically and culturally, than one might
imagine.[74] Provence, Languedoc, Rouissillon, and Catalonia
formed a continuum. Linguistically, Provençal, markedly different
from the *langue d'oïl,* fades subtly into Catalán before Castilian
asserts itself. Politically, parts of Provence would be shifted about
like men on a chessboard—but generally among counts of Barcelona or sovereigns of Aragon or local rulers who were themselves
counts of Barcelona or sovereigns of Aragon. So strong was this
unity that even today it reasserts itself in local nationalism and the
age-old yearning to abolish the Pyrenees. It was along this corridor
that Kimhi's legacy of rationalism and his approach to linguistics
and exegesis traveled.

Yet the Spanish émigrés did not find Provence a *tabula rasa.*
Following the incursion of secular sciences from Spain, Provençal
prowess in Talmud and midrash did not diminish. With characteristic adaptability, the new was incorporated into the old; the
sciences of the Gentiles grafted onto the tree of tradition. When
certain aspects of the midrashic tradition established by Moses the
Preacher became problematic in the light of contemporary intellectual currents, they were seldom rejected outright but were themselves subjected to a process of adaptation. Thus we find Samuel
Ibn Tibbon[75] and David Kimhi himself[76] working at a reconcilia-
tion of Maimonidean Aristotelianism with midrash which Moses
Ibn Tibbon and Yedaiah Ha-Penini of Beziers would carry forth
with increased vigor.[77] In a similar fashion, local and Catalonian

kabbalists would invest the ancient midrash with the new insights of kabbalism. One should expect this native "preoccupation with midrash, operating on different levels and with different methods of interpretation,"[78] which we shall find is characteristic of the mature David Kimhi, to be an important factor in his early education. Indeed in the *Open Book*, where Joseph Kimhi expresses his thoughts on the hierarchy of the sciences, he speaks of the compatibility—nay, interdependence—of talmudic and philological studies.[79] Unfortunately, however, we cannot look to him or to his son Moses for a detailed program as to how this synthesis was to be implemented. Provence produced few formal curricula. Two later writers, Joseph Ibn Caspi of Lunel (1270–1340) and Joseph Ezovi (thirteenth century) have left us educational programs[80]— the one in an ethical will, the other in a didactic poem. Yet even these do not provide a systematic or chronological presentation; they merely point the way and set general guidelines. But what Provence lacks, North Africa provides: Judah Ibn Abbas' *Lighting the Way,* a rationalist plan of study of the late thirteenth century. If we allow for differences in time and geography, this document proves in retrospect to be an almost perfect "Making of David Kimhi."[81]

Starting with the earliest years, Ibn Abbas echoes R. Joseph's association of rabbinic learning and the study of *peshat,* the plain sense of Scripture. He outlines: At the age of thirteen, after having thoroughly studied the Bible, "he will take up the study of grammar and philology through the works of the sage R. Jonah Ibn Janah . . . R. Judah Hayyuj and R. Abraham Ibn Ezra."[82] If we were to add the name of Joseph Kimhi to this list, we should have before us the four classic philologists that a later authority would see as the "pillars upon which Kimhi built his edifice."[83] Through their works, written in Hebrew or translated from the Arabic, the entire range of Spanish philology would be made accessible to him.[84] Ultimately David was to master the entire corpus. At this stage, however, besides simply "covering the syllabus," his brother Moses no doubt communicated to David that peculiar characteristic of all three Kimhis: the ability to single out the trees in the forest. David's skill at selection and synthesis, which he defined in a traditional statement of modesty as a "gleaning after the reapers,"[85] was no doubt nurtured even in the early years.

Along with study of grammar, there came, of course, its concomitant, the study of *peshaṭ*. In the literature of the period, the two are normally coupled. Joseph Kimhi had considered the grammatical aspects of Scripture propaedeutic to the study of the plain sense.[86] Later, on his road to truth, Shem Tov Ibn Falaquera's *Student* seeks out a linguist with whom he reads "books of grammar, philology, and the *peshaṭ* of biblical passages."[87] The effect of this persistent and all but automatic identification of the two on the budding exegete should not be underestimated. In practical terms, we shall see that whether a work was to be considered primarily exegetical or primarily grammatical depended only on its format. In the case of David Kimhi himself, his grammar, *Mikhlol,* and the commentaries would be the obverse and reverse of the same coin.

Following the biblical studies, we recall that rabbinics, the study of Talmud, formed the third phase of the trivium. Provence in this period was engaged in intensive study of talmudic literature. "Codes and commentaries, studies of existing codes or abridgements of the Talmud and treatises of the Talmud itself, custumals, and . . . voluminous responsa" have secured for their authors "honorific positions in the gallery of immortal Talmudic celebrities."[88] Yet with the influx of Spanish Jewry into Provence, the posture of many Provençals, especially those of the Kimhis' inclinations, would change. We find ourselves confronted with an uncertain transition from an ideal of study of the Talmud in its entirety to acceptance of the Spanish reality: study was confined to those sections of the Talmud concerned with daily practicalities, while considered restraint was exercised in the use of commentatorial literature. Even one who would counsel his son,

> But askest thou in what to set thy lore,
> In Grammar much, but in the Talmud more,[89]

suggests that the accessibility of codes and compendia renders overconscientious examination of rabbinic literature redundant.[90] It is in this very vein that our educator, Ibn Abbas, continues:

> Then he takes up the study of Talmud beginning with the [first] order, *Zera'im,* with the tractate *Berakhot* (Benedictions). It has become customary to do so because its content is readily understandable and because it serves as a good introduction.

> After that, he should proceed through the [other five]
> orders . . . However, if he wishes to limit himself to [the
> first three orders and certain essential tractates of the last
> three], he may do so. Let him always take the trouble to
> refer to the commentary of Rashi . . . and not bother to look
> at the *novellae* or *addenda* . . . which numerous people com-
> piled. They waste one's time and are irrelevant.[91]

A reading of David Kimhi's published works, with their lack of
emphasis on talmudics, might indeed lead one to believe that this
was his own experience. We shall see, however, that this relative
absence of talmudic materials was deceptive, that there was more
than would meet the eye. Other considerations make it highly
likely that Kimhi would have departed from the "rationalist"
stereotype to join the ranks of the talmudists in the first option:
the "Honors Course" in Talmud.

Only after the completion of the traditional trivium would the
student be ready to embark on the second phase of his education:
the sciences. First, young David would have to "*Know the God of
your father* (I Chronicles 28:9), that is, let him rely on tradition
until he can know Him by himself."[92] Many rungs would have to
be scaled on the ladder to metaphysics.[93] If one were too precipitate, the child would "become confused . . . Then he would begin
to deny the great portents and miracles . . . not to speak of . . . the
Torah and commandments which are based on reason . . . If one,
however, studies philosophy afterwards, he will not become confused . . . because he has already fixed a peg in a sure place."[94]
It is for this reason that Samuel failed to recognize the voice of
the Lord: "because he had not yet studied the science of divinity
even though he studied the other sciences."[95] Thus in the thir-
teenth-century course prescription, there is a five-year "transition"
period of study of ethical literature, such as the *Choice of Pearls*
so valued by Joseph Kimhi. Furthermore, regular weekly examination of the Torah commentaries is enjoined. It goes without saying
that these, as well as the commentaries of his father and brother,
would become part of David's stock-in-trade. The commentaries
of Ibn Ezra especially, with their philosophical elucidations and
obfuscations, would serve well to arouse the young student's
curiosity in what was to come:

> the sweet honey of the sciences. He begins with the propa-
> deutic: first, compositions on the principles of medicine.

> Then he takes up the study of mathematics with the work
> of Abraham Ibn Ezra which deals with most mathematical
> topics . . . [This is followed by] astronomy with the *Form
> of the Earth* of Abraham bar Hiyya the Spaniard and then . . .
> the study of the calculation and tables of the above-men-
> tioned author . . .

> Then he shall take up the study of logic in the writings of
> Aristotle followed by geometry, optics and music (even if he
> has already studied this in his medical studies in connection
> with the pulse, for this science serves a very useful function
> in explaining the body's motion . . .) Then he is to study
> the science of weights and then mechanics. All this will
> require ten years and the young man will then be twenty-
> eight. He will then take up the study of physics in the works
> of Aristotle . . . He will commit himself to this and to regular
> study of the propaedeutic sciences twelve [more] years until
> he is "forty−[fit] for discernment."[96]

One assumes that David passed this phase of his education satis-
factorily. There is ample evidence of his reading in all these works
and his learning in all these subjects,[97] including music, considered
"a great science which stimulates the intellective soul."[98] But now,
having attained the milestone of his fortieth birthday, it should
become his lot

> to turn aside from all worldly concerns and preoccupations
> and rally all his mental and spiritual resources and endeavor
> . . . to reach the last true area of philosophy: metaphysics,
> called the science of divinity. He is to persist in its study day
> and night . . . and rejoice . . . that he has reached all that the
> separate intellects can reach. . . Now he is truly worthy of
> being called a human being.[99]

To "turn aside from all worldly concerns," to become "truly
a human being" in the sense understood by the twelfth-century
intellectual, was an ideal to which David Kimhi would give frequent, resolute, and resonant expression. Yet David of Narbonne,
as David of Jerusalem before him, would find the path to this ideal
strewn with pitfalls.

Whether David actually waited until the age of forty to begin
the study of metaphysics is a moot point. It is more likely that he
exploited the prerogative of the intellectual: the double standard.
In any event, it is at the age of forty or thereabouts that we begin

to hear from him directly for the first time. At the turn of the thirteenth century, a scholar could make his way slowly. There need be no precipitate striving for tenure or royalties or—in the language of the period—"honor, wealth, or eternal fame."[100]

A Teacher of Talmud

The records are silent on the period in which David Kimhi was undergoing the process of becoming Radak (*Ra*bbi *Da*vid *K*imhi), of being titled with an acronym, the medieval Jewish equivalent of election to the *Académie*.[101]

Scant information is available concerning his family. That he had a son is known from the fact that he had a grandson.[102] But the curtain is drawn on the relationship with his children and his wife. One finds the expected remarks about feminine "simple-mindedness" and masculine superiority which are routine in medieval writing,[103] but he also tells us that women are more "tender-hearted" than men.[104] He reacts to physical beauty in general—masculine or feminine—in a stereotyped fashion.[105] As in the case of Absalom and Adonijah, it leads to vanity and rebellion.[106] Yet in rationalizing why the Patriarchs were determined on marrying women of particular beauty, he protests far too much:

> One may say that they were well intentioned since a beautiful woman arouses desire. [This was necessary . . . because they wished] to have many children. Further, they wanted their sons and daughters comely in appearance and resembling them. Further, a comely appearance delights one . . . [Such should be the appearance of her] who is always before one that his happiness may be constant. Man must be content in his world and in the portion which God gave him. Thus does God occasion a beautiful wife for the righteous man as He did for the patriarchs and the other righteous men who were content with their lot and brought forth children like themselves.[107]

Radak informs us that he was a teacher by profession. Even while he was composing the *Roots,* he wrote, "most of my time has been spent teaching boys Talmud." Teaching was a career which bore considerable esteem in his times. Despite the centrality of the book in the lives of Radak and his circle, Provençal Jewish literature frequently stresses the advantage of the live teacher over the passive written word. Menahem Ha-Meiri of Perpignan compliments the early generations of Provençal scholars by observing that they engaged principally in oral transmission of learning while writing very little. Their ability to dispense with written texts was considered a distinction.[108] Joseph Ezovi gives expression to these sentiments by counseling his son:

> To teachers, not to books entrust thy mind;
> Thy soul with living words, not dead, e'er bind.
> The written book appears expressionless,
> Thy teacher's wand doth give it rich address.[109]

Whether this respect for the teacher expressed itself in more tangible terms is difficult to know. Perhaps people found it easier then as now to pay tribute in verse rather than in tuition fees. Radak does, however, tell us that "among us are those who give stipends for the study of Bible and Talmud."[110] An early Provençal document, the *Torah Statutes,* outlines what were considered the ideal arrangements.

> They further enacted that a distinguished teacher be appointed over the subordinate teachers. He is to assemble up to one hundred young pupils in order to teach them Torah. He himself is to receive one hundred pounds and is to hire ten teachers at eighty pounds. The twenty remaining pounds are to be his allotment. He is not to teach the children but is to inspect and supervise the teachers preparing them in that which they are to teach. He is to rent a large house the rooms and lofts of which are [to be used] for teaching and every child must give his share of the rent. This house is called the small *midrash* [study-house].[111]

It would stand to reason that, if this were the arrangement in Narbonne, Radak would sooner or later have occupied this post of "distinguished teacher." Although we have no certain evidence that this was so, Picquet declares Radak to have been the head of the "synagogue" at Isle St. Ambroise.[112]

Radak was proud of his profession. He interpreted Proverbs 3:13: "*Happy is the man who finds wisdom and the man who yields* (AV: *obtaineth*) *understanding.*" This refers to one "who has learnt it so well that he can teach it to others."[113] He claimed that a "blessing would come to him who teaches Torah to others for all will bless him."[114] In the classroom, he probably showed little patience for longwindedness. If one keeps one's words brief, he observed, there is little chance of being misunderstood.[115] His polemical streak[116] reflects his intensity. One sees him as Elisha "concentrating on something exclusively, while pacing back and forth within."[117] He was open and not given to indoctrination. His brother would say, "Everyone choose for himself. Truth will point its own way."[118] Radak pursued this course. Although "there are many explanations which I did not see fit to record and those that I did record do not appear to me to be valid,"[119] he records them nonetheless. Nor did he feel compelled to know everything. He was willing to wait for the return of Elijah for the elucidation of apparently insoluble problems.[120]

According to Radak's own testimony, he was a teacher of Talmud.[121] As we have observed, there is little evidence for this in his literary works. As a talmudist, he seems to have engaged but little in talmudic code or commentary. Two short tracts, a commentary on the talmudic passage dealing with the compounding of the incense in the Temple (*piṭṭum ha-qeṭoret*)[122] and a commentary on the "Laws of Slaughtering" in Maimonides' *Mishneh Torah,* have been ascribed to him. In their present form, it is unlikely that they are the work of Radak, although they may hark back to works of his.[123] In any event, neither is of the sort that would set the world of rabbinics on fire.

In none of his works does Radak emerge with a clear stance as a *pasqan,* a decisor of halakhah (Jewish law). While he occasionally shows some independence and departs from the decisions of Maimonides, this occurs only in theoretical matters such as whether *be fruitful and multiply* (Genesis 1:28) is to be numbered among the 613 commandments[124] or whether the Ninth of Ab was observed during the Second Commonwealth.[125]

But the likelihood that Radak composed at least two halakhic tracts gives literary evidence of his concern for the area he professed to teach. Nor are his writings devoid of halakhic material where its use is appropriate. From frequent halakhic references in the Book of Genesis, the least "legal" of the books of the Torah, one has the impression that if Radak had completed the commentary on the remaining four books, his image as a halakhist would have been more clearly formed. On the basis of the available evidence, it is difficult to draw broad conclusions. In keeping with his interest in laws of slaughtering, Radak refers to the technicalities of sacrifices and the nature of the prohibition of the thigh vein.[126] Elsewhere he might dwell on the halakhic implications of a precept,[127] or the mere demands of the context might provoke a halakhic elucidation.[128]

As one might expect from a linguist-talmudist, the philological is sometimes woven into the halakhic. On the verse *they ate of the produce ('avur) of the land* (Joshua 5:11), Radak questions how the Israelites could have eaten new grain before the sheaf-offering on the Passover. He concludes that in fact they ate old grain since *'avur* is the produce of the past (*'averah*) year while the new grain, the produce of the coming (*ba'ah*) year, would be called *tevu'ah*.[129]

Indeed, halakhah even finds its place in the *Mikhlol* in the form of a statement concerning the importance of the proper reading of the *Shema',*[130] which was later cited by Joseph Karo, the sixteenth-century codifier.[131] One sees in the statement not only a zeal for the correct observance of the tradition but the sensitive ear of the phonetician.

> [The rabbis] decreed [that one must be precise] whenever he reads in the Torah or in the Prophets or in the Hagiographa. They enjoined this specifically in the reading of the *Shema',* but it applies equally to any passage to be read, for reading in the Torah, Prophets, and Hagiographa is obligatory for us . . . Their mentioning the reading of the *Shema'* specifically is for two reasons: (1) these portions speak of the declaration of the unity of God and the acceptance of the yoke of Heaven, and (2) all Israel, both the sages and the uneducated, read it twice a day. Therefore, they had to emphasize [the importance of reading it properly] because of those who are uneducated and are not skilled in reading . . . I have spoken at such great length concerning this matter because I have seen many err in reading, for they are not diligent in distinguishing letters of similar appearance or they slur over others where they should not.[132]

The halakhic was often accompanied by the hortatory. Radak does not seem to speak of a general laxity in the observance of the commandments as did his Catalonian counterpart Jonah Gerondi.[133] His principal preoccupations rather are the two very

central commandments of Sabbath and circumcision. Whenever
Scripture allows him the opportunity, he will enter into a discourse on the Sabbath. These are the most complete models of
sermons to be found in his commentaries. In a long hortatory
passage Radak expounds:

> *Take heed for the sake of your lives and do not bear a burden
> on the Sabbath day or bring it in by the gates of Jerusalem*
> (Jeremiah 17:21). The reason he was commanded to exhort
> them concerning the Sabbath even though they were guilty
> of other sins is that the observance of the Sabbath is funda-
> mental to belief in God, the creation of the world, and the
> signs and wonders, and to the maintenance of the entire
> Torah. Everyone who keeps the Sabbath with true faithful-
> ness does not quickly sin in other commandments. The
> rabbis said that everyone who observes the Sabbath accord-
> ing to its laws, even if he practices idolatry like the genera-
> tion of Enosh, is forgiven; for it is said *Blessed is Enosh* (the
> man) *who does this and the son of man who holds it fast,
> who keeps the Sabbath not profaning it* (*meḥallelo*) (Isaiah
> 56:6). Read not *meḥallelo* but *maḥul lo* (he is forgiven).[134]

> The first commandment Israel was commanded before the
> giving of the Torah was the Sabbath. Now see how great is
> the observance of the Sabbath! [The prophet] associated the
> destruction of Jerusalem with Sabbath observance. The
> rabbis found an allusion to this in the verse *I will kindle a
> fire in its gates and it shall devour the palaces of Jerusalem*
> (Jeremiah 17:27). They said:[135] "An outbreak of fire occurs
> only in a place where there is desecration of the Sabbath.
> They asked: 'What does *and it shall not be quenched* (*ibid.*)
> mean?' At a time when no one is available to quench it."[136]

In such a vein, with greater or lesser prolixity, Radak takes up
the theme of the Sabbath on various occasions,[137] enriching his
words with abundant rabbinic passages.[138] Yet despite the hortatory nature of these passages, it is doubtful that they were indeed
intended to remonstrate. In middle age, it is unlikely that Radak
would lapse into the error of the tyro preacher and objurgate the
loyal few who came to hear him as if they were sinners in Israel.
This is especially true of his discussions of circumcision, the
commandment which they "maintain more than any other"[139]
and which would be neglected only by those who had formally
rejected Judaism. Yet this commandment—with its various ramifi-

cations—was elaborated upon to a greater extent than mere
predicatory or educational purposes would require.[140] We shall
see that it is possible that Radak's stress on the Sabbath may have
stemmed very little from tensions in the inner life of the Jewish
community; rather it may have formed part of the implicit
polemic against the Christian adversary.[141]

The sermon in general was, of course, an established institution
in Narbonne. In 1200, the walls of Narbonne's synagogues and
study-houses still reverberated with the homilies of Moses the
Preacher.[142] Of sermons and preachers in contemporary Provence
we do not have an abundance of literary remains.[143] In neighboring
Catalonia, the sermon does not seem to have reached its full development until the time of Jonah Gerondi and Moses Nahmanides.[144]
Yet the preacher was a fixed institution in the Mediterranean
region. In the *Mishneh Torah,* Moses Maimonides reconfirmed
the importance of the rabbinic institution of the preacher.[145]
"It is necessary to appoint in every community a great scholar,
advanced in years, God-fearing from his youth and beloved by
the people, to rebuke the multitude and cause them to repent."[146] It is such that we find in Radak: the voice of a moralizer
who exhorts against the excesses of the flesh against the spirit, the
adumbration of the excesses of the individual against society.

Moderate in his preaching, Radak, like Maimonides,[147] cease-
lessly preaches moderation.[148] Not only drunkenness but any form
of overindulgence is to be censured.[149] God taught this lesson to
mankind when he condemned post-diluvian man to reduced
stature and lifespan.

> *The men of renown* (Genesis 6:4). They were renowned
> among the generations that succeeded them. The survivors
> of the flood saw that God does not look favorably upon the
> pursuit of pleasures and physical gratification . . . [leading
> to] overgrowth of the body or hyper-longevity. Thus it was
> that the lifespans of people after the flood became progres-
> sively shorter . . . while their bodies became smaller . . . By
> the time the Israelites came to Canaan, only the sons of the
> giant in Hebron were extant.[150]

Yet with it all, Radak is less concerned with the dimensions of
the body than those of the spirit. In truth, Radak admits that lusts

and sins of the flesh, especially sexual sins, are at least understand-
able. They stem, after all, from man's animal nature. But stealing
and murder, crimes of violence against one's fellow, do not.[151]
These are the crimes most reprehensible to the Lord. Violence,
the disruption of social order,[152] is the most heinous. The preservation of the fabric of society is essential to man's survival.[153]
It is because of this crime—violence—and exclusively because of it
that the generation of the flood was punished.[154] Indeed, God
takes cognizance of the Gentiles—not ordinarily subject to divine
providence—only when they engage in crimes of violence—especially, but not exclusively, against Israel.[155]

The routine attribution of violence to the Gentiles would lead
one to think that Radak's social critique is primarily outer-di-
rected. Yet there can be little doubt that he does not spare the
sensibilities of his fellow Jews. Although Provençal Jewry does
not seem to have had a counterpart to the courtier class in Spain,[156]
which provoked such moralists as Jonah Gerondi,[157] echoes of
social tensions can be heard in Radak's remarks.

He gives the remonstrances of antiquity a contemporary ring.
His sympathies for the poor are explicit and he often reiterates the
commonly cited equation of the poor ('aniyim) and the humble
('anavim).[158] It is the poor who can be relied upon to speak the
truth.[159] They are God's own people[160] and are "generally righteous in justice because they are oppressed. They [themselves] do
not oppress because they do not have the strength to do so."[161]
There is little if anything original in these remarks but their
frequency reflects Radak's deep concern. Wealth is not completely
denounced. It does have its advantages: those who are "wealthy
and not occupied in crafts have leisure to study Torah and science
and are generally wise and knowledgeable people."[162] Yet in the
wrong hands, wealth leads to idleness and idleness to irresponsi-
bility: "They are idle because they are rich. They spend all their
time drinking and listening to song. They devote none of their
leisure to Torah and science."[163] As is common among medieval
social critics, Radak inveighs against ostentatious display of
wealth. The catalogue of garments in Isaiah 3 seems to have a
familiar ring to him. After the sinners are purged from Israel in
the end of days, he tells us, "those that are left will be humble
and saintly—the reverse of what they were in the days of Ahaz
when they were proud and corrupt. Then women will not flaunt

their ornaments . . . for all of those will be eliminated in the
future. There will be no pride in men or women."[164] He scorns
the investing of energy in the building of "pleasure palaces as if
they will live in them forever."[165] Radak's interpretation of the
extravagance of Jews is revealing. He does not see it as mere self-
indulgence but as part of a frantic and misguided attempt to curry
favor with the Gentiles.

> Just as the harlot dresses in fine clothes, makes herself beau-
> tiful, and applies eye shadow so that they will all desire her,
> the Community of Israel persisted in the practices of the
> nations; worshipping their gods, wearing their clothes,
> *vaunting themselves and flaunting their fine clothes and*
> *carriages* so that they would love her and say: "she is like
> us and we love her."[166]

To Radak, as to the Spanish preachers,[167] any such assimilationist
gestures were anathema. Customs such as shaving, which Jews
"practice in those lands in which we live," are a "disgrace."[168]

Critiques of the leadership of the Jewish community are more
implicit than explicit. The prophet Samuel, who served both
medieval Judaism and Christianity as an ideal of spiritual leadership, is attractive to Radak by virtue of his reluctance to profit
from his duties.[169] "Judges," he tells us, "must hate lucre and be
of those who are content with their lot, who disdain worldly goods
and do not pursue gain."[170] Had Saul known true men of God and
not just sorcerers, he would not have been gauche enough to ask,
What shall we bring the man? (I Samuel 9:7).[171]

It need hardly be said that Radak, with his longings for the
Davidic restoration, was a confirmed monarchist. "Kings," he was
certain, "were generally wise men."[172] Yet he knew of their wiles.

> *Their hands are upon that which is evil to do it diligently.*
> *The minister asks and the judge is ready for a reward; the*
> *great man utters the evil desire of his soul* (Micah 7:3). The
> king himself will not demand bribery for he will be embar-
> rassed to do so but the minister demands it for him . . . The
> judge perverts justice so that the king will reward him with
> money . . . He who is called *the great man* is beneath the
> minister and exacts bribery from the litigants.[173]

Radak therefore envisioned this monarchy with clearly defined constitutional limits. His bill of rights is written—appropriately enough—around the antimonarchical speech of Samuel in I Samuel 8. With the aid of a number of rabbinic passages, Radak tempers Samuel's warnings and shows the limits of the monarch. If he drafts workmen, he must pay them suitable wages; if he commandeers private property, he is entitled only to the usufruct and not to the land itself. If this were not the case, Jezebel "would not have had to have recourse to all those machinations and to the shedding of innocent blood."[174] Radak condones the king's living in kingly fashion—provided that his luxuries do not come about through violence and oppression.[175] He himself was certain that the days of monarchical tyranny were over. In the future, *My prince shall no more wrong My people* (Ezekiel 45:8) for the temptation will no longer exist: "They shall have their own properties which will suffice them."[176]

Biblical narratives frequently serve as the starting point of moral instruction. The historical material in Scripture was especially challenging to biblical exegetes of all shades in this period.[177] Radak made only the most sparing use of philosophical allegory and did not know (or care to know) anything of the mystical. The purpose of these stories, he instructs us, is "to enable man to acquire good traits and reject the bad."[178] The binding of Isaac, indeed, "did not take place for the sake of contemporary generations but for the coming generations who believe in the divine written Torah of Moses and *in its narratives.* Thus they might see how great was Abraham's love for God and they might learn from him to love God with all their heart and all their soul."[179]

From the story of Abraham and the angels one learns of the importance of hospitality and the lengths to which the host should go.[180] The stories of Hagar in the wilderness and Joseph in Potiphar's house demonstrate how one should trust in God no matter how bad the odds seem.[181] God's "descent" to observe Sodom serves as an example of caution and judiciousness.[182] The account of Joseph's brothers at Genesis 42:21 shows that one should examine one's conscience if one finds himself in dire straits.[183] Radak was quite sure that all these narratives existed to teach a moral lesson and felt compelled to admit ignorance in the one place he could not establish it.[184] As homiletic material, these remarks are only incipient sermons. Yet they mark an important beginning in the Catalo-Provençal exegetical tradition which would ultimately lead to Gersonides' thorough and comprehensive listing of *to 'aliyot* (moral, philosophical, or halakhic lessons), which became a fixed feature of his commentaries. These *to 'aliyot,* listed systematically on every passage, deal not only with morals but with practice and belief.[185] For Radak too, even more important than the ethical lessons to be learned, was the fact that the narrative portions of the Torah were the greatest evidence of its credibility: "There are those who believe and those who do not believe. Since the day idolatry ceased, most of the world believes in the Torah of Moses our Master and in its narratives, although they disagree with us concerning the commandments claiming that they are allegories."[186]

Radak and the Rationalist Tradition

Radak's role as religious guide was not limited to questions of morals and ethics alone; it extended to belief as well. In Provence there were many perplexed in search of such a guide.

The Jew had met Perplexity in his wanderings; she was to become a tenacious if tiresome traveling companion. In tenth-century Baghdad, Saadia Gaon attempted to repel the intruder once and for all. He wrote his *Doctrines and Beliefs* less to convince his non-Jewish opponents than to convince himself and his corelligionists.[187] His was no easy task. The spiritual climate in Baghdad was so unrestrained that a visiting Spanish Muslim recoiled in dismay from what he saw.[188] Yet by the time he returned to Andalusia, he no doubt found that the contagion had preceded him. The Jew—always more susceptible to the ills of the world than the world itself[189] —sent to Baghdad for the vaccine. The *Doctrines and Beliefs* traversed the Mediterranean to bring succor to the Spanish dispersion. The diagnosis of Saadia and his popularizers was straightforward: unverified faith is too vulnerable. Without the validation of reason, profession of faith is not much more than a mouthing of words. Bahya Ibn Paquda, a twelfth-century Spaniard, received the tradition from Saadia. In his *Duties of the Heart,* an ethical work, he declares it "want of zeal for anyone to rely on tradition alone who can obtain certainty by means of rational demonstration."[190] From Bahya, the tradition passed on to Joseph Kimhi. Reason is ever the watchword. The doubting Jew need doubt no more. God "speaks to a mature man,

one who knows how to scrutinize his faith so he will not err."[191]
From Joseph, David learned that no one, and certainly not the
Jew, is exempt from this duty. Even good intentions, if unex-
amined, lead to downfall.

> [Our fathers] prospered in the service of [idolatry] . . .
> and thought that it could benefit or harm, inflict illness or
> heal. This has no basis . . . in science or medicine or reality
> at all. It was just the habit of one generation after another
> to think that [the idols] were at the root of things and that
> one need not seek after a Creator or Guide or Director. These
> are the "ways of the Amorites."[192]

For David as for Joseph, the "ways of the Amorites" had not
passed from the world, and the latter-day "idolators" were far
from well intentioned. Joseph Kimhi counseled his Christian
opponent to conserve his energy. He simply could not "profess
the belief which you profess, *for my reason does not allow me.*"[193]
     For David, as for Joseph, there was one highway that led out
of inconsistency and error, that led to God Himself:

> To my Father highways
> In my heart do I build,
> And sing of His praise
> Before my voice be stilled.[194]

These highways that Radak traveled, which formed the junction
between him and his God, were those that were paved by his
father, Joseph.

> *Happy is the man [whose strength is in You]* (Psalms 84:6).
> My father interpreted: They have strength, wisdom, and
> knowledge of Your unity. This is the essence of serving You.
> Thus David said to Solomon his son: *Know the God of your
> father and serve Him* (I Chronicles 28:9).
>   *In whose heart are the highways* (*ibid*). In their hearts, they
> have highways as a result of knowing You. They pass back
> and forth on those highways and increase in strength daily.
>   This interpretation is correct.[195]

Whatever the image—the "angel" for Ibn Ezra,[196] the "highway"
for the Kimhis—the link between man and God is the intellect.

Only the intellectual is religious: *"Bless the Lord O my soul* (Psalms 104:1) . . . In the lower world there is none that knows how to bless except the rational soul of man."[197] Only those fear the Lord who know Him and His power.

> *Then those who feared the Lord spoke with one another* (Malachi 3:16). When those who fear the Lord hear the words of those who deny God's providence in the lower world, they speak with each other. They consider and debate these things at length until they find *intellectually* that all His ways are just; that He is a faithful God without iniquity.[198]

To fear God means to fear nothing else: *"My heart shall not fear* (Psalms 27:3). For my heart and *my intellect* make me confident of God."[199]

The task of the intellect is not a light one. The road to God is long and dimly lit. Yet:

> The heart takes its place
> Like a king on a throne
> With a flame that does blaze
> To search the unknown.[200]

The search for the unknown can begin only with the known. Indeed the search for the unknown God begins with man himself, with meditation "on man's creation—how his limbs were formed, and how his sustenance was provided from the day he was born. This wisdom brings man to recognize God."[201] From man in this world the search proceeds to the heavens above.

> *Lift up your eyes on high and see Who has created these* (Isaiah 40:26) . . . Look at the mighty creatures, the stars. See with your intellect who has created these. They are creatures—not creators . . . The world is created, for nothing creates itself and there cannot be more than one Creator as is proven by the methods of science.[202]

There is no alternative but to "study books of science and to come to a rational understanding of creation in both the upper and lower worlds."[203] Science is the only safeguard against skepticism and heresy.

> [*Happy are they that dwell in Your house* (Psalms 84:5)]
> for those who dwell in Your house take strength in You for
> they seclude themselves there and occupy themselves with
> science to know You.[204]

Only they are "*those who fear the Lord* (Psalms 15:11) . . . for
they know from their science that there is no other in whom to
trust."[205]

In the tradition of his predecessors—Saadia, Ibn Ezra, Joseph
and Moses Kimhi, and Maimonides—Radak assumed the congruency of truth and truth, the interdependence of Torah and science.
For Joseph Kimhi, one without the other was like "a tent without
cords."[206] On the cords of Torah, Radak builds entire tent-camps.

> *This book of the Torah shall not depart out of your mouth*
> (Joshua 1:8) . . . This was a commandment to Joshua and
> to every man . . . to know the entire Torah *and afterwards
> study the sciences.*[207]

> *Everyone that thirsts come for water* (Isaiah 55:1) . . . "Water"
> is a metaphor for Torah *and science.* Just as the world cannot
> survive without water, it cannot survive without Torah.[208]
> Just as one who thirsts longs for water, so does the rational
> soul long for Torah *and science.*[209]

> *He who keeps the Sabbath* (Isaiah 56:2) . . . freeing his soul
> from mundane affairs, concerning himself with Torah *and
> science* and contemplating the works of the Lord.[210]

Radak does not go as far as some of his copyists in reversing
the order of the sequence "Torah and science."[211] In respect of
both time and veneration, the Torah has priority. The Torah
prevents true wisdom from turning into mere guile and craftiness.[212]
Practice of the Torah is a safeguard against misuse of intellect: "If
those who occupy themselves with science do not fear God and are
not perfect in his commandments, He will not reveal to them the
mystery of God."[213] With reference to the rabbinic debate over
whether study or practice is greater,[214] Radak remarks that the
rabbis "only considered study greater because it leads to practice. . . Study without practice is not beneficial but harmful both
to oneself and others."[215] Yet though commandments are an in-
dispensable foundation, they are little more than that. They "en-
lighten the heart" but are "the stepping-stone to the greater

glory."[216] *The upright in heart* (Psalms 36:11) "walk wholeheart-
edly and uprightly engaging in Torah and commandments."[217]
Yet "these have not acquired the science of divinity [and have]
knowledge of the Creator only through tradition . . . The sages,
who engage in Torah and commandments *and the science of the
divinity of the Creator* according to their ability—they are *those
who know You* (*ibid.*)."[218]

Radak's understanding of the intellect as the moderator of
faith, which he adopted from Hispano-Provençal rationalism,
was to gain reinforcement from other sources. When Samuel Ibn
Tibbon's Hebrew rendering of Maimonides' *Guide for the Perplexed* descended upon Provence, it fit Radak like a glove. Maimonides confirmed that which came before but in ways ever more
bold, daring, and profound. He "taught us and illuminated . . . the
darkness in which we walked before he came."[219] Maimonides is
a leading actor on Radak's stage. He is not always the hero of
the moment but he is always allowed to finish his lines. And
though he is given long monologues, his presence is felt even more
strongly behind the scenes. Whether he is a guide or a sounding
board, he expresses himself on all subjects. There are the affairs
of the upper world: God, spheres, and angels. There are the affairs
of the lower world: man, Torah, commandments. There are—
above all—the interworld affairs: prophecy, providence, the life of
the soul in this world and the next.[220] Yet as thoroughgoing and
pervasive as these expressions and manifestations of Maimonidean-
ism are, their principle significance lies in their representation of
a common commitment. They are an oath of allegiance—not to
Maimonides but to Radak's and Maimonides' common advocacy
of the rationalist conception of Judaism.

Radak's Role in the Maimonidean Controversy

Not all shared this advocacy. Not all understood. There were
those who really believed that the rule of *ratio* undermined faith
instead of bolstering it. They declared Maimonides a subversive:
a denier of resurrection, a denier of miracles, a denier of the plain
sense of the Torah, a new idolatry in a world full of idolatries:

> All mockery is forbidden except mockery of idolatry.[221]
> Why have you transgressed the word of the Lord and made
> the *Guide* a new Torah? You say, "We have the right of re-

demption and inheritance for Moses Maimonides commanded us this Torah as an inheritance" . . . You have proposed to raise R. Moses higher than the prophets and to place him at the head.[222]

Opposition to the *Guide* in Spain and Provence mounted.[223] Its dangers as a bridgehead to heresy were clearly spelled out: The *Guide* is "a support for every rebel who aspires to its teaching. It is a constant stumbling block and obstacle."[224] "It gives obscure counsel with its words and spins parables to the ignorant and the fools . . . They do not know the nature of this book nor do they understand its essence."[225] The end of this is that the children of these free thinkers will inevitably apostasize: "They will cast out the old in the face of the new."[226] Those who feared the worst undertook the worst. R. Solomon ben Abraham of Montpellier and his disciples Jonah Gerondi and R. David ben Saul had tried to incite the populace of Narbonne, Beziers, and other communities against the *Guide.*[227] Yet far worse, R. Solomon

> became corrupt and acted immorally and became a slanderer and informer. His end testifies to his beginning. May the heavens reveal his iniquity and the earth rise up against him. When the rabbis of France abandoned him, considering him a fool and recognizing him for a false witness, he turned unto the idols and the idolators. He entreated them and they agreed to help him in putting forth his hand against the Jews. He called first to the barefoot Minorites[228] and told them: "See how most of our people are heretics and apostates for they have been seduced by the words of R. Moses of Egypt who wrote heresy. As long as you are purging yourselves of your heretics, purge us of ours." They then ordered the burning of those books, namely the *Book of Knowledge* (of the *Mishneh Torah*) and the *Guide.* Yet his uncircumcised heart was not satisfied and he spoke also to the preachers, i.e., the *Predicadores* (Dominicans), and to the priests along the same lines until the matter came to the Cardinal himself. Thus were the Jews in Montpellier and the environs in great danger and were a sport and a mockery in the mouth of the Gentiles. The evil slander passed from city to city and they said: "See how the Law of the Jews is lost for they have become two factions on account of it. There is no law but ours."[229]

Radak of course was assured that Christianity had enough cause to be jubilant with regard to the Jewish question without the Jews themselves adding fuel to the fire. This outrage had to be stopped. Radak sought counsel. Had Samuel Ibn Tibbon been alive, he would have turned to him.[230] Instead he sought another kindred spirit who would aid him in arousing support for a general censure and repudiation of these malefactors.[231] Radak chose R. Judah Alfakhar of Toledo. If Alfakhar was selected because of his influence or "political" importance, it is not clear why. Indeed, Alfakhar's chief claim to historical prominence is Radak's contact with him.[232] One thing is certain however. He possessed all the qualifications: like Maimonides himself, he was a physician-courtier;[233] like Radak himself, he was a southern European intellectual who engaged in scientific pursuits. Unlike the scholars of northern France, "who have dealt strictly with all those who [engage in science]," [234] Alfakhar would surely sympathize with Radak's position.

It was thus in the winter of 1232 that Radak, accompanied by his nephew Joseph, began his journey to see Alfakhar. It was to be a cold journey in many ways—so cold indeed that even the fire of his own zeal could not alleviate the chill. The events of this campaign were fraught with genuine drama. It is unfortunate then that this is often vitiated by the melodramatic presentation of a man "old and weak as he was" [235] setting out on the open road for the first time. As Radak himself informs us, he was indeed ill.[236] Yet external realities were not always the most decisive for David Kimhi: the discomfort of the inner city did not prevent him from living there; nor, as we shall see, did the enlightened rule of Aimeri IV ease his anxiety over the exile.[237] So too old age and illness could not put a damper upon his vigor. Radak expresses astonishment that his namesake, King David, had fallen ill. After all, he wonders, "He was only seventy!" [238] And it is in the light of someone who was "only seventy" that this chapter in his life must be viewed.

Nor do we have reason to believe that he was a stranger to travel. Rather it appears to have been a normal and natural part of his life. He was, it seems, one of those many Provençal Jewish scholars "whose desire for learning was not flagged by incessant travel or other external hindrances. Travel was a means to attain knowledge." [239] True, he might cry that "the grievance of travel exhausts one and shortens one's life." [240] But that again is in the context of the "anguish of exile and hard masters." [241] He himself was never forcibly removed from the place of his birth as were his father and brother. Nor was he, like that most famous of Jewish *vagantes,* Abraham Ibn Ezra, compelled by circumstances to seek out his living where it lay and to wander from city to city and land to land.[242] Rather, Radak's peregrinations were voluntary (if not always pleasurable) and were of short duration and specific purpose.

Most of Radak's wanderings were prompted by his scholarship. As in the case of his modern counterparts, his journeys in this capacity had a double objective: research on the one hand and social and intellectual exchange on the other. His forays in search of biblical manuscripts led him far into Spain: most certainly to Saragossa for the *Jerusalem Codex* and possibly to Toledo for the *Sefer Hilleli.*[243] His very frequent references to such "reliable" or "precise codices"[244] would lead us to believe that he paid visits to many other manuscript depositories.

We know of no Languedoc Oriental Society the meetings of which Radak might have attended annually. Yet, *mirabile dictu,* the absence of a structured organization did not seem to hamper serious intellectual conversation. Most notable is Radak's friendship with the savant and translator Samuel Ibn Tibbon.[245] The former lends eloquent testimony to their relationship with his comment that, since Radak's passing, "I have found no one with whom to speak."[246] Samuel was the son of Joseph Kimhi's "competitor" in the field of translation, Judah Ibn Tibbon. The latter left his son a well-known ethical testament which reflects very much the same kind of preoccupation with books as that reflected in the writings of the Kimhis. Often quoted is the elegant "Let thy books be thy companions." But this is later followed by an admonition whose substance is "Let thy companions return thy books."[247] One can imagine—perhaps not altogether facetiously—the mature Samuel Ibn Tibbon still keeping his card file of books in circulation with David Kimhi making his semiannual visit to return old volumes and check out the new.

Setting our sights westward, the first town which we may posit as having entertained Radak is Gerona. It was a member of this distinguished Jewish community, a pupil of his father's—Radak tells us—that prompted him to embark on his career as an exegete.[248] While such expressions of commission or encouragement are often taken as pure literary devices, this was probably not the case in Radak's ambience.[249] One may cite the testimony of another of Radak's associates farther to the southwest in Barcelona. This was the home of the translator Abraham Ibn Hisdai, who became famous for his renditions of various philosophical texts, Maimonides' *Book of Commandments* and a Judaized *Barlaam and Joshaphat.* [250] In Ibn Hisdai's introduction to Isaac Israeli's *Book of Elements,* he renders more than token acknowledgement to his patron: "R. David ben Joseph Kimhi who entreated me and encouraged me. He had me do what I would not have done on my own account and accomplished with his enterprise what could not have been accomplished with mine alone." [251] The friendship between Radak and Ibn Hisdai was to be long lasting and was to come to expression at a time when it would be most needed. [252]

Beyond this, however, one has the impression that travel itself held a special attraction for Radak. He would evince a vivid interest in geographical problems in the Bible and in the identification of such realia as names of gates, towers, and towns. The verse *all Israel mourned Samuel* and *buried him in Ramah and in his city* (I Samuel 28:3), which formed a syntactical problem for his predecessors, was a geographical problem for him. "Since there were two Ramahs," he explains, "as it says *of Ramathaim* (lit. two Ramahs, I Samuel 1:1), it says *and in his city.* That is to say the particular Ramah that was his city." [253] Concerning the town Kiriathaim, which might be rendered in English as Doubleton, Radak wonders if perhaps there were not "two towers whereby they called it double." [254] Where Rashi comments on the River Chebar with a bland "name of river," Radak tries to identify the river and is concerned with whether or not it is the Euphrates. [255] In references to the various gates of the Temple cited in Jeremiah and Ezekiel, Radak cites the Targum and the rabbis as sources for elucidation.

[*Go out to the valley of Ben-Hinnom*] *at the entrance of the Harsit Gate* (Ezekiel 19:2) . . . Jonathan translated *in front of the gate of* qilqalta and *qilqalta* in the words of the rabbis means rubble. [256] In my view it is the gate mentioned in the Book of Ezra as the *Rubble Gate.* [257] The rabbis explained that it is one of the gates of the court, namely the Eastern Gate. They said that it is called by seven names: the *Sur* gate to which the impure would retire, as it says *Depart! He is defiled* (Lamentations 4:15); the Foundation Gate, for there they founded the halakhah; the *Harsit* Gate for it faced the

sunrise (as derived from the verse *Who commands the sun*
[*heres*] *and it does not rise* [Job 9:7]); the *'Iton Gate* (Ezekiel 40:15) for it serves as an entrance and exit,[258] the Middle
Gate (Jeremiah 39:3) for it is situated directly between two
gates; the New Gate (Jeremiah 26:10) for there the sages innovated halakhah; the Upper Gate (Ezekiel 9:2) for it was
above the Court of the Israelites.[259]

Indeed he brings so much material to bear at times that his commentaries take on the appearance of a biblical Baedeker.[260]

Radak envisioned travel as a source of delight in the days of
the Messiah. Ibn Ezra, always en route and perhaps a little weary
of it, could accept Isaiah's prophecy that *their seed shall be known
among the nations* (61:9) only on the condition that it be the
nations that come to see Israel and not vice versa. Radak, on the
other hand, saw in this prophecy the promise that the Grand
Tour would be a feature of the future restoration; that "the
young men will go at their pleasure to see the lands of the nations."[261]

> When they go about the lands of the Gentiles for business or
> pleasure . . . they will be known and distinguished because
> of all their glory and grandeur . . . They shall go about in
> finery and embroidered garments . . . It shall be said of them:
> "These are the children of Israel. These are the posterity
> which the Lord has blessed."[262]

The campaign of 1232, however, did not turn out to be a source
of delight. It is indeed doubtful whether Radak reached his final
destination, Toledo, at all, although it is likely that he got as far
as Burgos and certain that he arrived at Ávila.[263] The actual route
of his journey is problematic. If he wished to reach Burgos by the
most direct circuit, he could have followed the St. Gilles route to
Compostela, *mutatis mutandis,* the Interstate 95 of its time. This
would have taken him west to Carcassonne and Toulouse and
thence to Ste. Christine and Jaca; it would then join the other
three French routes at Puente-la-Reina where the *camino francés*
would lead him on to Burgos, via Estella and Nájera. Although
Radak would hardly be joining in the pilgrimage, the concept of
a pilgrimage as a visit to a shrine (rather than the very different notion of a pilgrimage to Jerusalem) was not unknown to him. In
his reading of biblical history, Mizpah and Gilgal were understood

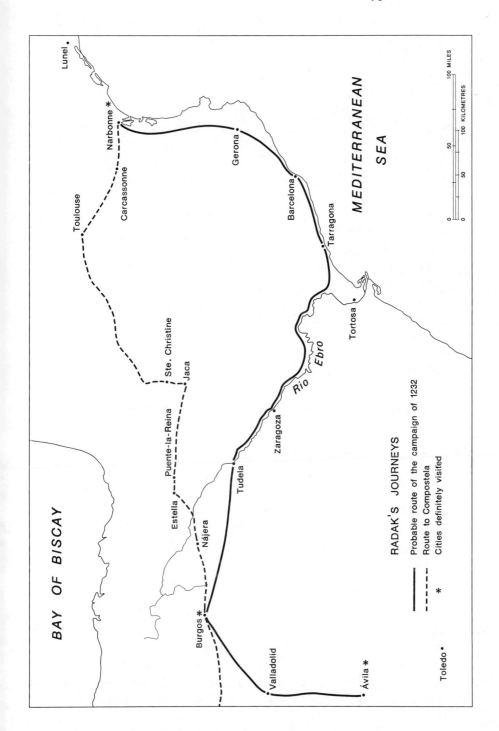

as shrines which were to be visited in time of need,[264] not, to be sure, because of relics preserved there, but because of incidents which took place there.

If Radak indeed followed this route, he should theoretically have had the added advantage of safety in numbers. *Omnis iniquitas et omnis fraus abundat in sanctorum itineribus* intones the *Liber Sancti Jacobi.*[265] "Risk not thy life by taking the road and leaving the city, in times of disquiet and changes," Judah Ibn Tibbon warns his son.[266] Joseph Kimhi too does not fail to remind his adversary that "the Christian goes out on the highways to meet travelers—not to honor them—but to swindle them and take all their possessions from them."[267] However, it is not altogether certain that Radak was very much interested in the shortest route. In his campaign of 1232, he was probably less concerned with going directly to Burgos or even to Alfakhar than he was with propagandizing among the various Jewish communities. An antagonist would term it "leading astray dwellers of the country and the joyous towns; provoking battles between city and city, kingdom and kingdom."[268] This fact plus the added consideration of safety assures us then that Radak followed the tried and true routes of Jewish travelers. After all, Joseph Kimhi tells us, "whenever a Jew stops at the home of his fellow for a day or two or [even] a year, he would take no payment for food from him."[269] David too would proudly observe that "our houses are wide-open to every passerby and to all who seek rest."[270] Why not then the route of Benjamin of Tudela himself with the direction reversed— Narbonne, Gerona, Barcelona, Tarragona, Tortosa, along the Ebro to Saragossa, Tudela,[271] and then westward to Burgos.

Radak's welcome in Burgos was short-lived. Some members of the community indeed received him favorably and gave him approbatory letters, which he immediately placed in circulation. However R. Nathan, a leader of the community and the father-in-law of Radak's antagonist, Joseph ben Todros, had Radak summarily expelled from the city. Presumably this was done with the backing of most of the community. R. Joseph claimed that "all those biased letters which I heard are being circulated from Burgos by R. David Kimhi . . . were not approved by the community nor were they written or signed with the knowledge of the rabbis."[272]

With this rebuke, Radak continued toward Toledo. At Ávila, fate intervened. Radak became ill and could not continue his journey. Reluctant to lose precious time, he sent his nephew ahead to inform Alfakhar of his mission. The reply was not long in coming. Radak had assessed his "ally" well. Alfakhar was indeed a student of the sciences, familiar with the *Guide for the Perplexed,* a coldly rational and analytic mind. All the greater then would be Radak's dismay at the letter he now received. He need read no more than the salutation in order to get the point:

> O David the Petty,[273]
> God rebuke you, you cur!
> We have no need of
> *agents provocateurs!*[274]

Alfakhar's letter is a summary critique of the *Guide* and Alfakhar was equal to the task. Rationally, he demonstrates the limits of reason. Proofs and syllogisms alone carry too great a risk of error because of their complexity. Where Scripture is uncertain— as in the question of anthropomorphism—then certainly reason should be employed to decide the issue. But can reason impugn the authority of the Torah in areas where the Torah is definitive? Is creation no longer creation? Are miracles no longer miracles? Is resurrection no longer resurrection? Are commandments no longer commandments?[275] Without stating it explicitly, Alfakhar implied what Radak knew well enough. Jewish allegorization of Scripture was potentially as dangerous as Christian. Aristotle can topple the foundations of the Sabbath as well as can the Church Fathers.[276] Alfakhar's acerbity is palliated by his words of respect for Maimonides. He grants not only that the Master is to be honored for the *Mishneh Torah* but that the *Guide* itself does have its virtues.[277] Its evil lies in its falling into the wrong hands, in its promulgation among those who cannot cope with it. Its end is heresy and apostasy.[278] Great then is the guilt of those who are accessories to this crime. R. Samuel Ibn Tibbon, the "first in this treachery," was well intentioned, but the "end was bitter."[279] Now that Ibn Tibbon has translated the *Guide,* David Kimhi could come and apply it.

> David . . . has made the Torah an example[280] and a reproach throughout . . . He went off and said that the great portents and miracles were riddles and parables. He mocked and there was none to call his shame. He has indeed counseled without

wisdom, undermining the foundation of the Torah. He has
sold all its precious pearls and verses to the Greeks . . . Let
Kimhi, the barren seed,[281] tell when the Holy Scriptures were
turned inside out according to Greek rules of hermeneutics.
So does Aram guide Ephraim and a chariot go forth from
Egypt. This must not be! From Zion shall the Torah go forth
and the word of the Lord from Jerusalem.[282]

Radak had clearly turned to the wrong person. Alfakhar viewed
the whole episode in terms of stereotypes, of heroes and anti-
heroes. R. Solomon was the white knight

whose name shines before the sun . . . , and was zealous for
God and His honor. He—with his disciple R. Jonah ben
Amittai—rejected you to avenge the Lord with all his heart,
all his soul, and all his might, with the holy vessels and the
trumpets of alarm in his hands. He sounds the alarm and the
call. He overcomes his enemies and vents his fury at those
who transgress religion.[283]

Radak was the rationalist rebel. It was as if Radak's devotion to
traditional learning were nothing. It was as if his minuscule allegorical commentaries were everything. All Alfakhar could and would
provide was stern counsel not to "remain in internal contention
and backsliding, ignoring the debates of Abbaye and Rava (talmudic studies) and attempting to ascend the Chariot (metaphysical
speculation)."[284]

This harvest of wrath was never reaped. It is not that Radak was
not impressed. The letter simply went astray and did not reach its
destination.[285] The traditional comedy of errors ensued. Radak
rebuked Alfakhar for not replying. Alfakhar replied with a second
letter expressing his surprise at what appeared to be Radak's im-
patience and confirming support once again for R. Solomon and
his disciples.[286]

Radak had now left Ávila and returned to Burgos. Here he received a report of Alfakhar's first letter from people who heard it
"from the mouth of the bearer of your letter who wanted to
vaunt my disgrace."[287] His reply was brief and to the point. He
spelled out R. Solomon's role in the betrayal of the *Guide* to the
Catholic clergy and hoped thereby to tarnish his image somewhat.

In the interim, word had spread concerning Alfakhar's harsh-
ness toward Radak and a reaction began to set in. Radak's ally in

Provence, R. Meshullam ben Kalonymos, wrote Alfakhar entreat-
ing him to "lift the reproach of the great sage R. David Kimhi
and to have consideration for his age. Do not condemn his teachings. Desist from your complaint against him."[288] Indeed, Alfakhar's behavior had such an impact that Joseph ben Todros, who
had heaped his own measure of abuse upon Radak, made a similar
appeal to Alfakhar.[289] Under the weight of public opinion, Alfakhar promised to restrain himself. He would curb his anger. He
would "remember David's humility and no longer persecute
him."[290] As a sign of his change of heart, Alfakhar decided to
send Radak a brief courtesy note. A model of self-righteous indig-
nation, it eloquently reveals the extent of his pacification.

> Open rebuke and abundant words are better than flattery and
> a soft tongue without concealed love. I said to myself that
> with a reproof to the wise, one can cleanse him whiter than
> snow. Rebuke your fellow and be not held sinful on account
> of your companions . . . I did not want to glory in your
> disgrace but to quiet your thunder and to restrain your fool-
> ish thoughts. Rather did I wish to glory in your praise and
> to support you in love . . . I wanted to . . . persuade you in
> the thought that I could be of use in lighting the path for
> your return.[291]

Radak, however, had no intention of returning; he had never
left. This he would now make clear. Despite Alfakhar's obtuseness
and desire to let the matter rest, there remained too much that
could not be left unsaid. Radak briefly responds to Alfakhar's
charges of Maimonolatry with the counter-charge that the anti-
Maimonists have sworn blind allegiance to R. Solomon, "placing
him in an inner chamber, and have made of him an image and
likeness contrary to the words of the true Torah, *for you saw no
form* (Deuteronomy 4:15)."[292]

But the question of personalities had now become peripheral.
The main issue was the stereotyped conception of the "Maimonists" as rebels and iconoclasts. If Alfakhar wished to use Radak as
an example of such backsliding, Radak did not object to presenting himself as evidence either. In answer to charges that he neglected "the debates of Abbaye and Rava," he affirms: "My feet
did not totter nor did I walk along an uncertain path. I am he who
devotedly chose the debates of Abbaye and Rava. They are my

lot. With them I have grown old . . . As all know, there is no rabbi in Spain more meticulous than I in observing the words of the rabbis."[293]

Yet, more significant, he was not an isolated instance of the successful fusion of rationalism and faithfulness to the Torah. This was characteristic of the Provençal communities in general.

> We are the ones who maintain religion, following without hypocrisy the words of the rabbis. We attend the House of God at dawn and even, standing in fear and trembling as befitting an Israelite. We are meticulous in the observance of religious law . . .
>
> We have inherited the legacy of our father Abraham of which God testified *to the end that he command his children and his household after him* (Genesis 18:19). Our houses are open wide to every passer-by and to all who seek rest. We weary ourselves day and night over the Torah and secretly support the poor. We do justice at every opportunity. Among us are those who provide books for the poor who have none and who give stipends for the study of Bible and Talmud.
>
> *Can you say of such as these that they are transgressors? Heaven forbid!*[294]

Radak's defense remains at the level of the practical. The rationalist should be judged by his deeds. As far as scientific pursuits are concerned, he follows the counsel of King Solomon "who taught us, *Do what your capabilities lead you to do* (Ecclesiastes 9:10) and *it is good that you take hold of the one—but do not let go of the other* (Ecclesiastes 7:18). Since I could," he tells us, "I did."[295] But, Radak claims, so did Alfakhar. In fact, Radak expected to discuss certain metaphysical points with the Toledan: " I wanted to meet you and ask you of certain problems face to face since I did not want to write them down."[296] It is this that lies at the root of the impasse. Radak conceived of a rationalist as one who lets his "reason" be a determining influence in his thinking and not just a support for preestablished notions. For Alfakhar, on the other hand, Radak's allegations of piety were unsupported by intellectual integrity. The rationalists' claim of credence in such basic principles as creation, miracles, and resurrection was given the lie by the mass of subterfuge and ambiguity characteristic of their thinking. Although Alfakhar's critique is directed principally against Maimonides, Radak might well be included in the indictment.

The Question of the "Supernatural"

Radak, for example, keeps one in suspense on the question of miracles. At times, he seems to accept the most fantastic of disruptions in the course of nature: the speech of the serpent in Eden[297] or the unusual longevity of the Jews in the future.[298] Of course, it is not terribly inconvenient to accept that which one was going to allegorize anyway or that which has not yet taken place. Yet others do seem to be accepted at face value: the miracles of the Exodus[299] or the floating axe-head of Elisha.[300] Even the rabbinic tradition of the *shamir*,[301] the insect that cut the stones of Solomon's temple so that iron would not have to be used, is "not to be questioned."[302] It seems axiomatic that God, who set the rules of nature, could disregard them: "Everything is in his hands, even to the point of changing the fundamental nature of things."[303] "God *forms the mountains and creates the wind* (Amos 4:13) and does what He wishes with the creatures."[304] In the words of Hannah: "*There is no rock like our God* (I Samuel 2:2). There is none as strong as our God for He changes nature as He wills. I was barren and it was not in my nature to give birth."[305] All this, of course, may stand in harmony with the rabbinic dictum, which Radak cites approvingly,[306] that certain miracles were preordained or "created" during the six days of creation.[307]

Yet beyond this, more drastic attempts at rationalization are evident. There is first of all the attempt to limit the miraculous quantitatively. Whereas Alfakhar claims that if one accepts one miracle, one might as well accept them all,[308] Radak demonstrates selectivity. Although he uses context as the decisive factor, the miracle of the walls of Jericho is still modified by the claim that only a part of the wall fell.[309] More significant, the "supernatural" is generally seen as coming about through "natural" means: "Even though He changes the order of the world in some miracles— such as the splitting of the Red Sea and the Jordan and the causing of the sun to stand still—He will not do so with most miracles. Even in granting victory in war to those who love Him, He does so through a cause which is usual in circumstances of war."[310]

Ultimately, "even though the Holy One, blessed be He, performs miracles and wonders with those who fear Him, they generally follow the course of nature."[311] Thus the acts of revival of Elijah and Elisha may have been brought about by natural means: "As we explained concerning Elijah, it states *he stretched out on the boy* (I Kings 17:21) . . . It is possible that he meant to transfer natural heat from his body through respiration for most miracles are performed with a minimum of invention."[312]

More than this, however, Radak seems to demonstrate the same kind of prevarication with respect to these miracles of resurrection as that evinced by Maimonides. Maimonides attributes his evasive interpretation to an "Andalusian,"[313] a ploy which fooled neither his antagonists[314] nor his protagonists.[315] Radak seems to do very much the same sort of thing. He rejects the insinuation that the child had never really died at all and insists that "he actually died as people think."[316] Yet later, he cites Jonathan's translation of I Kings 17:20, *Let not evil be brought upon the widow with whom I sojourn and let her son not die,* in the belief that "this supports that which we wrote concerning [the interpretation] that he did not die completely."[317] In the same way Radak insists that the ravens that fed Elijah are "ravens just [as it says]." He adds, however, that "there are those who interpret the word *'orevim* as *"merchants"* as in *"'oreve ma'aravekh"* (exchangers of your merchandise) (Ezekiel 27:27)."[318] Radak's ambiguity, intentional or unintentional, comes to effective expression in his treatment of the account of the witch of Endor. Radak begins with a straightforward elucidation of the "raising" of Samuel as if the account were to be taken at face value. He then—according to the Soncino edition of 1486—"sees fit to explain the necromancy according to that which is written concerning it (*le-fi mah she-nimza katuv bo*)." There follows a citation of rabbinic passages[319] on the topic plus some explanatory material of Maimonides.[320] At this point, Radak states that "we have seen a controversy among the Geonim in this matter. They are all in agreement that necromancy is nonsense and absurdity, lies and mockery." They all concur, of course, that the witch had no prophetic or mantic function. Samuel ben Hofni held the view that the entire episode was a staged performance and that the witch's "prophecy" was a combination of common sense and common knowledge. On the other hand, Hai Gaon and Saadia Gaon accepted the appearance of Samuel but insisted that the witch had no part in it. God raised him in order to inform Saul of his fate. Radak expresses wonder at these remarks:

> If God raised Samuel in order to inform Saul of his fate, why did he not tell him through dreams or through the Urim or through a prophet instead of this necromanceress? Further, if the "necromancy" was in fact a man speaking from his hiding-place, how could this escape Saul, who was a king and a sage in the company of sages? Who could say that he would err this way? It is not reasonable. The correct interpretation is ours.

Apparently then, Radak rejects both of the geonic interpretations in favor of his own. The immediate problem is, of course: What *is* his interpretation? He does not say. An examination of the manuscripts helps somewhat. In no manuscript (of over twenty I examined) does the passage quoted above, "Further, if the 'necromancy' . . . The correct interpretation is ours," appear. If this is deleted, it would appear that Radak in effect rejects only the interpretation of the Geonim Hai and Saadia and tacitly assents to that of Samuel ben Hofni. Yet a further complication ensues. A good number of the manuscripts agree with Soncino in reading "I see fit (*va-ʾani roʾeh*) to explain the necromancy according to that which is written concerning it."[321] Yet others read "I do *not* (*ve-ʾeni roʾeh*) see fit to explain the necromancy since one finds [the following] written concerning it (*le-fi she-nimẓa katuv bo*) . . ."[322] Radak's lack of explicit commitment to any one interpretation thus led the scribes to develop two different traditions concerning his intent. Indeed, one cannot claim with any measure of finality that Radak denied the possibility of a communication from Samuel himself. That a prophet could "prophesy" post-humously is seen from the letter which Elijah sent to Jehoram several years after the prophet's ascension (II Chronicles 21:12). Radak simply observes:

> This occurred after Elijah ascended. He appeared to one of the prophets through the spirit of prophecy and placed the contents of this letter into that prophet's mouth. He told him to write it down and bring it to Jehoram with the message that Elijah is sending him this letter. Jehoram, thus thinking that the letter is coming from heaven, would become contrite.[323]

There was, in effect, only one "supernatural" occurrence openly rejected by Radak: the corporeal ascension of Elijah itself. He states that it is "the opinion of our masses and indeed of our sages that God brought him bodily into paradise—just as Adam before he sinned—and that He took up Enoch in the same fashion." Radak grants that Elijah was raised in fire but maintains that only the spirit of Elijah ascended to paradise while his corporeal remains were burnt to ashes.[324]

Even without "rationalistic" considerations, Radak's involvement in an ongoing anti-Christian polemic would cause him discomfort enough in discussions of "bodily assumptions" and "resurrections."[325] *The* resurrection at the end of days, which formed such a pivotal question in the Maimonidean controversy, is, to be sure, affirmed in the most concrete terms. Although the whole concept of resurrection is scientifically untenable,[326] "According to the belief of the faithful seed of Israel, souls will return to their original matter . . . at the time of the resurrection which God promised us. It will take place miraculously and wondrously and not by natural means."[327]

Radak sees reference to resurrection in a number of passages.[328] That Ezekiel appears to be himself commanded to carry out the sàcrificial cult is taken as evidence that he will be raised from the dead to do so.[329] *They shall serve . . . their King David whom I shall raise up* (Jeremiah 30:9) may very well refer to the resurrected King David himself, in Radak's opinion.[330]

Yet whatever Radak's reaction to miracle and resurrection—affirming, denying, or both at once—his treatment is perfunctory and unenthusiastic. Ultimately Radak is far more impressed by natural law than by miracle. In a long aside, Radak points to the vulnerability of miracles. They can be easily denied. But the regularity of nature as proof of God's power cannot be gainsaid.[331] The thought of resurrection can only provide comfort for the future.

> It is true that reward and punishment is mainly a matter of the next world. However, what is discussed *here* is *not* a matter of the next world . . . They were not perturbed about the next world—*for they did not know what it is*—but about what they saw with their own eyes![332]

Radak was a man of the present.

II   Narbona: Exile

I find myself alone among a foreign
people like a bird separated from its
companions. It stays alone on the roof of
the house and will not enter the house lest
they catch it. It seems as if I—in exile—am
sitting on the roof of the house . . .
because I am not in my own land.[1]

A ten-minute stroll from what was once the Villa Juzayga
removes one completely from the confines of the city into the vineyards which are the pride and provisioner of the local population.
At dusk the vine leaves, which appeared citrine-green in full sun-
light, take on a new verdant richness; the terra cotta of the soil
deepens with the setting sun. The vineyards are cloistered with
crenellated walls of cane. Wildflowers with colors of the boldness
of a Gothic painting pattern themselves as in a twelfth-century
landscape of Eden. The Corbières loom in the distance, appearing
not to enclose but to emphasize the openness of the plain below.
Viewing this scene for the first time, one finds it strangely, dis-
quietingly, familiar. It seems that this same multihued panorama
has unfolded before—when the plain was the coastal plain of Israel
and the hills were those of Samaria. One feels the need to adminis-
ter a stern rebuke to the imagination for its excessess. But the eye
falls upon a piece of travel literature. It invites the tourist to visit a
nearby beach with its "paysages palestiniens."[2]

Rashi, living at Troyes, took the pluralization of the primordial
"seas" as a sign of diversity. Radak, near the shores of the Mediterranean, took it as an indication of unity.[3] Few are the places where
the unity of the Mediterranean is felt as palpably as at Narbonne.
It is as if the Lord had planted a small piece of the Land of Israel
in Languedoc so that the remnant of His people might prosper and
grow and study the Torah until the time of redemption. If one
were to rely on outward appearances alone, one might think this
was a place where David Kimhi might have felt "at home." That he
too could walk here with his father or his brother or his students
or his friends and dream that he was elsewhere. But then one turns
about and sees the towers of St. Just and the archbishop's palace
dominating this *paysage palestinien*. And one knows—just as Radak
knew—that he is not in the Land of Israel but that he has merely
stepped through the looking-glass. This is the irony of exile: it may

appear the same but the polarity is reversed. If in the Holy Land churches and mosques mar the landscape, it is only an illusion. "For these build it and the others destroy it . . . The builders have built in vain and the watchmen have watched in vain for . . . the Ishmaelites take it . . . from the Christians and they take it back again."[4] But St. Just and the archbishop's palace are otherwise. It would be here and in buildings like them that the prophet's words are reenacted every day: *"Fear not the reproach of men* (Isaiah 51:7). The nations reproach them on account of the perpetuation of the exile."[5] It is here in the cleric's chambers that Israel encounters her "enemy . . . wicked Rome under whom Israel's exile has lasted more than a thousand years and who thinks that the hope of Israel is lost. They rejoice at their misfortune."[6]

It is not the physical trials of the Exile—the Jewish tallage,[7] the despoiling,[8] the incessant wanderings,[9] the persecutions,[10] the deception[11] —that are the most painful. Nor is it even the taunting of the Gentiles;[12] their contemptuous cry: "I'd rather be a Jew than do that!";[13] their questioning whether a Jew is even a human being.[14] It is that they exploit the predicament of the Jew to desecrate the very name of God.[15] On the battlefield of the Book of Psalms, King/Rabbi David stands arrayed against the Philistines/ Christians warding off their barbed spears/tongues: "Throughout the exile, the enemies say to me *Where is your God?* If He were a true God and you served Him, He would save you and take you out of the exile."[16]

> *They profaned My holy name in that men said of them: These are the people of the Lord, and are gone forth out of His land* (Ezekiel 36:20). The Gentiles profane God's name when they say of Israel *These are the people of the Lord*—these had been called the people of the Lord but they went out of His land. He has left them in exile for some time and it is as if they profane Him by the perpetuity of their exile through their sins. The Gentiles say that God is unable to extricate them for they will say "How has God chosen a people and then despised them casting them from His presence?"[17]

"Where is your God," they cry, "let Him come and help you."[18] With each taunt, with each cry of *Where is your God?* it would seem as if "each one of them pierces me with a sword and murders me."[19] Notwithstanding the arsenal of dialectics and *testimonia* with which Radak would wage his counter-attack, his inner anguish would not be assuaged.

> We await redemption every day. It is not enough that You have not saved us but You have rejected us. You have left us in the hands of enemies to harm us. You put us to shame. We praise You to the enemies and tell them that You will most certainly save us. But salvation is far from us. They shame us when they say: "Where are your speeches? Where is one to save you?"[20]

From the shame and disgrace there is no escape—only helplessness, isolation, paralysis.

> *They have circumscribed me [like lions]* (Psalms 22:17). A lion marks off an area in the forest with his tail. Every animal that sees the circle will not go beyond it for fear of the lion. With their hands and feet withdrawn, the lion finds his prey within the circle. So are we in exile: in a circle from which we cannot emerge without falling into the hands of those who would prey [on us]. If we leave the territory of the Ishmaelites, we come into that of the Christians. So we draw in our hands and feet and stand frightened and terrified before them. We can neither flee by foot nor fight with our hands. It is as if our hands and feet were in chains.[21]

Outside the circle lies Jerusalem, the Land of Israel: the highest,[22] the choicest,[23] the most righteous[24] of lands; the land most beneficial to one's spiritual[25] and physical[26] well-being; the land of life;[27] the land in which God's presence dwells;[28] the place of perfection—moral, physical, spiritual. Better it would be to stand at the threshold of the House of God than to occupy a whole dwelling in the lands of the Gentiles.[29]

Yet Radak saw the road to Jerusalem as sealed. With all his journeys, he never seems to have attempted to reach this one place that was foremost in his consciousness. It is of course possible that he did not go simply because he could not afford it. The miracle of the manna was reenacted for Judah Halevi in the form of his patron Abul Rabia.[30] Radak, who relied not on miracles,[31] apparently had none performed for him. Nor would he take from another. As he tells of Samuel, *"Then he would come back to Ramah for his home was there* (I Samuel 7:17). Our rabbis

expounded: Everywhere he went, his home was with him; that is
to say, he would never have benefit of that which belonged to
another but only of his own."[32] Unfortunately, he came too early
for the travel grant, or perhaps too late. He tells us that the discrepancy in the sums reported in Kings[33] and in Chronicles[34]
concerning the gold sent by Hiram to Solomon was due to the
deduction of travel expenses.

Then too the perils of the journey were well known. For
"home consumption," Joseph Kimhi could speak of the fine and
temperate air of Jerusalem which would heal all those who needed
healing. Yet he tells the Christians that now, in the days of exile,
Jerusalem inflicts only illness upon those who visit her. If one sur-
vives that, then "the Ishmaelites seize him from the hands of the
Gentiles (Christians)."[35] Yet even if one could leap the barrier, it
would be of no avail. To live in the Land means to live in the
restored Land. One cannot go there alone.

> If these men, Noah, Daniel, and Job were in it, they would
> deliver but their own lives by their righteousness (Ezekiel
> 14:14). Daniel in his righteousness could save none but him-
> self but from exile he could not save [even] himself. How
> could he remain in the Land alone? [Even if he were with]
> his righteous companions, Ezekiel, Hananiah, Mishael and
> Azariah, how could they stay alone in a desolate land?[36]

There is an elusiveness about the unrestored Land. It eludes the
Gentiles, who fight over it.[37] It eludes the Jew, who searches for it,
who guards it only in his prayers.[38] There is a place called Jerusalem but it is not the real Jerusalem. It is only in the future that
"Jerusalem shall sit in its former place in the place known as Jerusalem today."[39]

So the Jew, so Radak, remains in the circle. He is the bird
stranded on the rooftop.[40] He is caught in an inescapable snare.[41]
He drowns in the depths of the waters.[42] He suffers endlessly.[43]
He stands at sword's point.[44] He thirsts in the wilderness.[45] He
dies.[46] Would that he could remain alive long enough to see the
redemption. He longs for life as much as that unknown descen-
dant of David in every generation longs to be the redeemer of
Israel.[47]

> Israel have been in exile so long that it is as if they say our
> bones are dried up and our hope is lost; we are clean cut off

(Ezekiel 37:11) and we will not see the redemption of Israel. How will we live to [the age of] a thousand or more? We ourselves are cut off.[48]

Radak is enshrouded in darkness[49] and yearns so for light. Light gladdens the heart![50] He is sensitive to the play of light and shade: he enjoys stained glass and envisages the possible creation of such an effect in the future Temple.[51] Individual colors are of lesser consequence. Where another's amplifications of the Chariot visions could serve as a sketch pattern for a manuscript illumination,[52] Radak dismisses the colors as being beyond his ken.[53] His is a world all black and white, the presence of light and its absence, with tones of gray filling the spectrum.

> *Woe to us, for the day declines, for the shadows of evening lengthen* (Jeremiah 6:4). The light has dimmed and the shadows lengthen and spread for we have no light but darkness.[54]

"Light," "morning," "day," are words of joy and redemption. "Darkness," "evening," "night," speak of anguish and exile.[55] "*We hope for light and there is darkness* (Isaiah 59:9). Every day we hope for light and salvation which is the light and there is darkness, exile—and the sorrows of exile are darkness and blindness."[56]

Darkness is exile and black the color of the religions of the exile. He superimposes contemporary reality on the biblical past (note the present tense):

> *He deposes the idolatrous priests* (*ha-kemarim*) (II Kings 23:5). The people who function before Baal are called *kemarim* just as the Targum . . . [calls] those priests who are idolators *kumraya* . . . for the *kemarim* wear black . . . as in the verse, *Our skin is as black (nikhmaru) as an oven* (Lamentations 5:10).[57]

If black is the color of the priest of Baal as well as that of Christianity, white is the color of the Torah, which the Gentiles ever blemish and blacken. Thus does Radak speak of the fourth chariot of Zechariah, which he refers to Rome:

> . . . *and the fourth chariot dappled (beruddim) red horses* (Zechariah 6:3). He showed him (the prophet) this hue in

association with the Kingdom of Rome since they think that they are in possession of the Torah of Moses our Teacher which is white as hail (*barad*). Yet they discolor it with corrupt beliefs just as the hailstones appear to be discolored or blackened.[58]

As exile dims the light, so does it impede the acquisition of wisdom.

Radak would have preferred to follow his conception of the Davidic ideal: exclusive devotion to the acquisition of wisdom. With his king, he longed to behold "*the graciousness of the Lord,* that is to say that he would have the leisure to visit and search out the separate intellects which are the angels of heaven from which the soul is derived and to which it is to return."[59] One suspects that even at the beginning of his literary career he already felt that longing for peace to which he was later to give expression. In the same way in which he depicted King David, he would seek "respite from having to deal with all these wars so that his body and soul would be free to dwell in the House of the Lord."[60] Radak would face many a war and fight many a battle both within and without the camp of Israel. Whoever his adversaries might be, he would continue to see them as Sauls or Philistines ever involving him in exiles or wars, ever distracting him from "the light of life."

> While I am still cast about in the exile, I have no leisure to engage in the ways of God. When You rescue me and I return to the Land of Israel and join the sages of Israel, I shall study and pass my time with them in matters of the soul which is the *light of life* and *walking before God.*[61]

". . . For in exile they had no leisure and could not devote their full concentration to the Lord their God."[62] King David had "no sages with him in his wanderings—only the poor and sorry few who accompanied him."[63] In the Land of Israel, on the other hand, not only will he be among sages, but to the astonishment of his foreign counterparts, he will be able to maintain his state almost routinely with most of his time devoted to the Torah: "All the other kings must toil and be concerned with affairs of state. When they see me concerning myself with Torah . . . they will speak against me."[64]

Indeed, the feeling that exile dissipates one's intellectual energies was hardly unique to Radak. It had been well articulated by Maimonides.[65] This sense of frustration was so generally shared in

pre-Kimhian Provence that it had practical consequences: an early
document, the *Torah Statutes,* probably of Provençal origin, limits
the size of classes to ten pupils

> even though the Sages said[66] that there should be twenty-five
> pupils to a teacher. But that applies to the Land of Israel,
> which by its very nature bestows wisdom, as well as to a time
> when Israel dwells in its own land and is self-governing. For
> the free soul is loftier, stronger, purer, clearer and more cap-
> able of intellectual achievement . . . while the subjugated soul
> is downcast, weak, arid and incapable of intellectual achieve-
> ment since it is subjected to hard and bold masters and all
> the fruits of her effort and toil go to one who toils not. It is
> endlessly troubled by hard labor and overcome by fear—and
> fear restricts wisdom.[67]

For Radak, exile seems to have tempered levity as well. Only in
an occasional anti-Christian remark will Radak attempt a pun or a
quip.[68] To be sure, the "holy spirit descends only in the midst of
joy"[69] but it is to be a restrained joy.[70] Exile has put a damper on
the holy spirit[71] and on Radak's spirits in general: "Even when I
want to enjoy myself, they make me miserable with their conten-
tiousness. They are like those who would give gall and wormwood
to a starving man and vinegar to one who thirsts."[72]

He had little heart for song: nonlliturgical poetry seems to have
made but slight impression on him. It existed, as did animals and
flowers, only to provide data for comparative philology.[73] One
wine song, quoted from Moses Ibn Ezra, makes his position clear.

> All men are fine,
> Save the publicans bold,
> Who pour out your wine,
> And take in your gold.[74]

Yet if there was no love lost on the publican, his wares enjoyed no
little esteem. Living in the midst of Corbières viticulture, Radak
praises the virtues of wine. Yet it is most virtuous in the glass of a
sage such as, say, himself. "Common people," however, "become
intoxicated and lose their senses."[75] He was apparently no stranger
to scenes of drunkenness and shows his contempt for it in graphic
descriptions.[76] He goes so far as to hold overindulgence account-
able for the first exile.[77]

If Radak had no call to secular poetry, he seems to have attempted at least one piece of liturgical writing. While this might not be worthy of special commendation by the literary critic, it is not without interest for the literary historian. Not surprisingly, its theme is once again light. Entitled in manuscript "An Excellent Prayer for Every Morning,"[78] the poem is an alphabetical acrostic which begins and ends every line with the word "morning." To Radak morning is a time of special grace, the time of prophecy. "*I repeatedly sent my servants the prophets to them early in the day* (Jeremiah 7:26). Every morning—for most of the admonishing would take place in the morning before one would go to work."[79] In this mood, he sings:

> At morning turn to me, O turn,
>   Afflicted and dismayed,
> Restore the prophet's vision—
>   For it was he *who said*
>   *There comes the morn.*
>   (Isaiah 21:12)[80]

Morning too is the most propitious time for prayer.[81] It is both the time when God's first born cries for relief from the weight of his yoke and the time when he shall joyously celebrate the redemption.[82]

> At morning shall my soul array
>   To you its finest paean,
> And I to You shall surely sing
>   At the very moment *when*
>   *Stars of morn together sing!*
>   (Job 38:7)[83]

Radak's prayer is a mosaic of verses describing the dark night of Israel's soul. Like a child stumbling in the blackness, "how his soul cries to You with no reply! How great is his terror before morning!"[84] Longing for the dawn of redemption when Israel's enemies shall be subjugated and shall learn to fear the one God, he cries:

> Make pure at morning those who wait,
>   The fallen tabernacle lift,
> Declare the guilt of those who hate,
>   To the right may they submit
>   At morning.[85]

Israel, "having raised our eyes and waited for the light at morn," calls for rescue from the pit[86] and the stumbling block, images of the exile.

> Show morning then to those dispersed,
>   Send them from the captive's pit,
> —No water to be found in it—
>   At eventide when they rehearse—
> > *Let come the morn!*[87]

But morning would not come and many were those who wearied of the waiting. They had waited too long now; to wait longer would be to wait in vain.[88]

The preachers—and Radak among them—could urge that God punishes those He loves so that their end be blessed;[89] that man is ultimately responsible for that which befalls him;[90] that God's ways are inscrutable;[91] that we are not to question Him;[92] that even Moses did not understand such ultimate questions as the "prosperity of the wicked in this world and the tribulations of the righteous in this world."[93] Yet the conventional consolations and theodicies made little impression. No longer could some believe that there is One "who watches over and sees . . . Some of our people say: *God does not see us* (Psalms 92:9)."[94] They "*walk contrary (be-qeri) to Me* (Leviticus 26:2): You will say that the chastisement I bring upon you is by chance (*be-miqreh*)."[95] The plaint over these misguided[96] deniers[97] and fatalists[98] reverberates. The lament over the latter-day "Epicureans" for whom *God has forsaken the earth* (Ezekiel 9:9) resounds.[99] Greater yet was the lament for those whose conclusions came to practical consequences. A later apostate, Abner of Burgos, still echoes the claims which Radak combats.[100]

> I saw the poverty of the Jews, my people, from whom I am descended, who have been oppressed and broken and heavily burdened by taxes throughout their long captivity—this people that has lost its former honor . . . and there is none to help or sustain them. . . . When I had meditated on the matter, I went to the synagogue weeping sorely and sad at heart. And I prayed . . . And in a dream, I saw the figure of a tall man who said to me, "Why dost thou slumber? Hearken unto these words . . . for I say that the Jews have remained so long in captivity for their folly and wickedness and because they

have no teacher of righteousness through whom they may recognize the truth."[101]

These forsook the Torah and apostasized.[102] They abandoned the concept of God's "unity and became like one of the nations under whom they live."[103]

Yet these, great or few as their numbers were,[104] were not at the heart of the issue. In Radak's estimate, at least, there were only a "few who left the fold."[105] These, the Peter Alphonses or the unnamed apostates that Radak received as a legacy from his father,[106] were not even worthy of his contempt. *They* were never even Jews to begin with. *They* are the seed of the "rabble who converted" in the desert[107] and are merely reverting to type.

The true Israelite maintains his faithfulness:

> *They that sow in tears shall reap in joy* (Psalms 126:5). Despite all their misery, Israel in exile sow—and their sowing is the performance of the commandments. They perform them in tears because of the anxiety of the Exile and hope that God will take them out of Exile.[108]

No, they do not give ground.[109] But they do not hold their ground with ease. It is not a question of a few turncoats: "*Many* of Israel despair of the redemption because of the length of the exile."[110] "They falter over God's actions when they see the tranquility of the wicked [= Gentiles] and the sufferings of the righteous [= Israel]."[111] "The House of Israel are in exile so long that they despair of redemption saying: *Our bones are dried up and our hope is lost*" (Ezekiel 37:11).[112] *None* seems to be immune to these doubts. The audacity of even loyal Jews hardly knew any bounds. David himself dares to reveal:

> *My feet were almost gone* (Psalms 73:2). My own feet almost slipped away from the faith when I saw the tranquility of the wicked. I almost said there is no justice and no judge. *My steps had well nigh slipped* (*ibid.*) I was almost completely bolted from my faith.[113]

Before God, he claims: "You have the power to relieve our anguish. [Yet] You do not do so but leave us in Exile for so long. It is as if You lead us astray from Your ways."[114]

Some found such sentiments unspeakable. One pious and learned gentleman in Spain could not bear to read the eighty-ninth psalm because it contained the verse, *You have cast off and rejected* (v. 39). Some exegetes, such as Abraham Ibn Ezra, obligingly took the edge off the passage for the benefit of such delicate temperaments.[115] But not Radak. He was

> bewildered by their bewilderment. The Psalms were said through the holy spirit. There can be nothing in them which is incorrect. If the poet wonders about the length of the exile, he did not say that God has forgotten His promise. Yet he does wonder about this exile because it has lasted so long . . . that they have almost despaired of redemption. So the poet asks in bewilderment why this is and what is the source of the wrath. Moses, our master, said, *Remember Abraham, Isaac, and Israel Your servants to whom You swore* (Exodus 32:13). Thus the poet says: "How can You do this since You swore?" Isaiah the prophet said: *Why do You make us err from Your ways?* (Isaiah 63:17). Elijah said: *You turned their heart backward* (I Kings 18:37). Shall we say that they all spoke improperly? They merely spoke figuratively. The poet said: "You have sworn to him and cast him off these many years. It seems as if You no longer remember."[116]

Radak sees no place here for exegetical ingenuity. Be the answers what they be, the questioning, the uncertainty, the doubting are in earnest. There is justice in the "claim against God because of the shame you bore among the Gentiles throughout the long exile"; in the claim that "if we sinned, we have received more than enough punishment. It has reached the point that our hope is lost because of the length of the exile."[117]

In endless tones and shadings, this claim was to be blocked on to the fabric of Radak's life. It was to be a peculiar fabric: the woof—centuries of Jewish experience and learning; the warp—the consciousness of domination by an alien faith in an alien land. Wool and linen together.

III   The Way of *Peshaṭ*

As previously noted, Radak's activities as teacher and preacher did not come to literary expression until his fifth decade.[1] However, once his pen was put to parchment, it seems never to have been stilled again in his lifetime. Apart from the occasional halakhic works he may have written,[2] his literary activities were centered upon philology and biblical exegesis, the family specializations.

The *Mikhlol*

Radak began with the *Mikhlol,*[3] a grammatical work in two parts: the morphological and syntactic section, the *ḥeleq ha-diqduq* or the *Mikhlol* per se, and the lexical portion (*ḥeleq ha-'inyan*), generally known as the *Shorashim* (*Roots*).[4] In hindsight, the interdependence of Radak's two *magna opera,* the *Mikhlol* and the commentaries, is so obvious that one might indeed believe that the former was consciously written as a prolegomenon to the latter; that all the while Radak, the conscientious pedagogue, was systematically planning his syllabus.

The *Mikhlol* was conceived as an attempt to fulfill

> the wishes of those who are wiser and greater than I [who were dissatisfied] with the works of the authors who preceded me because of the great effort [involved in reading them] and because of the great difficulty involved in understanding those which were translated from Arabic into Hebrew. I saw that I would benefit from the composition of this work by reviewing what I had learned in my youth and by acquiring new knowledge. So I overcame my indolence and undertook to see this work through with the help of Him Who gives fortitude to the tottering and succor to the weak.[5]

Over and above the personal benefit which Radak hoped to derive—the chance to review and consolidate his own knowledge—

Radak's stated aim was the imposition of order on the confusion
which prevailed because of the plethora of works bequeathed to
his generation by such philologists as R. Judah Hayyuj, Jonah Ibn
Janah, Abraham Ibn Ezra, his father, and his brother. In this
activity, Radak styled himself "the gleaner after the reapers"[6] and
rarely has an author's self-assessment been taken so seriously by
his critics. For A. Geiger, Radak was industrious but plodding.[7]
Graetz, with his accustomed certitude, found that "if any value is
to be set on his grammatical, lexicographical and exegetical works,
we must ignore the fact that Ibn-Janach, Moses Ibn-Gikatilia and
Ibn-Ezra lived before him, for with these he cannot bear comparison. David Kimchi did not establish one original point of view."[8]
One may debate this point, as do those who are most familiar with
the *Mikhlol* and most qualified to judge it.[9] To his contemporaries,
certainly, Radak was anything but conventional. An entire treatise,
the *Shield of David*[10] of Elisha ben Abraham ben Mattathias, was
written to defend Radak against the strictures of his successors.[11]
Yet to argue the question of Radak's originality of capacity for
grammatical innovation[12] is largely to miss the point. His concern
and his achievement went beyond the promulgation of new grammatical theories or refinements. Rather, his accomplishment in the
field of philology was the recognition that the era of new contri-
butions and refinements had reached its conclusion; that virtually
all that the Middle Ages had to learn about grammar had been
learned. Radak did not come to plant trees in an already crowded
forest but to find the forest. In the epilogue to the *Book of Roots,*
Radak states the obstacles and the means of overcoming them.
There were essentially two difficulties—the first: the fact that many
of the early treatises were written in Arabic, which made them
inaccessible to the members of the Provençal communities; the
second: the sheer quantity of material available. The prolixity of
the Spanish grammarians had already been lamented by Ibn Ezra.
One could "occupy himself all his life reading the books of R.
Judah (Hayyuj), the first grammarian; and the ten books of R.
Marinus (Ibn Janah); and the twenty books of R. Samuel the
Nagid—of which Solomon said, *of making books there is no end*
(Ecclesiastes 12:12)."[13] The brevity and conciseness of Ibn Ezra
himself and of the elder Kimhis were in large measure a corrective
to this. Yet succinct and pellucid though they were, their dis-
advantages outweighed their advantages. "Although they are all

fine flour," observed a later critic, "not one of them provides sufficient knowledge[14] . . . to quench the thirst of the students."[15]
Radak, ever the good Maimonidean, followed the golden mean and
"took the middle course, for his works are lengthy in comparison
to the books which the latter scholars wrote. Yet when compared
to the earlier scholars, they are the epitome of brevity."[16] These
would then be the features that would mark the *Mikhlol:* synthesis
of divergent sources, clarity of language, manageability of length,
topical order, an air of finality and conclusiveness. Radak's aim is
revealed in the very title he adopted for his work: the *Mikhlol,*
the *Summa*. The latter twelfth century saw the appearance of
several *summae* in Jewish literature. The best known of these is the
legal code, the *Mishneh Torah,* of Maimonides. To compare every
effort at compilation and consolidation in this period to the
Mishneh Torah would betray an excess of zeal.[17] Yet the introduction to the *Mikhlol* has a familiar ring:

> . . . Ever since our ancestors were exiled into foreign countries
> they forgot the sacred tongue and trained their children and
> grandchildren to speak the language of the respective nations
> among whom they dwelt. We have now left only that which
> is transmitted in writing, namely the twenty-four books [of
> the Bible] and [the few words] of the Mishna . . .
>
> Our learned predecessors have indeed paved the way and
> have taught us the principles of our language. Juda Hayyuj of
> Fez, finding the people slovenly and indiscriminate in their
> use of Hebrew, composed two enlightening treatises on verbs
> containing weak and double letters.
>
> Jona Ibn Janah, subsequently, wrote more copiously on
> Hebrew grammar, to our knowledge, than any of his prede-
> cessors. Others added grammatical treatises of their own, and
> the student will find himself at sea in the midst of so much
> grammatical literature, which requires a lifetime for its
> consumption.
>
> Now, although one should not be ignorant of the science
> of grammar, he ought to devote his time chiefly to the study
> of the Torah, the Talmud, the commentaries, and to the
> practice of the laws. The knowledge of grammar necessary for
> understanding the structure of the language and for employ-
> ing it correctly in speech and in writing should therefore be
> acquired through a short cut . . .
>
> The Lord has stirred my spirit and strengthened my heart
> to write a book concisely. I come thus like the gleaner after
> the reaper, following the footsteps of my predecessors, but

abridging their material. I called this book *Mikhlol,* for I
intend to include therein succinctly both the grammar and
the lexicography of the Hebrew language and to make it
easily and readily available for the student . . .[18]

Note the structure of the passage: a formulaic lament over the confusion and travails precipitated by the Exile, resulting in the
inability to handle a certain subject adequately; the vastness of the
literature, which renders it nearly impossible to master it; the senti-
ment that indeed other tasks more demanding than the one at
hand remain to be done; a statement of willingness to meet the
challenge and overcome obstacles; the bestowal of a name on the
work indicating its comprehensiveness and reflecting its potential
for rendering other works superfluous.

Despite the obvious generic and qualitative difference between
the *Mikhlol* and the *Mishneh Torah* of Maimonides, certain parallels
between the introductions to the two works emerge. Like Radak,
Maimonides too complains of "vicissitudes" and the "pressures
of hard times."[19] Radak speaks of the loss of the Hebrew
tongue;[20] Maimonides of "wisdom." Where Radak complains of
being "at sea in the midst of so much grammatical literature,"[21]
Maimonides lists the many works of rabbinic literature which
require "a broad mind, a wise soul and considerable study"[22] and
speaks of the recondite nature of the geonic writings which "only
a few individuals properly comprehend."[23] Both men proceed with
spirits stirred—Radak to present Hebrew grammar through "a
short cut,"[24] Maimonides to present halakhah in so concise a
fashion that if he "could put the entire Talmud in one chapter, I
should not put it into two."[25] Both sought to return to writing in
the tongue of the Jews and to present the material in clear
Hebrew.[26]

More striking are the parallels between the respective fates of
the two works. Both the *Mikhlol* and the *Mishneh Torah* were censured for their presumption. Maimonides' critics refrained from
using the term *Mishneh Torah,* the "second Torah," because they
felt that it arrogated too much authority to the code.[27] Indeed, it
is not unlikely that Radak was sensitive to this criticism. In his
writings, he gives as the etymology for *Mishneh Torah* not the
"second Torah" but the teaching (*limmud*) or the expounding
(*perush*) of the Torah.[28] Almost as retribution, Radak's critics
were also apparently reluctant to use the name *Mikhlol* and referred

to the work only by the author's name or by the term "composition" (*ḥibbur*).[29] In some ways, too, similar criticisms were
leveled against the two works. Both were criticized for their failure
to cite the sources of their material.[30] In the case of the *Mishneh
Torah* a large literature came into existence which attempted to
correct this alleged deficiency. The *Mikhlol* too, which was more
intent on text than on footnotes, was the target of similar objec-
tions, and we find Solomon Ibn Melekh's *Mikhlol Yofi* prepared to
correct this. "In this book," remarks Ibn Melekh, "you will often
find that where he wrote 'some explain,' I mention the holder of
that opinion."[31]

Yet there are striking differences in the fate of the two works
too. Whereas the *Mishneh Torah* would provoke a vast new literature of code and commentary on the Talmud which continues
until the present day, the *Mikhlol* settled the issues of Hebrew
grammar for centuries. No grammar of significance—with the pos-
·sible exception of the *Ma'aseh 'Efod* (completed 1403) of Profiat
Duran—would again be written in the Middle Ages. Indeed, when
the Christian scholars of the Reformation began their study of
Hebrew, it was largely to Radak that they turned. Directly or indi-
rectly, they were all his disciples: Reuchlin, Münster, Pagninus,
Luther, the masters of the King James version.[32] Radak so master-
fully and thoroughly settled the problems and issues of biblical
grammar that they would never again form a central concern of a
major Jewish exegete of the Middle Ages or the Renaissance.
Nahmanides, Bahya ben Asher, Gersonides, Abravanel, Sforno
were all free to explore new questions and cruise uncharted waters.
If Radak was an epigon, he was one of those epigons who open a
new era.

The Commentaries

With the exception of the *Scribe's Pen,* a masoretic work which
will be discussed in its proper context, Radak was occupied after
the *Mikhlol* with the writing of his biblical commentaries. There is
no real evidence by which to date these except in relation to one
another. He seems to have begun at the end of the Bible with the
Chronicles commentary and concluded with that on Genesis,[33] so
that the order would be Chronicles,[34] Psalms,[35] Former Prophets,[36]
Latter Prophets,[37] and Genesis.[38] The philosophical commentaries

to the Hexaemeron (the account of creation in Genesis)[39] and the Chariot vision of Ezekiel[40] appear to have been in existence at the time of the composition of the general commentaries.[41] Radak, like other exegetes,[42] does not seem to have set his commentaries aside once they were completed, for they show signs of reworking and revision. Thus while he referred in his commentary to Chronicles to "what we are going to explain in Kings,"[43] he mentioned elsewhere in the same commentary that "we have explained this matter in the Book of Kings."[44]

There are occasional references to commentaries other than the above-mentioned. At one extreme, we hear of expositions of all the "twenty-four sacred books."[45] On a less ambitious scale, Solomon Ibn Melekh tells us that while he has "in fact not found any commentaries of R. David Kimhi to the four [latter] books of the Torah, nor to Job, Proverbs, Daniel or Ezra," he claims to have heard that he "will find . . . [them] someplace."[46] Others have spoken of Torah commentaries;[47] still another of having seen a commentary on Job which "is not yet in print."[48] It is difficult to evaluate these statements. It is possible that in certain instances a specific commentary is not meant but that the grammatical writings, *qua* exegetical works, are intended. It is not impossible either that some of these "commentaries" consisted of extracts from the *Mikhlol* and *Shorashim.*[49] Solomon Ibn Melekh did precisely this in his *Mikhlol Yofi,* and more than one such project has been undertaken in modern times.[50]

The commentary to Proverbs has been particularly elusive. Ibn Melekh included it among the commentaries that he "would find someplace." Gedaliah Ibn Yahya refers to it, although less than enthusiastically.[51] Later David Ibn Yahya (ca. 1440–1524) claimed to have actually used it.[52] Yet, though beckoning, it has mockingly withdrawn at each approach. Take, for example, Ms. Parma 2348, which purports to contain a fragment of Radak's commentary on Proverbs.[53] This fragment turns out to be of a most rudimentary nature and does little more than parse the verses—hardly up to Kimhian standards. Pass on then to Ms. Escorial G-II-6. This codex boldly asserts on the title page that it houses "the commentary on the five scrolls by Rabbi Solomon . . . and the commentary to the Book of Proverbs and the Commentary to Chronicles of Rabbi David Kimhi." Clearly a case of false advertising. In the words of the cataloguer: "in spite of the note, the commentary to Proverbs

is not to be found in the codex, which does not seem otherwise
incomplete, although burned at the edges in the fire of 1671."[54]
The commentary on Proverbs would have remained the proverbial
closed book had not Umberto Cassuto reexamined Ms. Vatican
Ebr. 89, which contains a Proverbs commentary ascribed to
Joseph Kimhi. Cassuto concluded not only that this text is wrongly
ascribed to the father but that it is indeed the work of the son.[55]
A close reading of the commentary will confirm his findings.[56]
Radak would not have been at all appalled at his commentary's
falling into oblivion. In his introduction, he stresses that an
"author's name should be made known so that the public may
know whether he is sufficiently wise and competent in science so
that one may rely on him."[57] With Radak's persistent belief in the
principle of "measure for measure," such a turn of events should
have proved inevitable.

External Form and Characteristics

Radak's exegesis, the product of a mature scholar, was the literary expression of a long and many-faceted career. Teacher, linguist,
homilist, talmudist, and rationalist all converge in the written
words. Radak, for example, like Rashi, was a practicing pedagogue.[58] Both men left this fact indelibly stamped on their writings. Yet the difference in style and manner of presentation of
these two masters is considerable. Rashi's commentaries are in the
form of seminar notes which have been reworked, reformed, and
repolished by him or, in some cases, by his students. Rashi's
perush has been used for centuries as a text for elementary instruction. Yet while it is a commentary which may be used to advantage
by children, it is not a children's commentary. Its precision of
reference, its verbal economy, its subtlety, and its discretion render
it a text which has always initiated more questions than it has
answered and raised more problems than it has solved. Each
remark has prodded countless generations of students, teachers,
and supercommentators into exegeting the exegete and explaining
the explicator.[59] Such has never been the fate of Radak: no super-
commentary has ever been called forth; further clarification is
seldom, if ever, needed. Those who would wish to explain this feature of Radak's writing might feel themselves justified in associat-
ing it with his practical experience in the classroom. One could
suggest too that it has something to do with an attempt to project

to a wide and popular audience. I would suggest, though, that
these are not the causes of his lucidity but rather its effects.

Paraphrase, Targum, and Vernacular

I have spoken before of the group of exegetes that could be
termed the school of Joseph Kimhi. The chief characteristics of
this school lie less in Joseph's exegetical acuities than in his exegetical preoccupations. It is often quipped that the problem in the
study of the Book of Psalms lies in the difficulty of finding the
connection between the chapters; in Proverbs the connection
between the verses; and in Job the connection between the words.
Joseph Kimhi, and later his son Moses, undertook to comment on
the two most syntactically difficult books of the Bible: Proverbs
and Job. This concentration on material of complex structure went
hand in hand with the development of an exegetical approach
ideally suited to it: the paraphrastic method. Instead of merely
talking *about* a passage, they would allow the verse to explain itself
by restructuring and paraphrasing it, moderating it and amplifying
it. Radak adopted this technique throughout all his commentaries,
steadily perfecting and refining it as he proceeded from Chronicles
to Psalms and on to Genesis. In this way, Radak does not limit
himself to the annotation of an *incipit,* which yields a series of
notes. Rather he builds his remarks around the biblical text itself
so that text and commentary are interwoven. The impression is
thus created that the commentator has withdrawn and that the
Bible has undertaken to explain itself. A key word in this connection, reappearing time and time again, is *kelomar, that is to say,*
the sign of equivalence between a terse and potentially obscure
biblical passage and the leisurely, pellucid, Kimhian paraphrase.

> *And by the ministry of the prophets have I used similitudes*
> (Hosea 12:11), *that is to say,* I have placed similitudes and
> parables at the disposal of the prophets as in the parable of
> Isaiah *My well-beloved had a vineyard* (Isaiah 5:1) and the
> passage *Your origin and your nativity* (Ezekiel 16:3ff.).[60]

Or:

> *They buried him in Ramah and in his city* (I Samuel 28:3).
> Since there were two Ramahs—as it says *from Ramathaim*

(the two Ramahs, I Samuel 1:1)—it says *and in his city, that is to say,* that Ramah which was his city.[61]

More often than not, however, *kelomar* is omitted and the verse itself is set into the commentary as tiles into a mosaic. This reaches its greatest effect in poetic passages:

> *O Lord, my strength, my stronghold, and my refuge* (Jeremiah 16:19) . . . You are the *Lord* Who are *my strength* against those who fight against me. I shall take *refuge* in You *in the day of trouble.* Those whom I reprove over idolatry do not want to turn from their evil way. But I know that the time will come when even the most distant nations will repent *and will come to You from the ends of the earth*—coming to You in this place—*and will say "Our fathers have inherited nothing but lies and nonsense" . . .* (Jeremiah 16:19).[62]

To study such a passage in the original Hebrew and to observe the expansion and translation from the lofty biblical idiom into the elegant but straightforward rabbinic dialect is to become aware of the significance of another aspect of Radak's commentaries: his extraordinary use of Targum, the Aramaic translations of the Bible, "Onkelos" on the Torah and Pseudo-Jonathan on the Prophets, which were read and studied by Jews long after Aramaic had ceased to be a spoken language. Virtually all the Jewish exegetes used those ancient translations extensively.[63] Abraham Ibn Ezra paid Onkelos, the alleged translator of the Torah, great compliment in the introduction to his Torah commentary. Yet Radak paid the Targumim even greater honor through his actual treatment of them. He cites them copiously,[64] comments upon them and discusses textual variants in them as if they were the biblical text itself;[65] explains their language and methodology;[66] paraphrases them in Hebrew;[67] and expresses great astonishment when the Targumim come up with something he cannot agree with.[68] If then he tends to cite the "good and fitting interpretations"[69] of the Targum so frequently, it is not surprising. Since translation is a form, indeed the most sophisticated form, of paraphrase, the Targum was the first proper exegete, the model and prototype of the Kimhis themselves. And if, after all, the Targum strayed at times from the way of *peshaṭ* and adopted a midrashic view,[70] no matter. Radak himself was known to succumb at times, was he not?

Translation as a form of paraphrase came to expression not only in citations of Targum but in the use of *le'azim,* vernacular translations of Hebrew words. Such translations were common among Hebrew exegetes in northern[71] and southern Europe and were a natural consequence of Jewish bi- or multilingualism. The era when the Israelites, such as those in the Land of Goshen,[72] knew only Hebrew was no more. Indeed, those monolingual Goshenites themselves represented only a minority.[73] Multilingualism seemed to Radak to be the natural state of affairs. He could have made much of the midrashic tradition that the Assyrian Rab-shakeh's knowledge of Hebrew indicates that he was an apostate from Judaism.[74] Yet he refrained from so doing because "there are many people who speak the language of another nation."[75] Radak himself spoke the language of another nation, Provençal, and enriched his writings with frequent references to it. The evolution of these *le'azim* as they pass from manuscript to manuscript can be fascinating. Radak's Provençal may metamorphose from one to another dialect of Catalán, Castilian, Italian, or of Provençal itself in accordance with the origins of the scribe.[76] Preserved in the writings of Radak is an unexplored thesaurus of Old Provençal justly to be compared with the Old French glosses of Rashi.[77]

Usually, but not exclusively,[78] it was the specific and concrete, rather than the general and abstract, which was subjected to romanization. Plants,[79] animals,[80] metals,[81] and tools[82] were given definitive identification through translation. Compared to some, Radak was rigidly scrupulous in accounting for all these aspects of biblical realia.[83] Yet despite occasional reflection on the maternal emotions of bears[84] or the respiratory mechanism of the wild ape,[85] it is clear that Radak is far more interested in names than in their bearers.

Provençal was but one segment on Radak's linguistic sphere. David Kimhi, son and brother of Andalusians, recruited the tongue of Al-Andalus as well. Provence was never Arabic-speaking; yet the erudite—drawing on eastern sources—still employed the language. We thus find Radak quoting one of several Arabic explanations of Moses the Preacher.[86] As befits a non-Arabic-speaking land, however, these explanations were generally limited to what might be derived from the cognate relationship of the two Semitic languages, especially with reference to etymology. The battle over the legitimacy of this procedure had long been settled in Spain.[87] In the tradition of that country, Radak brought such parallels often. Yet beyond this, he employed Arabic as he had Provençal: as a source of *le'azim*. The advantages of this, even to the non-Arabist, are clear. Arabic nomenclature can pinpoint a particular item (again usually a plant or an animal) for him as effectively as Latin nomenclature does for the non-Latinist. One wonders then what Radak's accomplishments in Arabic actually were. Because this was the mother tongue of his parents and elder brother, one might assume that he had at least some passive acquaintance with it.[88] Yet too much more cannot be expected. Second-generation Provençals acquired a proper command of the language only after a considerable expenditure of energy and concentration: Samuel Ibn Tibbon, Radak's friend and an accomplished Arabist, seems to have had a difficult time learning the language.[89] Radak himself shows no evidence of excessive discipline in this regard. Although much of his Arabic is cited without acknowledgment to other sources,[90] a good deal of it appears to have been derived from his colleagues.[91] Even his knowledge of Hebrew-Arabic phonetic correspondences was not faultless. He correctly relates Hebrew *tabbahot* (cooks) to Arabic *tabbākh*[92] but at the same time connects Abishag the *sokhenet,* David's "companion," with Arabic *sukhn* (warm)[93] —an interpretation which is contextually appropriate but philologically unsound and based upon a confusion arising from an overdependence on Judeo-Arabic orthography.[94]

The tour of Radak's linguistic globe is not complete without considering Aramaic, which covers a hemisphere. Although this tongue had long since ceased to be spoken by Jews, it remained their second literary language in all parts of the dispersion. In Provence, Targum was cultivated in elementary education—not necessarily because of its intrinsic interest—but because of its use as a medium of Aramaic instruction.[95] In such a context, Radak's use of Aramaic would be extensive.[96] He used it along with rabbinic Hebrew, as he did Arabic, in matters of comparative philology.[97] And he also drew upon this language for *le'azim,* in the functional sense at least, with frequent recourse to all its dialects and documents: biblical Aramaic,[98] Targumim,[99] rabbinic,[100] and geonic literature.

On occasion, all these would converge in polyglot profusion in the context of one of Radak's marathon definitions—with perhaps some Old French or even Italian thrown in for good measure.

I will plant in the wilderness the cedar, the acacia-tree, and the myrtle, and the oil-tree; I will set in the desert the cypress, the plane-tree and the larch together (Isaiah 41:19).

The *oil-tree* is that which is called *pin* in the vernacular and the oil that exudes from it is tar. Thus did Jonathan translate it [literally] as "oil-tree." We can not say that this is the olive-tree because in Ezra the two are mentioned as distinct: *Bring olive branches and oil-tree branches* (Nehemiah 8:15).

Jonathan translates *tidhar* (plane-tree) as *murnyan* and in rabbinic literature *tidhar* is *shaga*.[101] Rashi translated it as *sap*[102] in the vernacular [Old French]. Jonathan translated *te'ashur* as *'eshkero'in* and in rabbinic literature *te'ashur* is *shurbina*.[103] Rabbi Jonah [Ibn Janah] wrote that it is *shurbin* in Arabic.[104] The author of the *'Arukh* [Nathan ben Yehiel] explained that *'eshkero'a* in Arabic is *baqam,* which is that which is known in the vernacular as *bois*.[105] In that case, he does not agree that *berosh* (cypress) is *bois*.[106]

Yet with all this, Radak's recourse to foreign languages was as limited as it was extensive. It was after all restricted to lexical data.[107] Questions of syntax or idiom were seldom raised.

Ultimately it was Targum that played the major role in the exegetical process itself in the context of Radak's use of paraphrase. The combination of the two in conjunction with narrative explanation creates the effect on the reader that every nuance and intent of the scriptural text has been conveyed. See, for example, how Isaiah's laconic parable of the cottage in the vineyard takes on form and substance under Radak's hand.

The daughter of Zion is left as a cottage in a vineyard, as a lodge in a garden of cucumbers, as a besieged city (Isaiah 1:8). Most of the cities were desolate in the days of Hezekiah. The king of Assyria had invaded all the fortified cities and *Jerusalem was left alone like a cottage* in the wilderness and like a *lodge* which is in a cucumber field about which there is no other house or cottage. *Cottage* and *lodge* are synonyms for the lodge where the watchman lodges.

Jonathan [the Targum] translated: "like a cottage in the vineyard after they have harvested it, as in a lodge where one passes the night in a garden of cucumbers after they have gleaned it (*'avayuhi*)." The word *'avayuhi* means they have searched it to the point that no cucumbers are left in it . . . that is to say, the daughter of Zion is left alone as a cottage in the vineyard after the grapes have been gathered and the watchman has gone away, and as a lodge in a cucumber garden after they have gleaned the cucumbers and searched the garden until none are left and the watchman has left. In this way Zion is left with no watchman, for the Holy One, blessed be He, Who guards Israel has removed His presence from them.[108]

Having elucidated the meaning of the verse through his expansive paraphrase, Radak goes on to clarify a fine point.

It says *as a cottage in a vineyard, as a lodge in a cucumber garden,* not as a cottage in a garden. For in a garden booth, a watchman is always present. When they harvest this fruit or that vegetable, another is left and so throughout the year. But in the vineyard and the cucumber garden, after they pick the grapes and cucumbers, nothing is left to guard and the watchman leaves.[109]

Radak knew too how to exploit paraphrase effectively in the context of dialogue, becoming, as it were, a script-writer: in the encounter of King Saul with the Witch of Endor, he sets the stage and provides the witch with lines drawn not from the Bible but from rabbinic tradition:[110]

Saul said to her: *Have no fear* (I Samuel 28:13): "Don't be afraid of whatever it is you're afraid of. I won't kill you but will keep my word to you. But what did you see that let you know I'm Saul?"
The woman said: *I have seen a great man rising from the earth (ibid.).* "I have seen a great man rising from the earth in an abnormal fashion: right side up. That's how I knew that you are King Saul and that he rose this way out of respect to you."[111]

Concern for Structure and Order
Radak's concern for clearing every ambiguity, indeed the sheer amount of space his words occupy on the printed page, reveals his inclination for comprehensiveness and all-inclusiveness. Radak betrays himself when he sets out in his commentary on Jeremiah *not* to comment "on every passage verse after verse as I did in the Book of Isaiah"[112] and then leaves very little unexplicated. Even the fact that he labels verses which need no comment with "it is evident" is sufficient to indicate at least his feeling of responsibility

for the interpretation of every verse.[113] Nor does he limit himself
to reordering the internal structure of a verse. We shall see that the
whole question of context was pivotal in Radak's approach and
that he was concerned with the syntax of verses no less than with
the syntax of words. He points out, for example, that the story of
Jeroboam's *lèse-majesté*[114] and subsequent banishment is not told
according to the order of events. He consequently reconstructs the
story while at the same justifying the sequence of the biblical
narrative, which "placed the explanation as to why [Jeroboam]
grew arrogant and lifted up his hand against the king between *he
lifted up his hand against the king* (I Kings 11:26) and *Solomon
sought to kill Jeroboam* (v. 40)."[115] Inversions in order or sequence
are always noted. We find that the descendants of Shem's younger
brother, Japheth, are listed before those of his own because "the
essential concern of the narrative is Abraham, who is descended
from Shem, and because of him the genealogy is presented in
greater detail."[116]

Awareness of structure and order is evidenced in poetic contexts
as well. Radak wonders why *He that gives breath to the people
upon it* (Isaiah 42:5) is placed before *and spirit to them that walk
therein* (*ibid.*) since man was created after the animals. This is so,
however, because "he is the chief of the creatures."[117] In his commentary on Psalm 104, which relates the creation of the world,
Radak traces each step in the cosmic process, its order and its flow.

> *You set a bound [which they should not pass over]* (Psalms
> 104:9). After You gathered the waters, You set sand as a
> bound so that they not pass over and destroy the creatures on
> dry land. *That they not return to cover the earth* (*ibid.*), as
> they had originally covered the earth . . . This was through
> the power and wisdom of the Creator and His mercy on His
> creatures. When the waters were gathered in one place, the
> waters, which had evenly covered the earth, rose . . . and
> stood as a heap as it says, *He gathers the waters of the sea
> together as a heap* (Psalms 33:7). Although water naturally
> flows down, He restrained its nature so that when waves strike
> the shore they do not cross over the bound which is the sand
> on the shore.[118]

On a broader scale, Radak evinces extraordinary skill in inter-
weaving a "harmony" of related biblical passages, such as that at II
Kings 18:4.

Hezekiah king of Judah sent to the king of Assyria to Lachish "I have offended; turn away from me; that which you put on me will I bear." The king of Assyria appointed to Hezekiah king of Judah three hundred talents of silver and thirty talents of gold.

After [Sennacherib] seized the fortified cities of Judah and set his face towards Jerusalem, as is written in Chronicles *and that he was purposed to fight against Jerusalem* (II Chronicles 32:2), Hezekiah sent to one of the Judean cities, Lachish, where the Assyrian king was located, as follows: *"I have offended; turn away from me; that which you put on me will I bear."* This is to say, "I have offended in that I have rebelled against you and not served you. Turn away from me . . ." He did indeed turn back at that time after he was given that which he imposed, namely, three hundred talents of silver and thirty talents of gold. After a time, he returned to Judah after Hezekiah ceased to send his yearly tribute, as Rab-shakeh said to him, *"Now whom do you trust, that you have rebelled against me?"* (II Kings 18:20).

[The Assyrians] then came to Lachish, whence they dispatched messengers with a small armed force to Jerusalem. [Rab-shakeh] spoke as he spoke and, since his words were not accepted, returned with his escort. The Rabbis say that Shebna and his party then came to terms with [Sennacherib] and the verse *Do not call a conspiracy everything that the people call a conspiracy. Do not have their fear of it or their dread of it* (Isaiah 8:12) applies to them.[119] Rab-shakeh found that [Sennacherib] left Lachish and went warring with Libneh. Then he heard say that Tirhakah, king of Ethiopia, went to war with him and he departed from there. He sent emissaries to Hezekiah a second time and frightened him by saying that when he returned from his war with the king of Ethiopia, he would come against Jerusalem with all his armies. He went and fought with Ethiopia and Egypt and, with all his prisoners, came to Jerusalem and besieged it. That night an angel of the Lord went forth and struck the Assyrian camp. The Israelites then went forth and despoiled them. Concerning this it is said *I have given Egypt as your ransom, Ethiopia and Seba for you* (Isaiah 43:3), and also, *The labor of Egypt, and the merchandise of Ethiopia, and of the Sabeans, men of stature, shall come over to you and they shall be yours; etc.* (Isaiah 45:14). Those who were saved were converted to Judaism as it is said: *Surely God is in you, and there is none else. There is no other God* (*ibid.*). Concerning them it is said *In that day there shall be five cities in the land of Egypt that speak the language of Canaan, and swear to the Lord of hosts, etc.* (Isaiah 19:18).

I have explained this entire affair in one place at one stroke
since it is not set forth in its entirety in one place, not in this
book, nor in Isaiah, nor in Chronicles.

What Radak has done for us here is to record one of his lectures
in the same way that, as we have seen, he recorded his sermons.
While such lectures were not the rule in the commentaries, they
were not altogether unusual. Radak was careful, of course, to avoid
the lengthy and often irrelevant excursuses of the geonic period.[120]
The Spaniards, with Ibn Ezra at their head, reacted sharply to the
tendency of certain geonic scholars to expatiate on a biblical text
as a vehicle for the propagation of science and philosophy[121] and
aimed toward a maximum of relevance and a minimum of verbiage.
Lengthy digressions were not, however, unknown in the commentaries of Ibn Ezra himself in the case of an especially intriguing or
problematic subject.[122] Radak, as we have seen, preferred to dis-
tribute his remarks evenly and at a moderate pace rather than to
concentrate all his energies on selected verses. Yet he is ready, when
need arises, to go beyond his accepted limits and elucidate a bewil-
dering point. In the historical books especially, Radak attempts to
deal with contradictions in the text,[123] historical questions such as
why there were no ironsmiths in Israel in the time of Saul,[124] and
genealogical problems.[125] Theological dilemmas have their place.
Much space is devoted to an analysis—itself somewhat puzzling—of
the account of the Witch of Endor.[126] The problem of retributive
justice, a pivotal concern for Radak, provoked several inquiries.[127]
Above all, Radak is concerned with the stock problem of attempting to justify acts which do not, especially from the post-biblical
point of view, befit biblical heroes.[128] He asks how Jonathan could
have deceived David by telling him that Saul would not harm him
(he believed that Saul's threat stemmed only from temporary mad-
ness);[129] he questions David's apparent neglect of mourning prac-
tices after the death of his son (the entire story took place before
the burial when mourning rites are not yet observed);[130] with
obvious polemical intent, he initiates a discussion stressing that
Jeremiah was not told not to take a wife "at all but just not to
take one from Tekoa."[131]
    The length of the apologetic varies with the severity of the
"offense." His apology for Rachel's insistence on keeping the tera-
phim and calling them gods[132] is relatively brief. Only in passing

does he note that Abraham probably paid for the lamb he found in the thicket, lest anyone think that he would have offered as a sacrifice property that was not his own.[133] Yet long defenses are in order when David's marital arrangements and liaison with Michal come under scrutiny,[134] and certainly when he discusses the problem of Solomon and his wives.[135]

Rationalism

For the most part, however, Radak the apologist reveals himself somewhat unobtrusively. Radak the rationalist, on the other hand, announces himself with considerable fanfare. He prefaces his Psalms commentary, for example, with the rabbinic discussions of the authorship of the Psalms and the statement that they were composed through the holy spirit.[136] Midway through this discussion, Radak launches into an exposition of the difference between inspiration by the holy spirit and prophecy that reflects Maimonidean discussions of the topic.

> We shall now briefly explain the difference between prophecy and the holy spirit. Prophecy comes to one who is a sage and of perfect character. Prophecy may come to him in a dream. Should prophecy come to him in the waking state, his senses will be nulled and he will not be aware of the happenings of this world. In his prophetic vision, it will seem to him that a man is speaking to him or saying certain things to him. He might see certain images in the vision or hear a voice speaking to him instead of seeing a form.
> The holy spirit involves no nulling of the senses whatsoever and [comes to] the perfect man who is occupied with divine affairs. [Such a person] speaks in ordinary fashion but a sublime spirit moves him and has him utter praise and thanksgiving to God or rational or moral teachings. He might also speak of the future with divine assistance to the rational faculty . . . It is with this faculty that the Book of Psalms was uttered . . .
> Even though those who uttered it are called prophets . . . their "prophecy" was as we described it for prophecy is classed in different levels. Even though Daniel saw visions and apparitions in both the dream and waking states, his power and knowledge in those visions did not reach that of Isaiah, Ezekiel, or the other prophets. For this reason, his book was not included among the prophetic books but among those books called writings, that is, written in the holy spirit.[137]

Radak's commentaries are liberally interspersed with philosophical interpretations where pertinent. The entire spectrum of
rationalist investigation in the Middle Ages is broached: physics[138]
and metaphysics,[139] prophecy[140] and providence,[141] and philosophic rationalizations of the commandments.[142] The eightfold
alphabetical acrostic of Psalm 119, which speaks of the statutes
and commandments of the Torah, would prompt Radak into an
epistemological discourse establishing the foundations of tradition.
In this passage, very similar to one in the introduction to his
father's *Open Book*,[143] we learn that

> this psalm deals with commandments, judgments, statutes,
> and the like all of which are constructed with intellect and
> wisdom. The ways of acquiring wisdom and the human
> virtues are seven. Of them it is said *she has hewn out her seven
> pillars* (Proverbs 9:1). These are the five senses to which the
> human virtues are related, as the sage R. Solomon Ibn Gabirol
> explained.[144] What he failed to do is to connect the senses
> with the ways of access to wisdom. With four of the senses, it
> is obvious; with the eyes man sees scientific books; with the
> ears he hears scholars; with the mouth he voices what he
> learned and teaches others; with the hand, he writes books.
>   What must be clarified is the sense of smell. It is related to
> wisdom since the nostrils are proximate to the two anterior
> brain cavities in which the imaginative faculty is located. The
> sixth way [of access to wisdom] is the reporting of observers.
> Although not perceivable by the senses, it[s truth] is obvious
> to one. The reporters tell, for example, that Constantinople
> is in the world. Even if one has not been there and seen it, it
> is evident to him that this is the case since everyone who has
> been there testifies to its existence without exception . . . The
> seventh way is that of rational proof and knowledge. This is
> the firmest of them all.
>   [Yet] there is another way not warranted by reason. How-
> ever, it is a great and certain pillar for those who embrace the
> Torah. This is the eighth way, that of tradition, in which we
> must all necessarily believe. Through it, the fact that Moses
> wrote the Torah at God's word, the creation of the world,
> the stories of the Patriarchs, the great portents which our
> fathers saw in Egypt or in the desert, the splitting of the sea
> and the Jordan, the assembly at Mount Sinai, the halting of
> the sun and the moon for Joshua, and the rest of the wonders
> recorded by the prophets, which our eyes did not see and our
> ears did not hear and which are not recognized nor examin-
> able by the intellect, are all verified and affirmed within us.

The reports of the reporters are indeed verifiable but this is not. It is rather to be affirmed from books which are a legacy from generation to generation. It is confirmed with us and fixed in our hearts, as if our eyes saw, our ears heard, our intellects recognized, etc., for sometimes the senses deceive and the intellect errs when proofs are not certain. Tradition, however, is a legacy from generation to generation and has not been denied by a member of any nation; nor do any of the books contradict [one another] concerning it. Therefore tradition is as certain with us as the intellect.

Also obvious is Radak's frequent citation of rationalist texts and authorities from the *Book of Creation*[145] to Maimonides[146] and Samuel Ibn Tibbon.[147] Radak lends a philosophical tone to his Genesis commentary by "dropping" a variety of such sources in the first two chapters alone: Abraham Bar Hiyya (Genesis 1:21), Abraham Ibn Ezra,[148] Isaac Israeli,[149] Joseph Ibn Zaddik (Genesis 2:7), Judah Halevi (Genesis 1:2), Joseph Kimhi (Genesis 1:26), Maimonides,[150] Saadia Gaon (Genesis 1:2), the *Book of Creation,*[151] the "investigators,"[152] the "astronomers" (Genesis 1:16), and the "experimental scientists" (Genesis 1:25).

Peshaṭ and *Derash*

The central question of course is not the number of philosophical asides which grace the commentaries but the cumulative effect that Radak's rationalism had upon his exegesis in terms of developing his own conception of *peshaṭ,* the plain sense of Scripture. To answer this question, we must consider the locale of Radak's activity: Provence. This area has been given short shrift in characterizations of the region and its representatives. Radak has suffered more than most. The thinking generally runs as follows. Provence, we are told, lies between France and Spain. Its Jewish culture is consequently a blend of French rabbinics and Hispano-Arabic science.[153] Finally: "In no one did the two currents of Jewish thought find a more complete union"[154] than in Radak.

The facts, I believe, suggest otherwise. Radak, to be sure, was steeped in rabbinics. Yet we have seen that these were not necessarily French rabbinics.[155] Rashi does figure prominently in the commentaries,[156] but Rashi was well known and widely studied by virtually all of world Jewry. More significant is that other exegetical trends which were gaining momentum and thrust in northern France did not seem to be well known to Radak: the enterprise of such men as Samuel ben Meir, Joseph Bekhor Shor, Joseph Kara, and Menahem bar Helbo, who set themselves the task of "disencumbering [Scripture] from 'aggadah (homiletical explanations) and employing only the *peshat*."[157] Their program to realize Rashi's wishful expression of the need to record "the *peshatim* which come to light daily"[158] does not seem to have been of great assistance to Radak in his own search for an approach to *peshat*.[159] On the other hand, what is of greater significance in the *argumentum ex geographia* is the proximity of Provence to Catalonia. Radak's rationalism was Spanish and both aspects of this rationalism, the philosophical and the philological, would find themselves side by side with the midrash and homiletics that was Narbonne.[160] That "the two currents of Jewish thought" were liberally represented in Radak's commentaries cannot be questioned. Midrash, grammar, and, to a lesser extent, philosophical observations account for a large share of the commentaries. Yet whether they found a "complete union" is not so easily decided. Despite the mass of midrashic material in the commentaries, one repeatedly encounters a paradox when one reads the commentaries, especially the earliest, on the historical books; it seems as if homiletics or rabbinics is not Radak's concern. In his introduction to Chronicles Radak frankly informs us that his commentary is a new departure: an attempt to achieve a sound level of *peshat* exegesis over against the midrashic *status quo* which prevailed in Narbonne. At the start of his commentary on Joshua he announces that he "will bring a number of (*qezat*) *derashot*" but only "for those that love *derash*." Here it appears that he will cite midrashim primarily for their diversionary value, much in the spirit of Joseph Ezovi's counsel:

> Now here, now then, list to the Midrashim;
> How oft they brighten words that seemed dim.[161]

Thus we find:

> There are *derashot* as to why the [prophet] said: *Hear* to the heavens and *give ear* (Isaiah 1:2) to the earth—the reverse of what Moses said.[162] One of them is that Moses was close to the heavens and therefore said *Give ear O heavens*. Since he

was far from earth, he said *Let the earth hear*. Isaiah came
and said *Hear O heavens* since he was far from the heavens
and said *Give ear O earth* since he was close to the earth.[163]

Yet it is hardly the case that all or even most of the *'aggadot* that
Radak cites are introduced for entertainment or escapist value.
Even more puzzling: if Radak was bringing midrashim for the
"lovers of *derash*," it would appear that he himself was chief
among them. The word *qezat*, "a number of," is more flexible in
medieval Hebrew than in modern. Reflecting Arabic *ba'd*, it
signified "some," not in the sense of "a few," but in the sense of
"not all." To this extent Radak was true to his language. He did
not bring *all* of the midrashic corpus. Yet as one peruses the commentaries, verse after verse, chapter after chapter, and book after
book, one almost feels that he tried to; that he was indeed honor-
ing his oath of fealty to the lords of *peshat* only in the breach.
Read on though and rest assured. When Radak voices his vexation
with the midrashic mind, he proves that it is not only the nations
who know how to rage. On the colorful midrashic account which
has the ark carrying its bearers across the Jordan, he fulminates:

> The rabbis explained this altogether differently . . . I am
> puzzled by what made them come up with this *derash*. It is
> not the verses because we have already explained them all as
> we understand them. Even if [the verse] is taken as they say,
> [there are other problems] . . . How does the ark come to
> carry its bearers and cross over? If there were such a miracle,
> would not Scripture say so explicitly . . .? Again, even if one
> takes their words at face value . . . why did they need such
> a miracle? *Was it so hard for them to explain it as we
> did . . .?*[164]

Although he concludes with the standard disclaimer, "They knew
what they were saying since their understanding was broader than
ours,"[165] the words do little to temper either this critique or
others. Of the *derash* that Rebekah went to consult Shem when
she went to seek the Lord (Genesis 25:2),[166] Radak states bluntly:
"Is it believable that Shem was alive?"[167] His censures were varied:
he might label a midrash incomprehensible,[168] superfluous,[169] far-
fetched,[170] irrational,[171] or simply erroneous.[172] Yet his greatest
eloquence lies in his understatement. The Targum builds up a pic-

ture of Deborah's diversified commercial interests in dates, olives, vineyards, and white sand[173] on the basis of the single datum that *she lives beneath the palm tree of Deborah* (Judges 4:5). Radak can only laconically remark that "according to the *peshaṭ* she had a house under a palm tree."

To Radak *'aggadah* is now guesswork:

> *Jeroboam the son of Nabat* (I Kings 11:26). They said in the midrash that Nabat is identical with Micah who is identical with Sheba ben Bichri.[174] Yet Sheba ben Bichri was from the tribe of Benjamin and Nabat from the tribe of Ephraim.[175]

> We cannot provide reasons for all the deficient and *plene* spellings. There are too many of them.[176]

> There are many *derashot* on these names and if we were to explain homiletically why they were so called, no book could contain them.[177]

Now gratuitous:

> There is a midrash which says that the Holy One, blessed be He, said to Joshua *You shall cause this people to inherit the land* (Joshua 1:6), i.e., when you are with them. Here when he was not with them, they failed. However, since Scripture gives the reason, i.e., that they failed because of their sin with the *spoil,* we are not to look for another reason.[178]

Now simply fanciful:

> *Hide there three days* (Joshua 2:16). The rabbis said: This indicates that the holy spirit descended upon Rahab for if . . . not, how did she know that they would return three days later?[179] According to the *peshaṭ,* she said what seemed reasonable. From Jericho to the Jordan it is a day or perhaps a bit more and she thought that with the going, coming, and searching, the entire journey would last three days.

Yet all these overt expressions of disagreement represent only the peak of the iceberg. Numerous aggadic passages are cited without such disapprobatory remarks. More often, Radak will quote the passage and state "and according to the *peshaṭ* . . ."[180] or "after the manner of *peshat*."[181] Even more common is the reverse, where he will cite his own *peshat* and add "and midrashically" or "in the midrash"[182] or "our rabbis expounded (*dareshu*)."[183] This steady juxtaposition of *peshat* and *derash* amounts in effect to a process of labeling. Without having recourse to an analytic exposition of the nature of *peshat*, Radak is able to illustrate his conception of it simply by contrasting it with the midrash. Thus where Rashi might cite a midrash as his sole explanation or add a *peshat* interpretation without an introductory formula, Radak would take pains to be certain that the reader knew one from the other. On the passage *I shall spread My net over him and he shall be taken in My snare; and I will bring him to Babylon in the land of the Chaldeans* . . . (Ezekiel 12:13), Rashi simply cites the midrash that Zedekiah "had a tunnel from his house to the plains of Jericho and he went out through the tunnel. What did the Holy One do? He brought a gazelle before the Chaldean army which went before them over the tunnel and they pursued it. When Zedekiah went out from the tunnel . . . they saw him going out and they apprehended him."[184] Radak cites the same midrash; but he prefaces it with, "I will place the [desire] of pursuing and catching him in the heart of the Chaldeans. And in the *derash* . . ."[185]

Again, Rashi cites the *derash* on David's cry *My son, my son* (II Samuel 19:4), which states that David repeated this phrase eight times, raising Absalom through the seven divisions of hell and finally into paradise.[186] Radak too cites this passage but prefaces it with the explanation: "Mourners repeat their words, as in *My bowels, my bowels, I writhe in pain* (Jeremiah 4:19)." Finally, in the list of David's musicians in Chronicles, it is stated that there were six sons of Jeduthun but only five are named.[187] Radak remarks

> but we have found one that is not here . . .: *the tenth is Shimi* (I Chronicles 25:17). It is found in the *haggadah* that when David divided them, Jeduthun had five sons and his wife was pregnant with Shimi. He saw through the holy spirit that he too would be head of a ward. It therefore says *six*. Yet it is possible to say that he was small then and was not yet fit to sing and be head of a ward until he grew up . . . He was therefore counted in the number of the lot since they were teaching him and he was to become head of a ward.[188]

Frequently, Radak was as critical of midrash halakhah as he was of midrash *'aggadah*. While not especially original in this, he reflects contemporary rationalist critiques of midrash halakhah.[189] *The cloud upon the ark cover* (Leviticus 16:2) in which God appears is the Cloud of Glory and not the incense that the high priest brought into the sanctuary on the Day of Atonement.[190]

Radak took the rabbis to task for certain aggadic passages with halakhic content:

> *The king had taken counsel [with his princes and all the con-gregation in Jerusalem to keep the Passover in the second month]* (II Chronicles 30:2). I am puzzled by the rabbis' saying that Hezekiah intercalated Nisan in Nisan[191] and that they did not agree with him. Scripture says: *The king had taken counsel with his princes and all the congregation.* They have no proof from the text. It is possible that they agreed in Adar to declare a second Adar instead of Nisan. They would [thereby] observe Passover in [what would have been] the second month, Iyyar, but which would now be Nisan, [the time of] observance of Passover.
>
> As to their disagreement as to why Hezekiah sought divine mercy,[192] this is stated explicitly! It is because many of them ate the passover in ritual defilement as it is written: *They ate the passover otherwise than it is written* (II Chronicles 30:18).[193]

Radak chose to skirt the halakhic problems concerning the relationship of Judah and Tamar and the punishment of the latter by declaring that levirate marriage was the practice of the ancients[194] and that the sentence of burning passed upon her was the current way of handling the problem.[195] Similarly, the sons of Jacob observed the prohibition of the thigh sinew, not as a divine injunction, but as a family ordinance in the manner of the Rechabites.[196]

Such examples, which might be multiplied a hundredfold, show evidence of Radak's rebellion against the traditions of his spiritual forebears—the Narbonnese *darshanim*. And indeed, precisely because it was a family quarrel, it caused Radak, on more than one occasion, to relax his accustomed restraint. Those who have turned toward the obvious in seeking to understand Radak's apparent rejection of *'aggadah* have not been entirely wrong. Radak received

his exegetical training from two Spanish *pashṭanim* who would
guide him in the paths marked by Hayyuj, Ibn Janah, and Ibn Ezra.
Spanish *peshaṭ* did not develop against a background of reaction
against midrash and *'aggadah* to the same extent that French *peshaṭ*
did.[197] Yet it could not make its peace with it. Ibn Ezra wearied
at the endless ingenuity of the *darshanim* in Christian Europe.
Their inventiveness may provide charming material for schoolchil-
dren, but no serious student of the Bible can rely on it. Confronted
with the *'aggadah* that the Torah begins with the letter *b* in *b*eginning because it is also the first letter of *b*lessing, Ibn Ezra retorts
with a *b*ounty of *b*iblicisms *b*ordering on *b*ombast, *b*aseness, and
*b*lasphemy all *b*eginning with *b*. "And the end of the affair is,"
quoth the master punster in his introduction to the Torah, "that
there is no end to *derashot*." Yet in acknowledging the influence
of the Spanish *pashṭanim* on Radak's attitude toward midrash, one
runs the risk of overlooking other factors which had equal or perhaps greater influence on his development. "That there is no end
to *derashot*" or to "*'aggadot*" was not the cry of the Spanish
pashṭanim alone. Jewish intellectuals of all breeds—"rationalists"
and Talmudists, Orientals and Europeans—found aspects of the
'aggadot problematic or embarrassing. Their fanciful quality and
more especially their anthropomorphisms proved to be a source of
difficulty from the geonic period on.

Thus do we find R. Abraham ben Isaac (Rabad of Narbonne)—
one of the spiritual pillars of Narbonne in Radak's youth—dwelling
on this point in his code, the *'Eshkol*. Although he was hardly cut
from the same cloth as Abraham Ibn Ezra, Rabad expresses hesitation over the question of the extent to which *'aggadot* are "binding" and has recourse to the decisions of the Babylonian Gaon Hai:

> Everything written in the Talmud . . . is more correct than
> what is not included in it. Although *'aggadot* written in the
> Talmud, if they prove untrue or distorted, need not be con-
> sidered authoritative, because of the general rule that one
> does not rely on *'aggadah,* yet we are obliged to remove
> wherever possible the distortion of any statement included
> in the Talmud. For if that statement had not contained some
> [worthwhile] hermeneutic interpretation, it would never have
> been incorporated in the Talmud. But if unable to remove the
> distortion, we shall treat it like any of the rejected laws.
> Statements not included in the Talmud, however, require no
> such exertion on our parts.[198]

In essence, he concludes, "we accept that which is certain and verifiable by reason in them but there is no end to *'aggadot*."[199]

Those of a more philosophical or, more precisely, Aristotelian
bent found themselves in an even deeper quandary. Maimonides'
ambivalence was characteristic. He expressed the hope that he
might someday write a commentary to the *'aggadot* and thereby
exonerate them from criticism. He never did so, however, for, in
the words of his son, he "lost heart."[200] A later Provençal Maimonidean, Joseph Ibn Caspi, echoes these reservations and points
to a solution.

> There are many haggadot the literal wording of which
> posits ideas inadmissible rationally, or attributes to God
> corporeality, change, or any other affection. Perchance thou
> mayest eat to satiety from these evil viands, these deadly
> poisons—I refer to the before-mentioned haggadot as
> literally interpreted. God deliver thee! Therefore my son,
> understand that most of the haggadot found in the Talmud
> and other rabbinic books, which on the surface seem to imply
> the ideas I have named, are figures of speech, with an inner
> meaning, which we can sometimes discern, sometimes not . . .

> Should any of the rabbinic teachers desire to explain liter-
> ally and not metaphorically any of the haggadot which are
> opposed to reason, or attribute corporeality or other inad-
> missible quality to God, as in the instance when "the children
> of Israel did impute things that were not right unto the Lord
> their God," do not assent to such a teacher, accept not the
> saying nor its utterer, for it is the opinion of a single unsup-
> ported authority.[201]

Radak, straddling the period between Rabad of Narbonne and
Ibn Caspi, is swept into this whirlpool and bravely struggles to stay
afloat. He too was embarrassed by certain "irrational" midrashim.
As an example, one may illustrate such embarrassment with one
striking instance of omission. In his commentary on Psalm 91,
Radak cites the beginning and end of the passage in the *Midrash on
Psalms* dealing with this psalm. The former[202] discusses the
Mosaic authorship of the chapter while the latter[203] is a long con-
solatory passage. The central portion of the midrash,[204] replete
with demonological references and allusions, is not cited. Instead
Radak observes:

*Of the pestilence that walks in the darkness, nor of the de-
struction that waits at noonday* (Psalms 91:6). The authors of
the *derash* explain the *darkness* and the destruction *at noonday* with reference to demons as they do *a thousand may fall
at your right side* . . . (Psalms 91:7). The scientists do not
admit the existence of demons and have disproved them for
they do not exist.[205]

Radak closes with a variety of possible rationalistic explanations
of the psalm. He notes too that the rabbis called this psalm the
"Song on Mishaps,"[206] which is a "great mystery for those who
understand."[207] The "mystery," of course, is the lesson on divine
providence taught by Maimonides in his *Guide for the Perplexed,*
where these very demonological verses are taken to refer to "mishaps" due to the laws of nature and those that are caused by our
fellow men.[208] Similarly, in the apparition of the Witch of Endor,
the witch exclaims that she sees *'elohim* rising out of the earth.[209]
This word, plural in form, may traditionally be understood, according to the context, in one of three ways: God, gods, or distinguished men. Post-biblical readers would presumably agree that the
only appropriate meaning is the third and that it refers to Samuel.
There is, however, a further complication. The verb *rising* is plural
in form also. Rashi and the midrash allow themselves free rein:
"[There were] two angels. *Moses and* Samuel. For Samuel was
afraid [thinking] 'Perhaps I am summoned to judgment' and
raised Moses with him." Radak simply notes that "the plural form
of *rising* is like the plural form of *'elohim,* that is, the plural of
majesty. And in the midrash . . ."[210]

The "irrational" character of such midrashim was under attack
not only by Jewish rationalists but by Christianity. Starting with
such figures as Peter Alphonse and Peter the Venerable in the early
twelfth century, we find Christians—and in particular apostates
from Judaism—exploiting midrashim, such as those which speak of
God in an anthropomorphic manner, to embarrass Judaism. A. L.
Williams summarizes a list of such "absurdities," cited by Peter
Alphonse:

. . . A body is ascribed to God. He wears phylacteries. He is
only in the West. He is limited in space. He is angry at the
first hour of the day, though no one has known the precise
hour of the day except Balaam. God weeps once every day,

and His tears fall into the Great Sea. Because of His weeping
He roars like a lion three times a day, and beats the sky with
His feet, and whispers like a dove, grieving for His temple. He
prays every day that His pity may surpass His anger.[211]

In reply, such an apologist as Meir ben Simeon, a Narbonnese contemporary of Radak, was forced to remonstrate to the Christians:
"Sir! You know, as does every wise man, that one takes the words
of a sage literally if they are rational and sensible. But if they are
not rational and sensible when taken literally, then we must take
them figuratively."[212]

Even more problematic, however, were midrashim of another
sort. Narbonne, we must remember, had attained rather early on an
independence from the Babylonian centers. This independence
manifested itself not only in halakhic authority but indeed in literary traditions and use of sources. In the realm of midrash, we find
Moses the Preacher incorporating in his encyclopedic collections
midrashim stemming from "extrarabbinic, even heterodox
groups."[213] Such midrashim could be cleverly used to support the
teachings of the Christian church. Thus a contemporary of Radak,
an anonymous Spanish apostate, quotes the remarkable 'aggadah
concerning the return (le-haḥazir) of the pig (ḥazir) to Israel as
proof of the ultimate abrogation of the commandments.[214] Worse
still, even well-known talmudic passages were resourcefully
exploited to prove the truth of the Christian faith. Thus Peter
Alphonse cites a passage in the tractate Yoma that speaks of several bad omens which manifested themselves in the Temple forty
years before its destruction. Since that is approximately the date
of the death of Jesus, he saw these omens as a sign of divine retribution for the crucifixion.[215] Thus, anti-Jewish treatises pro-
gressively waged their war against the Talmud on two fronts: on
the one hand, proving the tenets of Christianity from rabbinic
sources; on the other, denying the latter's heresies.[216]

This activity increased in momentum throughout the thirteenth
century. In 1263, Moses Nahmanides would stand at Barcelona
debating these points with the Christians. Before the clerics were
vast collections of passages arranged by such Hebraists as Raymond
Martini, many of which would be attributed by them to none
other than Moses the Preacher.[217]

Radak did not openly respond to these affronts. Nor did his

father Joseph react to Christian use of midrash in the extant portions of the *Book of the Covenant*. Yet the fact that it was an
issue among the polemicists of the "Defence committee"[218] of
Narbonne is evident from the treatise of Radak's younger contemporary and fellow townsman Meir ben Simeon, who devotes a
chapter of the *Obligatory War* to Christian use, or misuse, of
'aggadah.[219]

The Jews, in their fashion, were not left tongue-tied. Using the
time-honored polemical technique of turning the tables, they
charged that it is not the Jew who is the aggadist, the *darshan,* the
betrayer of the text—but the Christian. It is the "sages of the
Gentiles who say that the Torah—everything said in Genesis, the
commandments and precepts—is riddle and allegory. Each takes
away and adds as he sees fit."[220] Joseph Kimhi's *min (infidelis)*
attests: "You understand most of the Torah according to the
litera while we understand according to *figura*. Your whole reading
of the Bible is erroneous for you resemble him who gnaws at the
bone while we [suck at] the marrow within. You are like the beast
who eats the chaff while we [eat the wheat]."[221] An early thir-
teenth-century apostate affirms: "Whatever Moses said he said
mystically or *allegorically,* I give you the testimony of the prophets
who came after Moses that the Law cannot be understood except
through the apostles."[222]

Jewish reaction—from Joseph Kimhi[223] to Meir ben Simeon[224] —
against *figura* is decisive. Radak joins the fray. He lashes out at the
"Christians who say that the Torah is an allegory (*mashal*)."[225]
"*You have founded them forever* (Psalms 119:152) for the commandments have no time limit as the Christians say";[226] "the
covenant and the testimony have been written and taught and no
commandment is to be taught after the Torah of Moses."[227] He
advances the prophet's injunction *Remember the Torah of My
servant Moses as I commanded at Horeb* (Malachi 3:22) as a reply
to the Christians who say it was given literally (*ke-mashma'ah*)
for a limited time and that Jesus came and explained it *spiritualiter*
(*ruḥanit*).[228] In a summary statement he rejects the view that

> the Torah given at Mount Sinai was valid only until the advent
> of Jesus; that until his time it was [to be taken] *corporealiter*
> (*gufanit*) and that when he came, he ordained that it be
> taken *spiritualiter* (*ruḥanit).* Their words are wind and vanity

for the commandments—which they say are allegory and not
to be taken literally—were specifically commanded by
God . . . If the commandments were allegorical, they would
be ambiguous and everyone would have a different opinion
concerning them. Scripture says, *for the commandment which
I command you this day is not hard for you nor is it far off*
(Deuteronomy 30:11). If the [true meaning of the] commandments were concealed and esoteric, they would be too
hard and far off.[229]

The problems raised by aggadic departure from *peshaṭ* on the
one hand and Christian allegorical or figurative departure from
peshaṭ on the other converged to challenge the very exegetical integrity of the Jewish commentator. Ultimately he must practice
what he preaches. Thus we find that in the case of Meir ben
Simeon, his

refutations of christological interpretations of Scripture rest
on the whole fairly and squarely on the literal exegesis of the
relevant passages, almost to the exclusion of any rabbinic support for, or evidence against, his own statements. However
grossly inconsistent he appears to be in connection with the
interpretation of uncomfortable talmudic "blasphemies," as
far as the Bible is concerned, we note again and again his
insistence on *mashma'uth ha-miqra* or *peshuṭo shel miqra,*
that is, the primary meaning of the text.[230]

At this same juncture stood Radak. An aggadist of the aggadists,
a disciple of Moses the Preacher, a "lover of *derash,*" Radak would
yet opt for the "way of *peshaṭ.*"

Grammar and Masorah

Up to this point, we have seen Radak's conception of *peshaṭ,* the
plain intent of Scripture, defined in negative terms alone—as a
critique of midrash. Radak's methods in establishing *peshaṭ,* however, although not formally catalogued, are clarified through their
usage. The distinction between his conception of *peshaṭ* and his
conception of *derash* was based upon, if not defined by, certain
technical exegetical principles. It is to the play between exegesis
based on these principles and "midrashic" exegesis as understood
by Radak that I now turn.

We have seen grammar and *peshaṭ,* the plain meaning of Scripture, associated in the Spanish tradition to the point of identification.[231] For Ibn Ezra, the error of the *darshanim* was their failure
to weigh their interpretations in the grammatical "balance." Joseph
Kimhi, we recall, juxtaposed the "plain sense interpretations"
(*peshaṭeha*) to the "grammatical interpretations" (*diqduqeha*).[232]
Indeed, the primary purpose of the study of Hebrew grammar in
the Middle Ages was the proper understanding of Scripture. The
active aspect, the ability to write prose or poetic compositions, was
a professed[233] but secondary goal. Grammatical works were
prolegomena to biblical commentaries. More precisely, they were
themselves biblical commentaries—arranged not by chapter and
verse but under morphological and lexicological rubrics. If one
were to unravel these texts and reweave them on another loom,
the result would be—as is Solomon Ibn Melekh's adaptation of
Radak's *Mikhlol*[234]—a commentary on a good part of the Bible.

Virtually every major biblical exegete in the Spanish tradition—Ibn Balaam, Ibn Janah, Hayyuj, Ibn Ezra, Joseph and Moses
Kimhi—was a grammarian. It will come as no surprise that *peshaṭ*
commentaries written in this tradition contain of necessity a
generous proportion of grammatical material. Some exegetes, such
as Abraham Ibn Ezra, aimed for a measure of order. Ibn Ezra
intended—with less than perfect success—to place the explanation
of the "words" of the grammar before the explanation of the context.[235] In this way, he unwittingly showed accommodation to the
tastes of the modern reader, who is accustomed to seeing the contextual and "higher critical" aspects of a commentary presented in
essay form with the philological and "lower critical" material
assigned to notes. Radak showed no such consideration. His commentaries are a *mélange* of grammar and *peshaṭ,* grammar and
derash, grammar and textual criticism, grammar and homily, grammar and philosophy. No sooner does one get caught up in the
sweep of a biblical passage than he is faced with the fact that "it
says *meḥallelo* with a masculine suffix even though *shabbat* is
feminine because the Sabbath day[236] is intended"[237] or that "the
affix *bet* in *be-ven* is for additional emphasis."[238] To the reader,
the effect may be disconcerting:

> *As for your birth* (Ezekiel 16:4). He tells you the circum-
> stances of your birth. It is the time of the death of Joseph

and all his brethren and the entire generation. Israel was grow-
ing and gaining rapidly because at that time Israel had no
guardian or protector other than God, *On the day you were
born* (*huledet*). This . . . word is written with a *vav and* a
dagesh and it is an infinitive of the verbal pattern *hof'al*.[239]

Such "interruptions" are reminiscent of the tiresome walking con-
cordance in David Frischman's "Ibn Ezra says . . . ,"[240] who could
correctly but irrelevantly recall a grammatical point in Ibn Ezra at
every turn. Yet the location of these remarks, interspersed as they
are throughout the main trend of thought, is not at all haphazard.
On the contrary, they are most strategically placed. Standing
where they do, they are to be read as signposts and caution lights:
*Have due regard for the principles of textual criticism and philol-
ogy! Do not stray from the path of sound exegesis! Do not abandon the* peshaṭ!

As we have seen, the grammatical portion of Radak's exegesis
was prepared before he began the commentaries. Just as he had
consolidated his grammatical knowledge in the *Mikhlol,* Radak set
aside a special work, to be discussed below,[241] devoted to masoretic questions. Masorah, the tradition of textual transmission of
the Hebrew Bible, was as central an exegetical concern of Radak's
as was grammar. Whereas the centrality of the latter is betrayed
by the frequent grammatical interjections in the commentaries,
that of the former is indicated by the very choice of the place
Radak chose to begin his exegesis: the Book of Chronicles. For
the rabbis, the "Book of Chronicles was given only so that it might
be expounded midrashically."[242] Its long genealogical lists, its
departures from the former prophets, its own midrashic tendencies,
its textual problems,[243] were all ideal subjects for midrashic treatment. "In this book," we are told, "there are many obscurities and
many things which conflict with the books of Samuel and Kings."[244]

By the end of the twelfth century, little had changed in the
approach to these obscurities. Radak writes:

Since this book is a historical narrative, it has not been
generally studied. I have not seen any exegete attempt to
comment upon it. I have, however, found some commentaries on this book here in Narbonne, but I am ignorant
of the names of the authors. I have seen that they generally
follow the method of *derash*. One learned disciple of my

father's in Gerona asked me to expound it and I saw fit to fulfill his request.[245]

Whether Radak's response to his father's pupil is merely a literary device or not, it is in fact a response to a historical need. The one attempt at a *peshaṭ* approach to Chronicles, composed in North Africa,[246] seems to have been unknown in Radak's circles. Whereas his brother Moses had attempted to rescue the books of Ezra and Nehemiah from the hands of the *darshanim,*[247] Chronicles remained at their mercy. In the commentary on Chronicles, we shall see that Radak formulated, explicitly or implicitly, the attitude to masorah and textual criticism which served as a guideline to his work throughout his exegetical career.

The labors of the Masoretes had served to establish the general unanimity of readings of biblical manuscripts. S. Baron informs us that "after 1200, even the minor regional variations largely disappeared from Mediterranean communities, so that the numerous manuscripts . . . showed but microscopic variations."[248] Some saw this as a glass of water that was half full: Ibn Ezra placed his confidence in the Masoretes, "the guardians of the walls" who "purged the text of foreign matter."[249] The Tiberian Masoretes had completed the task and there was no need to proceed further. For those who did persist in masoretic pursuits, Ibn Ezra did not hide his disdain: "they are like camels who carry silk. They do not benefit the silk nor does the silk benefit them."[250] Ibn Ezra's utter confidence in the Tiberian tradition prevented him from giving much consideration to the "microscopic variations" to which Baron refers. It was inevitable that this itinerant scholar would see such in his travels in "Spain, France, and across the sea"[251] but he pays them scant attention. U. Simon observes that it is a moot question to ask whether "his confidence in the labors of the Masoretes led to his lack of interest in textual questions, or whether his lack of interest in textual problems led him to see the work of the Tiberians as the last word."[252] R. Abraham too spent much of his career in Muslim Spain, where the Jews were frequently accused of tampering with the biblical text for the purpose of obliterating alleged references to Mohammad.

We find Jewish apologists proclaiming:

... We indeed find today the Torah, written in exactly the same text without the slightest change, publicly displayed in all Jewish communities from India to the ends of Spain and Morocco in the civilized world, and from the borders of Ifriqiya, Ethiopia, and Yemen in the south to the last cities of Almagos in the Arctic Ocean to the north. Not one segment of the people differs [in this respect] from another, down to the three small letters *nun* which, occurring in the earliest texts, are still found in all recensions throughout the world.[253]

This polemical motif together with Ibn Ezra's aversion to overconcentration in any discipline[254] helps clarify his position vis-à-vis masorah. R. Abraham's contemporary, Joseph Kimhi, with his theory that even the "trivial" sciences needed their specialists, was more moderate. R. Joseph, the grammarian, spoke little of masorah. Yet for him the question of variant readings and manuscript traditions was of more than "academic" interest. He found the question of textual "variants" a serious question, if not in the Jewish study house, then in the debating chamber with Christians.

R. Joseph would be called upon to show how

Jerome your translator has corrupted the text by saying *The Lord said to my Lord ('adonai)* (Psalms 110:1). In our text, the most authoritative, it is written, *The Lord said to my lord ('adoni).* The vowel sign is *ḥiriq* indicating a reading of *'adoni* (lord) and not *pataḥ* calling for a reading of *'adonai* (Lord) as you say.[255]

Reacting to the Vulgate, which challenges the authority of the masoretic text, R. Joseph denies the possibility that the readings of the Vulgate represent a legitimate alternative to that of the masoretic text. He argues that Jerome's text was based on

the Book of Origen, the most ancient and authoritative [text and the one] from which your text was translated. Everything is dependent upon it. For it was dictated by the prophets, and Jerome the translator relied upon it, translated from it, and trusted it, with the exception of a few words which he did not understand or which were contrary to his belief and which he altered, changing the root of the faith to worm-wood.[256]

The "distortions" of Jerome continued to be a matter of inter-est in the time of Radak. He too announces that "Jerome your translator erred"[257] in repointing the Hebrew text of Psalms 110:1 in order to achieve a trinitarian interpretation. He cites the exam-ples given by his father and adds others. Jerome had accused the Jews of misinterpreting Isaiah 2:22, which according to his tradi-tion reads *Desist from the man whose breath is in his nostrils for he is highly esteemed.* Jerome bemoans the fact that the Jews read *bammah* (*in quo*) instead of *reputatus* (*bamah*) while still referring the verse to Jesus. It thereby appears "not to praise Christ but to consider Him as nothing."[258] Radak, with a sense of irony that came to the fore on the battlefield, observes: "There is an allusion to Christianity in this verse: [the Christians will abjure their faith and say to each other:] Desist from this man whom you have wor-shipped until now for you have served a man and not God as you thought but breath was in his nostrils, so little was he to be con-sidered."[259] Radak rails against the Christians who "corrupted *ka'ari* (like a lion) and read *karu* (they dug)" in Psalms 22:17 "in order to read *they dug* (pierced) *my hands and feet,* to indicate that they stuck nails in his hands and feet when they hanged him."[260] More inventive is his interpretation of "Shiloh" in Gene-sis 49:10. This opposes the variant of the Vulgate[261] and indeed that of the Targum[262] and proposes a root *shyl*[263] to yield the interpretation "his son" so that the term might be referred to David.[264]

Awareness of the Christian challenge to the text of the Bible was present in Radak's commentaries even when not stated explicitly. A case in point is Abraham's encounter with the angels in Genesis 18:3. The rabbis of the Talmud debated whether the ambiguous *'adonai* was to be considered sacred (O God) or profane (O lords). Although the rabbis decided in favor of the former,[265] post-talmudic exegetes recoiled from the anthropomorphic overtones of that interpretation.[266] Later commentators expressed open aware-ness of the Christian interpretation. Ibn Ezra remarks: "Some say that God is three persons, that is, three who are one, indivisible. They have forgotten the verse: *the two angels came to Sodom*

(Genesis 19:1)."[267] Here Ibn Ezra rejects the association of the three angels with the persons of the Trinity and objects that, if this be the case, two parts of the Trinity had separated from the third.[268] There is however an additional consideration in Ibn Ezra's discussion of the word *'adonai*. Ibn Ezra distinguishes *'adonai* with the vowel *patah* and *'adonai* with the vowel *qamaz*. He understands the former as a simple plural, *my lords;* the latter as the plural of majesty, *Lord*.[269] On the basis of this, "*'adonai* is not sacred but is like *rabbotai, my masters*. The *nun* is therefore written with *patah* not with *qamaz* . . . and in those codices in which *nun* is written with a *qamaz* it is to be understood [elliptically] as *prophet of the Lord*."[270] Faced with these manuscript variants, Ibn Ezra preferred the version with *patah* but did his best to explain away the alternative. When we examine Radak's remarks on this passage, we find that he does not even express awareness of the textual discrepancy. Following his father,[271] he tells us that the word does not refer to God but that it does not refer to the three angels either. It is directed, rather, to only one of the angels, their leader. In fact, the form should have had a singular suffix, *'adoni, my master*. However, we are told, *'adonai* was written as a plural of majesty as in Judges 6:15.[272] Apparently, then, Radak seems to be ignoring the version with *patah* lest it be taken as a basis for the rendering of the Vulgate. That this interpretation had an anti-trinitarian thrust is supported by Radak in his comments on Genesis 19:18.

> *O not so my lords.* The rabbis said, "Every *'adonai* written . . . in connection with Lot is sacred with the exception of this one. It says *in saving my life* (v. 19) and it must therefore refer to One who has the power of life and death."[273]
> Their words are puzzling, for it says *Lot said to them* (v. 18), i.e., plural. Further an angel has the power of life and death as an emissary of God, as do even the prophets, such as Elijah and Elisha."[274]

Here, where only *two* angels are involved, *'adonai* may be understood as plural.

For Radak, the readings of the Vulgate had no basis in reality; they existed only in the imagination of Jerome: "Jerome your translator erred."[275] "How can they maintain the error of one against [the testimony] of many? For from east to west [all manuscripts] concur . . . Do they not say that our Torah[276] is evidence for them? If so, let them believe in it."[277]

Radak had answered the Christians as Ibn Daud answered the Muslims. Yet he knew that the picture of textual uniformity which he presented had its flaws. By the time of Radak, scribal error and discrepancies resulting from the rapid proliferation of Hebrew manuscripts[278] had greatly increased. Throughout both the Iberian peninsula and Provence, a general concern for closer inspection of manuscripts in the light of masorah was felt. Meir ben Todros Abulafia of Toledo warned scribes of "erring"—choosing the wrong reading—in the discrepancies in new manuscripts which had recently appeared [279] and composed his *Masoretic Tradition as Hedge for the Torah* (*Masoret Seyag La-Torah*) to hedge out these errors. In Posquières, Joseph Kimhi's pupil Menahem ben Simeon demonstrated a keen interest in masorah and manuscripts.[280] In Narbonne, Radak complained of "many of the scribes and experts in vowel-pointing, readers and students who have no understanding or grasp and wander off course walking in darkness as a result of their lack of effort and excessive indolence in acquiring knowledge of what has been written in the books of the Masoretes."[281] Yet even if the scribes had studied the "works of the masorah" at length, it is doubtful whether the situation would have been greatly alleviated. These works, like the manuscripts which represented them, often contradicted one another. The tenacity of the variants is demonstrated by the fate of Maimonides' attempt to decide the issue once and for all by promulgating in the *Mishneh Torah* the acceptance of the Ben Asher tradition as manifested in the manuscript now known as the Aleppo codex.[282] Rather than this book's exerting its authority on the manuscript traditions, however, the reverse occurred: European copies of the *Mishneh Torah* were harmonized with the variant traditions.[283] This phenomenon would later affect manuscript copies of Radak's commentaries as well.[284]

Nor was it the modern variants alone which contributed to the confusion. Divergent traditions from the rabbinic period, recorded in midrash and Targum, were a thorn in Radak's side.[285] Rejecting an interpretation of Ibn Ezra based on a variant reading which conflicts with "all the correct texts I have seen,"[286] Radak notes

that this reading is the basis of certain midrashic interpretations.[287]
Whether a variant reading really underlay the midrash,[288] as Radak
felt, or it was simply the result of an application of the midrashic
device of 'al tiqre,[289] his reservations are unequivocal. Both the
midrashic tradition and Ibn Ezra[290] read *For your sake was I sent
(shullahti) to Babylon* (Isaiah 43:14). Yet both together could not
stand against the weight of the fact that "I have the tradition that
it is to be read *shillahti* (I have sent)."[291] Radak brings few such
rabbinic departures from the masorah and fairly consistently
avoids even citing midrashim based on 'al tiqre. Yet interpretations
of the Targum which are clearly based on variant readings of the
text[292] are cited regularly, along with appropriate expressions
of "astonishment": "It would appear that Jonathan translated 'el
as if it were written with a *zere* meaning *these* . . . as did Ibn Ezra.
I am astonished at this for in no manuscript have I seen it vocal-
ized with anything but a *segol*."[293] "It is astonishing that Jonathan
read it as if it were written with a *shin*."[294] "It is surprising that
Jonathan translated 'im as if it were 'am . . . we do not know if he
had such a reading."[295]

The combined challenge of Vulgate, midrash, Targum and contemporary scribal confusion led Radak to take the study of
masorah far more seriously than had Ibn Ezra. Going beyond the
latter's prescription to "understand a bit of masorah,"[296] he refers
time and again to masorah and masoretic works—Ben Asher and
Ben Naphtali, Orientals (*madinha'e*) and Occidentals (*ma'arava'e*),
the "Masorete," the *Mahzora Rabba,* the *Book 'Okhlah ve-
'Okhlah*[297]—and even introduces masoretic observations of his
own.[298] With respect to manuscript evidence, he cites *testimonia*
of others: R. Hai Gaon, Ibn Ezra, traditions of the *Codex Severus,*
the *Codex Damascus,* and the *Sefer Bavli* as cited from Ibn Janah.[299]
Not relying solely on secondary sources, he refers to his own findings in the "correct manuscripts," which he compares with the
masorah and one another.[300] If Ibn Ezra happened to find variants
in his travels, Radak seems to have traveled in order to find variants. He speaks of the *Sefer Yerushalmi* in Saragossa[301] and the
Sefer Hilleli in Toledo.[302]

In determining the authority of evidence, one of the criteria was
age. In his discussion of the verses Joshua 21:36f., not found in
Jewish Bibles, Radak remarks:

There are certain manuscripts which are emended [adding these verses] . . . and I have not seen these two verses in any exact, ancient manuscript except that some of them are so emended. I noted that R. Hai was asked concerning this matter and he replied: "Even though [the cities] are not enumerated here, they are enumerated in Chronicles."[303] One can see from his reply that they were not written in their Bible texts.[304]

But it was generally the masorah that was decisive. Even when the variants seemed more likely in the context, the masorah was to be preferred.

> *Now, my lord the king, now (ve-'attah) you do not know it* (I Kings 1:18). Many scribes have erred on this word and written *ve-'attah (and you)* with an *'alef* since it is more likely in the context. But it is clear to us that it is *ve-'attah* with an *'ayin* from the correct codices and from the masorah.[305]

It might happen too that Radak would fail to show one manuscript preference over another. He does not decide the discrepancy concerning the word *namotu* (Psalms 17:5) "in that some texts have the *tet* with a *dagesh* in which case the verb is of the class *mediae geminatae*, while some texts read it without the dagesh so that the verbs would be of the class *mediae vav*."[306] Elsewhere he interprets a passage twice: *Nstm* in Zechariah 14:5 is interpreted both as *nastem* and *nistam*. Isaiah 29:13 is explained on the basis of both alternatives, *niggash* or *niggas*,[307] even though the masorah clearly states that it is to be read with a *shin*. In this last case, the Targum reads it with a *sin* and this clearly parallels Isaiah 58:3, where Radak rejected a targumic reading (there preferring *shin*).[308] Apparently, in the case of Isaiah 29:13, we are dealing with a conflict between two sets of "correct manuscripts" to which Radak lends full credence.

This admission that there may be two readings of equal reliability (or unreliability) in contemporary manuscripts parallels Radak's attitude toward the problem of *qere* and *ketiv*: the appearance of two forms for the same word—the actual written form (*ketiv*) and the one that was to be read (*qere*). In Radak's perspective, the Masoretes faced precisely the situation he encountered in his own time. He saw their task as he saw his: one of restoration,[309] of the reestablishment of the correct tradition. Yet there were instances where they, just as he, could not decide between two divergent readings.

> These differences in reading apparently developed because, during the first exile, the texts were lost, the scholars were dispersed, and the biblical experts died. Thus the members of the Great Assembly who *restored* the Torah to its former estate found differences in the texts and followed the reading of the majority as far as possible. When they could not come to a decision, however, they wrote one reading down without pointing it, or they wrote it in the margin and not in the text, or else they wrote one in the margin and one in the text.[310]

Radak's treatment of a particular instance of *ketiv* and *qere* depends on the degree of difference between the two. If the readings are indeed disparate, Radak generally relates to the phenomenon of *ketiv* and *qere* as he would to alternative contemporary readings and explains them both.[311] Thus at Psalms 24:4, the *qere, nafshi,* would render the verse *who has not taken My name in vain* while the *ketiv* would have it: *who has not vaunted his soul in vain.* Again the *qere* at I Kings 12:33, *millibbo,* renders *in the month he devised of his own heart,* while the *ketiv, millevad,* results in *in the month which he devised other than the festivals of the Lord.*[312] More frequently, however, Radak treats *ketiv* and *qere* as if they were two synonymous expressions. His frequently cited note "the idea is repeated in different words"[313] is adapted to "*qere* and *ketiv* and they are equivalent."[314] Thus we see that at Jeremiah 28:1 the *ketiv, bi-shenat,* represents the bound form of the noun, while the *qere* represents the free form—a difference with grammatical but no semantic significance. At Genesis 39:20, we learn that the *qere, 'asur,* is a passive participle while the *ketiv, 'asir,* is an adjectival form; or that the *qere* and *ketiv* are equivalent but the *qere* is a more euphemistic expression.[315] Radak dwells on any special characteristics that one of the forms might have—"and the *qere* is *ba-sadeh* without the definite article as is the general usage"[316]—but the emphasis is on harmonization. In an ingenious attempt at such, Radak demonstrates how the *ketiv* and *qere* complement each other to reveal the full meaning of the verse.

In the verse *that the waters which came down from above stood, and rose up in one heap, a great way off from Adam, the city which is beside Zarethan* (Joshua 3:16), the *ketiv* is *be-'adam* (in Adam) while the *qere* is *me-'adam* (from Adam). This means that if the waters had not risen in one heap but had remained level, they would have entered Adam the city and would·have flooded it. Even though it was far, there was a great deal of water. Now, however, that they have risen in one heap, the waters are indeed far from Adam the city, as far as the Jordan itself.[317]

Radak's concern with such problems as *ketiv* and *qere,* masorah, and scribal difficulties led him to devote a special work to this subject just as he had to grammar. The *Scribe's Pen* (*'Et Sofer*)[318] was more systematic than the *Masoret Seyag la-Torah* of Meir ben Todros Abulafia. The latter listed all words whose roots had a masoretic peculiarity, while the former, a brief work, was organized under three chapters: (1) the writing of the text, dealing principally with problems of *ketiv* and *qere*;[319] (2) vocalization;[320] (3) the *ṭe'amim,* or the masoretic accents.[321] The *Scribe's Pen* is characteristically Kimhian, not only in its organization but in the fact that the second chapter, the lion's share of the book, is a summary of Hebrew morphology. In this we come full circle. Without a grammatical foundation, knowledge of the masoretic lists will avail the scribe no more than knowledge of midrashic traditions will avail the exegete.

> If your knowledge of Torah be thorough,
> But no interest in grammar you've showed,
> Then you've guided your ox through the furrow,
> With nary a whip nor a goad.[322]

Exceptions and Rules

Midrash thrives on the aberrant. A superfluous letter or word, a morphological anomaly or a syntactical peculiarity all challenge the ingenuity of the *darshan*. It is true that the rabbinic tradition that the "Torah speaks in human language" was as old and authoritative as the tendency which declared open season on all extraordinary linguistic phenomena. Yet the one tradition could not dominate the other nor did it really care to.[323] However, for the medieval *pashṭan* who had to draw a clear line of demarcation between midrashic and scientific exegesis, the situation was otherwise. Abraham Ibn Ezra criticized the midrashic exegesis of Christian Europe as "unbalanced"[324] (*she-lo yabbiṭu be-mishqal moznayim*). His meaning is plain: Ibn Ezra entitled his first grammar *The Balance*.[325] Grammar is the foundation of *peshaṭ;* it is the great corrective to the excesses of midrash. Yet—and herein lies the difficulty—it is precisely the "ungrammatical" character of biblical language which renders it so readily susceptible to midrashic exploitation. According to Ibn Ezra, some of these anomalies might best be left ignored. They are few and far between and "we pay no attention to them."[326] Others made peace with the regularity of irregularity in biblical Hebrew. The eleventh-century grammarian Ibn Janah went as far as to suggest the possibility of textual "emendations" medieval style.

> Often, by means of forced theories of grammar and rhetoric, [Ibn Janah] attributed to the received text, where modern scholars declare it to be corrupt, the *sense* of the emendations proposed—on the basis of the context—by the moderns. Thus, since the Hebrew words for "wood" and "bones" are very similar, modern scholars do not hesitate to read "wood" instead of the first "bones" in Ezekiel 24:5, while Ibn Janah obtains the same sense by claiming that among Biblical writers it is a deliberate rhetorical device to say *'atsamim* "bones" and mean *'etsim* "wood."[327]

Like Ibn Janah, Radak was willing to "pay attention." But like Ibn Ezra, he found Ibn Janah's quasi-emendations too radical.
"*Shevi'i* (seventh) cannot be *revi'i* (fourth) at all as Rabbi Jonah claims, for this metamorphosis cannot be and is impossible."[328] Other means would have to be employed:

> *Manoah said to the angel of the Lord:* Who (*mi*) *is your name?* (Judges 13:17). He did not say *mah* (what) as is the custom, since he was a great and noble prophet in Manoah's eyes. A great man is known by his name to him who has never seen him. Here the name is equivalent to that which it represents.[329]

In other words, such forms are not "emendable." Their departure from the norm is quite deliberate and is meant to convey an additional nuance of meaning. If the *ketiv* of *tavoti* ("you have come," I Samuel 25:34) contains both past and future affixes, it is only to indicate the alacrity of her coming.[330] At Ezekiel 8:16, the verb *mishtaḥavitem* is a combination of third plural present and second plural past because "he found *those* men *worshipping* the sun toward the east and asked those who were coming in, "Have you worshipped?"[331]

Radak found that with problems of morphology, just as with problems of *qere* and *ketiv,* a little ingenuity went a long way. It was otherwise in the realm of the syntax. Here, where the exception often prevailed over the rule, even the aloof Ibn Ezra was forced to take an interest. The approach of the Spanish philologists to syntactic difficulties was fairly uniform. For some time, through thoroughgoing classification and systematization, they had attempted to prove that what was aberrant only *appeared* to be so. Since most of these deviant constructions were found to repeat themselves with impressive frequency, it was to be concluded that there is no such thing as a true anomaly. There is a common form and there is an uncommon form; but the uncommon form is never so uncommon that one might, for example, feel justified in the assumption that it was articulated to serve as a pretext for an *'aggadah*. Of course, this approach is not necessarily rooted in its entirety in an anti-midrashic polemic. The very need to allay any suggestion that Scripture is imperfect in grammar or style would suffice for its development. Then too, medieval grammarians, exposed as they were to a plethora of Hebrew, Arabic, and Aramaic dialects, seemed to come to the realization that norms in language are not static and that grammatical regularity is at best a deceptive concept. In this sense, with greater inclination to description than prescription, they had more in them of the modern linguist than the classical grammarian. If it is true that Augustine's training as a rhetor led him to "interpret the Bible as if everything in it were said exactly as it should be said,"[332] we may say that Radak's training as a grammarian made him interpret Scripture as if everything in it were said as it *could* be said. Whether it be a peculiar syntactical usage or a morphological mutation, Radak regularizes the regular, makes normative the nonnormative, and legitimizes the corrupt.

The first stage in this process involved recourse to statistics. At each occurrence of an anomaly, Radak would list similar examples and perhaps refer to the *Mikhlol* for exhaustive treatment.

Will they cry unto Me. "My God, we know You Israel"
(Hosea 8:2). Israel which was placed second should have
come first so as to read *Will Israel cry unto Me . . .* There are
many such examples of *hysteron proteron* in Scripture, such
as *a place for a there grave* (Ezekiel 39:11), *withal I until
escape* (Psalms 141:10), etc. . . . as we have written in the
Mikhlol.[333]

Similarly, if one encounters a singular form instead of an expected
plural, Radak lends reassurance that "this occurs in Hebrew in
many places."[334] Again, if the bound form of the noun is used
instead of the free form, "there are similar cases."[335] "There are
many similar examples"[336] becomes the catchphrase. It is applied
to problems of vocalization[337] and orthography as well: Radak
demonstrates the "regularity" of the unusual occurrence of a
quiescent *'alef* at the end of a verb form; first, by indicating a
parallel; then by declaring that this is the same phenomenon as
that found in the pronoun *hu* (he) of which occurrences in Scripture are legion.[338]

   Yet the collection of the data, as scrupulous as it was, was only
the first step in the regularizing process. The second was that of
classification and the formulation of rubrics under which a given
irregularity could be subsumed. By Radak's time, such exegetical
principles—most of which were rooted in rabbinic hermeneutics—
had been widely catalogued and studied in Spain. At around the
time of Radak's birth, the Aragonese scholar Solomon Ibn Parhon
could include a large and well documented list of these in his
Maḥberet He -'Arukh.[339] All of this material was free grist for
Radak's mill. For terminology and formulation, he could draw on
one and all. Thus the principle of "ellipsis" may be expressed by
the *ḥesron* of Ibn Janah[340] or the *derekh qeẓarah* of the midrash
and Ibn Ezra.[341] *Hysteron proteron* will be referred to sometimes
by expressions based on the rabbinic *'en muqdam u-me'uḥar*[342]
and sometimes by the Spanish philologists' *hafukh.*[343] In the application of these principles, too, Radak was ambitious and far-
reaching. Take for example the principle of ellipsis. This concept,
which allowed that a difficult passage may be interpreted on the
assumption that some element is lacking, is applied broadly by
Radak. That "it is usual in Scripture to omit something when the
matter is clear"[344] is to be considered axiomatic. This principle
may apply to a word or an entire phrase:

He placed at the head of the columns (II Chronicles 3:16). Since the chains were already mentioned, they were omitted here and Scripture depended on the perceptive reader to understand. This is biblical style in several places.[345]

With the application of this principle, the obscurity of a passage such as *I will take vengeance and not strike a man* (Isaiah 47:3) fades if one realizes that the preposition *ka* (like) is missing—as in Proverbs 17:22: *A merry heart benefits like a good medicine.* One may read: *"I will take vengeance and not strike like a man . . . but will take vengeance."*[346]

Radak is especially adept in the ways of prepositions—their unwarranted presence[347] as well as their unwarranted absence, their willingness to enter alliances[348] as well as their readiness to exchange roles.[349]

> *. . . and Bela the son of Azaz [the Reubenite] . . . who dwelt in Aroer (be-'aroer) . . .* (I Chronicles 5:8). There are those who explain [the preposition] *bet* (in) of *in Aroer (be-'aroer)* as standing in place of *mem* (from) for Aroer did not belong to the Reubenites but to the Gadites, as it says, *the sons of Gad built Dibon and Ataroth and Aroer* (Numbers 32:34). This is correct. Similarly, we have found *bet* instead of *mem*: *that which remains of the flesh (ba-basar) and of the bread (ba-leḥem)* (Leviticus 8:32) . . . One can also explain *be-'aroer* as *at the border of Aroer,* for the city itself belonged to the Gadites who built it, while its borders belonged to the Reubenites.[350]

Like his predecessors, Radak notes the precise function of each *lamed,*[351] *vav,*[352] or *kaf.*[353] Prepositions are key elements in the comprehension of a passage and Radak spares no energy in elucidating their functions.

> *The sin of Judah is written with a pen (be-'eṭ) of iron and with a point (be-zipporen) of flint. It is graven upon the table of their heart and at the horns (le-qarnot) of your altars* (Jeremiah 17:1). One might explain that the *bet* of *be-zipporen* (with a point) doubles[354] for another *bet* and that *be-shamir* (with flint) is implied as well. That is to say, it is written with an iron pen and with a point and with flint. Having mentioned the instrument with which he would write, he now mentions the material upon which he would write. Even

though he said that it is *upon the tablet of their heart,* their
heart is the flint . . . The composition of the verse is then: *It
is written with an iron pen and with an iron point . . . on flint
for it is graven on the tablet of their heart which is flint.* The
bet of *be-'et* and *be-zipporen* is the *bet* which is called *bet
instrumentalis*[355] while the *bet* of *be-shamir* is the auxiliary
bet.[356] *Upon the horns of your altar* is expressed with *lamed*
instead of *bet,* as in *before you by the sword (le-harev)*
(Leviticus 26:7) and many other cases.[357]

In passages such as these, with his accustomed balance of grammatical analysis and paraphrase, Radak proceeds to shed light on
the obscure. Yet, unlike most of his predecessors, he does not rest
content with classification alone. Radak, we must recall, was an
apologist by nature.[358] And though one thinks of his apologetics as
hovering above the lofty escarpment of faith and doctrine, they
cannot always be prevented from overflowing into the basin of
syntax and prepositional phrases. Here too, Radak could not limit
himself to stating the case; he had to rationalize it as well. We look
in vain for an expository treatment of these problems; Radak was
no more inclined to produce a discursive essay on the theory of
language than he was on philosophy. It is left to the reader to
synthesize and extrapolate from one or the other stray remark. Yet
a consistent view does emerge. One begins to understand that
language in general, and Hebrew in particular, has its own inner
logic that can explain any seeming inconsistencies in Scripture. Returning once again to the realm of the preposition, Radak develops
a consistent theoretical rationale as to why certain prepositions—
'ahare (after), *'ashre* (happy is . . .), *lifne* (before)—end in a plural
suffix (*-e*), while others such as *'ahar* occur in a singular form.

   'Ahare (after) has a plural form on the pattern of *'ashre*
   (happy) except that *'ashre* is always plural and never appears
   as a singular. This is not the case with *'ahare* for one finds
   after ('ahar) these things (Genesis 15:1) and so forth. *'Ashre*
   is plural because it has to do with many goods; for man will
   not be rendered happy by one good which he possesses or one
   success which happens along. Therefore the word is always
   plural. The plural form of the word *'ahare* (after or behind) is
   like the plural form of *lifne* (before or in front of) since the
   back corresponds to the face (*panim*). Now *panim* (face) will
   never be found in a singular form since he who sees them
   and faces them will always encounter a plurality and will not

be able to see one organ on the face apart from the others. For the organs of the face are all paired: the eyelids, the eyes, the nostrils, the cheeks, the lips, the teeth. This is not so with the nape of the neck, which is behind the face and is a single unit . . . Thus the entire human form is developed with various organs in front but is uniform in the back.[359]

An even more striking attempt at demonstrating the logical consistency of a grammatical anomaly is found in the area of syntax of the verb. Thus does Radak deal with the occurrence of a verb in what would normally be considered a passive form when an active verb is required.

> Your wound *sickened* (*naḥlah*) (Nahum 3:19). Scripture uses the passive *nif'al* verbal form in speaking of the wound even though it should be active. It is the man who falls ill while the wound causes the illness . . . However, because of the many ills in the wound, it is acted upon by them, i.e., it is full of them.[360]

That such considerations could represent more than a mere scholastic exercise in ingenuity is evident from a passage such as Ezekiel 14:4. There the occurrence of an apparently passive form, *I the Lord have* been *answered,* instead of the active, *have answered,* creates theological confusion. Here too Radak overcomes the problem.

> Now God is the agent in answering the one who cries to him . . . while the man who cries is the one who is answered. . . How then does it use of God a passive form [as if to say *I was answered*]? We declare the reason to be that the term *ma'aneh* (answer) has two senses. The first is the commencement of speech, as in *Job answered (said)* (Job 3:2) and *You shall answer (recite) before the Lord* (Deuteronomy 26:5). The second is in the sense of response, which is the most common . . . Thus when the passive is used, He is responsive to the one calling upon Him.[361]

Akin to the intricacies of active and passive is the problem of transitive and intransitive. Radak observes that the verb "to weep." ostensibly an intransitive verb, takes a direct object in Hebrew as well as other languages "since the weeping is done *for* the object so that it is as if he had received the action."[362]

If Radak could feel such confidence with respect to relatively difficult linguistic phenomena, it is not surprising that he would take more usual anomalies as self-evident. We recall, for example, that inversions in Scripture are routinely explained by the common-place principle of *hysteron proteron.* Thus such a passage as *as stubble devours the tongue of fire* (Isaiah 5:24) need only be re-shuffled to calm the most anxious spirits. Yet how to calm the *darshanim* who will capitalize on such a passage?[363] Turning to them with the same techniques as those cultivated in religious polemics, Radak bluntly counters the midrashic "Why?" with a pashṭanic "Why not?" The meaning of the verse is so evident, he claims, that "one cannot be misled . . . It is known that fire devours stubble. It is the same with *water causes fire to boil* (Isaiah 64:11) and *stones wear the waters* (Job 14:19)."[364] In other words, where the meaning is obvious, there is no reason *not* to expect inverted word order.

Biblical inconsistency in the use of gender and number provokes some remarkable explanations:

> *Bring it to him* (II Samuel 14:10). Since he is addressing a woman, he should have used a feminine suffix . . . Yet he uses a masculine suffix since he was addressing one of the pages . . . for the woman could not bring it without the assistance of one of the king's pages.[365]

With the midrash before him, Radak struggles with *The woman took the two men and hid him* (Joshua 2:4).

> *She hid him*—each one separately so that they would not locate them if they came up on the roof. In the *derash*[366] it says that the two spies were Caleb and Phineas. Phineas stood before them and they did not see him since he was like an angel. *She hid him* refers then to Caleb alone.
>
> It is possible to explain that [the suffix "*o*" (him) in the word] *tizpeno* (she hid him) refers to the preposition *'et* [marking the direct object in the phrase *She took 'et the two men*], which includes both of them.[367]

Apparently then Radak takes the entire phrase, "*'et the two men,*" as the object of the second verb, as it is of the first. Elsewhere, such sophisticated perceptions are not needed. Sometimes it is sufficient to point out that "the verb agrees with the noun adjacent to it" rather than with its actual subject.[368]

Yet the vast majority of such cases lie between these two approaches. Radak will show that grammatical disagreement is not necessarily an anomaly but a deliberate device to achieve greater precision. As we have seen in the above-cited example from Joshua, the juxtaposition of singular and plural forms conveys the concept of "each of them." Thus *our sins has testified against us* (Isaiah 59:12) refers to the testimony of each individual sin.[369] Similarly, and in tacit agreement with midrashic traditions,[370] *there cameth men unto me* (Ezekiel 14:1) refers to their "full unanimity and agreement."[371] In the same fashion, Radak approaches the problem of why verbs referring to Israel appear now in the singular now in the plural, now in the masculine gender and now in the feminine. This problem too is susceptible to rationalization. When the verb form is masculine singular, it is the nation as a whole which is spoken of;[372] if it is a question of masculine plural, Scripture refers to the individual members of the nation.[373] Feminine plural, on the other hand, has reference to "assemblies (*qehillot*) of Israel."[374] In the question of feminine singular, however, grammatical theory borders on political theory: whereas the masculine refers to *'am* or *populus,* the feminine is said to refer to the *kenasah.* This word, a rare back formation from *keneset [yisra'el],* the community of Israel, appears to reflect such a concept as *congregatio* or *communitas.* It differs from the *'am* in the sense that the latter exists under all conditions while the former applies only to the organized commonwealth in the Land of Israel.[375]

Biblical Stylistics

Concern with syntax went hand in hand with awareness of style. Radak's own limitations as a poet did not render him any the less sensitive to literary device in Scripture. The stylistic phenomena, the rhetorical figures, the modulations of language were not discovered for the first time by the litterateurs of the Middle Ages. They were preceded by the rabbinic *darshanim,* who were interested in these stylistic features, not for the purpose of formulating the canons of an *ars poetica,* but as raw material for the production of midrashim. Seeming redundancies, omissions, and repetitions of words were classic bases of midrashim. To the Targum, each *holy* of Isaiah's *holy, holy, holy* (Isaiah 6:3) bears a particular connotation: "holy in the highest heavens the place of His Presence; holy on earth the work of His hands, holy for ever and ever." "The artistic charm," in the words of a noted student of midrash, "is thereby sacrificed for the sake of the theological lesson to be learned from the text."[376] Not all the rabbinic sages were completely in sympathy with this approach. Some maintained the view that the "Torah speaks in human language"[377] with no hidden teachings to be uncovered by midrashic techniques. These were the forerunners of such medieval *pashṭanim* as Joseph Kimhi's pupil Menahem ben Simeon, who was unequivocal in his statement that "when you observe the words of Ezekiel, you will see that he repeats things two or three times. He did this to make them contrite and frighten them. It is also for emphasis."[378] Yet not all *pashṭanim* maintained this attitude consistently. Joseph Kimhi himself takes Jeremiah's *the Temple of the Lord, the Temple of the Lord, the Temple of the Lord* (Jeremiah 7:4) as referring to the three parts of the Temple, the *'ulam, hekhal,* and *devir.*[379] Thus he agrees with the midrash in principle if not in specific content. In the same way, Radak, following the Targum, sees Reuben's *excellence of dignity and the excellence of power* (Genesis 49:3) as referring to "three distinctions . . . the priesthood, primogeniture, and kingship."[380] Yet by and large, Radak maintained the posture established in his approach to syntactic analysis and saw these phenomena as devices to be subsumed under stylistic rules: "The repetition is for emphasis, for it is usual for Scripture to repeat words two or three times to stress a point."[381]

To be sure, the appreciation of biblical stylistics was not at all original with Radak. For example, the Spanish poet and savant Moses Ibn Ezra, who lived a hundred years before Radak, set forth these "ornaments of poetry" in the last chapter of his work on poetics.[382] Ibn Ezra had intended to prove that the foundations of Hebrew poetry were to be seen in Scripture itself and were not merely derivative from Arabic poetry.[383] Although his own primary objective was not biblical exegesis, the exegete could indeed apply such material as Ibn Ezra's for his own ends. In the case of Radak, this was, of course, the reinforcement of *peshaṭ*. Thus Radak once again attempts to wean the reader away from a midrashic approach with his point-counterpoint presentation of the alternatives. When Scripture speaks of the angel's addressing Hagar in the wilderness, the expression *he said* is used three times.[384] "This is the custom of

Scripture at certain places . . . for emphasis, as we have written many times in the *Mikhlol* . . . and there is a *derash* that God sent her three angels one after the other."[385] In the threefold repetition in Nahum's *The Lord is a jealous and avenging God. The Lord is avenging and full of wrath; the Lord is avenging* (Nahum 1:2), the rabbinic sources refer the three expressions to the three exiles.[386] For Radak, they remain "emphatic repetition."[387] Radak constantly stresses that the purpose of repetition is emphasis.

> *On the affliction of Your handmaid* (I Samuel 1:11). [*Handmaid* appears] three times in the verse as [does *Noah* in Genesis 6:9] . . . for this is literary style in Scripture. They expounded on it: "Hannah said: Women were commanded three commandments and I did not transgress one of them"[388] . . . The repetition emphasizes the prayer and entreaty.[389]

From repetitions and duplications of words, it is a short step to synonymous expressions. Here we find Radak approaching this phenomenon—well exploited by midrashic teachers—in the same manner he approached syntactic problems. Just as those phenomena were categorized under syntactic rules, he proposed stylistic principles to dehomilize the biblical text. In Hannah's prayer for a son, two forms of the verb "to look" (*ra'oh tir'eh*) are used in the verse: *If You will look, looking at the affliction of Your handmaid* . . . (I Samuel 1:11). For the rabbis, the presence of the two forms alludes to an ultimatum which Hannah delivers before God.

> *If You look, looking at the affliction of Your handmaid.* R. Eleazar said: Hannah said before the Holy One, blessed be He: Sovereign of the Universe: If You look, it is well, and if You do not look, I will go and shut myself up in the knowledge of my husband Elkanah, and as I shall have been alone they will make me drink the water of the suspected wife (Numbers 5:11–31). You cannot falsify Your Law, which says, *She shall be cleared and shall conceive seed* (Numbers 5:28).

For Radak, all this is superfluous: "it is customary for two forms of the verb to be employed, viz., *if you listen listening* (Deuteronomy 11:13). The fact is that this combination is for emphasis." When it is a question of two different but synonymous expressions being used, Radak develops the principle of "the thought is repeated in different words for emphasis" (*kafal ha-'inyan be-millot shonot*). Occasionally, Radak proves the point:

> *If You remember me and do not forget Your handmaid* (I Samuel 1:11). They expounded the midrash: *Remember me* (*zekhartani*) refers to males (*zekharim*) and *not forget Your handmaid* refers to females.[390] *A man child* (*ibid.*) means males and her saying *no razor shall come upon his head* (*ibid.*) proves that she spoke of males for this would not be said of females.[391]

Yet in general the principle is stated without apologetics and with high frequency, becoming one of the hallmarks of his commentaries.

Radak's confrontation with the midrash may be seen in yet another context. The midrash makes the statement of Jacob's departure from Beersheba—*Jacob went out from Beersheba and went towards Haran* (Genesis 28:10)—a redundancy meant to teach the impact of the righteous on a community:

> The departure of a righteous man from a place makes an impression. When the righteous man is in the city, he is its splendor, its brilliance, its glory. When he leaves, so leave its splendor, its brilliance, and its glory.[392]

For Radak:

> The custom of Scripture is to record the beginning and end of an event and to omit that which occurred in the interim. For example, in *he arose and went to Aram-naharaim* (Genesis 24:10) and *the bud that shall yield no meal* (Hosea 8:7), the intermediate actions were omitted since the text was intent on making its point.[393]

What was to the midrash an incidental reference becomes—despite its brevity—a narrative in its own right. There is stylistic ellipsis as well as syntactic ellipsis. "It is the way of Scripture to omit words when the context is obvious."[394]

We also find the opposite phenomenon of apparently superfluous words[395]—especially the particles and prepositions out of which midrashim were so often woven.[396] We have seen what the rabbis could do with a superfluous *'et*.

Cursed be the man that rises up and builds this city, Jericho (*'et yeriho*) (Joshua 6:26). The rabbis explained this to indicate that they should not build it and call it by another name or build another city and call its name Jericho.[397]

For Radak, the *'et* appears "for greater explicitness."[398] "For greater explicitness" becomes a general principle which also explains the appearance of *'et* with a passive verb[399] or other stylistic phenomena.[400] Such principles or stylistic rules proliferated in the commentaries. Radak speaks of the customs of Scripture as a traveler would speak of the customs of the communities he visited. "It is the custom of Scripture to begin with the last-mentioned subject as in *I gave to Isaac, Jacob, and Esau and I gave Esau Mount Seir . . .*" (Joshua 24:4).[401] "It says *deceitful [brook]* (Jeremiah 15:18), stating the adjective and not the substantive. This is scriptural style in many places, e.g., *like a flock [of ewes] all alike* (Song of Songs 4:2), *and his food a fatted lamb* (Habakkuk 1:16)."[402] "*You were wroth and we sinned* (Isaiah 64:4). *After* we sinned. Similarly, *it bred worms and rotted* (Exodus 16:20), *after* it rotted. Similarly, *[and made the sea dry land] and the waters were divided* (Exodus 14:21), *after* the waters were divided."[403]

This "underplaying" of stylistic phenomena did not, however, imply that they were entirely devoid of significance or effect. Radak notes, for example, that there are figures characteristic of prophecy,[404] or of mourning and lamentation (*derekh ha-meqonen, ha-qinah, 'avelut*).[405] Especially effective use of language is labeled "elegance" (*derekh zahut*)[406] or "poetic eloquence" (*derekh melizat ha-shir*).[407] Radak points out the use of metaphor (*hash'alah*)[408] and alliteration (*lashon nofel 'al lashon*) such as *ve-ha-memale'im la-meni mimsakh* (who lavish libations on Luck) (Isaiah 65:11).[409] He shows the reader how Jeremiah makes use of a rhetorical imperative:

Set up a standard (Jeremiah 51:27) is not commanded to any individual in particular but to whoever is there. It is purely rhetorical like *See the smell of my son* (Genesis 27:27), *Say to the king and the queen-mother* (Jeremiah 13:18), *Strengthen the weak hands* (Isaiah 35:3), *Say to them that are of a fearful heart* (Isaiah 35:4), etc. . . .[410]

Hyperbole and exaggeration (*haflagah, guzma*) are frequently noted. *Every man of Judea* (Jeremiah 44:26) is not meant literally but "refers to most of them."[411] *He saw that there was no man* (Isaiah 59:16) is considered a generalization, "for it cannot be possible that there be none in Israel righteous enough to be worthy of redemption."[412] David's reply to Nathan that the rich man who mistreated the poor "*deserves to die* (II Samuel 12:1) is hyperbole, for one does not incur death for stealing. Yet because he did something base, he said that he is deserving of death."[413] Hyperbole can also develop into irony: "*Come to Beth-el and transgress* (Amos 4:4). The command is not to be taken seriously but is an exaggeration (*gizzum*) like *Rejoice, O young man* [*in your youth*] (Ecclesiastes 11:9)."[414]

Yet even these indications of artistic usage are given within the framework of rules and examples. It is always the "style" of the prophet, of the mourner, of Scripture itself. Scripture is always written in the natural, ordinary style appropriate to the context.

Radak did not provide any broad theoretical justification for this approach. He did not have to. In his introduction to the Decalogue, Abraham Ibn Ezra had attempted to prove that any homiletic exploitation of the fact that there are two divergent versions of the Decalogue can not be relied upon. The version in Exodus, he insisted, was the original uttered at Mount Sinai, while the second in Deuteronomy was the paraphrase of Moses. There are differences of course—just as everyday conversation undergoes minor transformations when it is repeated at a later occasion. Just as in ordinary speech and writing, "Scripture preserves the *sense* but not the words."[415] Without direct reference to Ibn Ezra, Radak accepted and reiterated this point of view:

> In the repetition of these things, there is a change in the words but the sense is the same. It is the custom of Scripture that in repetitions, the sense, if not the words, is preserved. Even in the Ten Commandments, the foundation of the Torah, the words are changed in the repetition in Deuteronomy but the sense is the same.[416]

Here Radak, as had Abraham Ibn Ezra, eloquently reinforces the notion that Scripture is written as an ordinary human document possessing the same characteristics that are found in normal speech and writing. Scripture follows conventional linguistic patterns and is not, as midrash would have one believe, subject to caprice. This assumption, established through Radak's complex of stylistic and syntactical rules, was to be given expression elsewhere as well.

Obscurities and Discrepancies

Although the solutions proposed by modern biblical criticism would have jarred the rabbinic or medieval mind, the problems raised would have had a very familiar ring. In their own way, the ancient commentaries came to terms with passages contradictory to others and to traditional attributions of authorship.[417] The midrash and Rashi too noted the existence of "J" and "E" passages, but their approach differed radically from that of the critics.[418] It is true that in Ibn Ezra one finds the beginnings of textual criticism in the modern sense,[419] but Ibn Ezra was a fairly isolated phenomenon. His followers, including Radak, did not proceed along these lines.

On another level, however, Radak's commitment to the solution of text-critical questions was unreserved. This commitment was given expression in his choice of the Book of Chronicles as the subject of his first commentary. This was the book containing "the many obscurities and discrepancies with Samuel and Kings."[420] These "discrepancies" included contradictory data in names, dates, and other factual information. Again, these were to be fuel for aggadic fires and Radak proceeded, as was his wont, to control the conflagration.

The lion's share of his deliberations was taken up with the problem of names. Contradictions between names as reported in Chronicles and the other historical books are many and varied and range from orthographical alterations to complete substitutions. For each type of problem, Radak had an appropriate solution. Here too a rule might be formulated. On minor changes, he states that "metathesis in names is common in Hebrew, as you will frequently see,"[421] for the "Hebrews were not too strict about this."[422] On another occasion, "it would appear that they were not very particular about whether the name was Dishan or Dishon."[423] In sum, "You will see that in Hebrew they are not overly concerned about differences of one or two letters in most names of people or cities. They call nations by two dissimilar names, one name in one place and another name in the other."[424]

As with nations, so with individuals and places. Here too the
darshanim found much clay for their wheel, but Radak was clearly
weary of their interpretations. "In the listing of the cities of the
Levites, you will find that the names vary from those found in the
Book of Joshua as I explained to you concerning the names of
people . . . There are many *derashot* on the changes of names and
there is no need to mention them."[425]

Following earlier precedents,[426] Radak would find rational solutions. For one thing, it was the custom in biblical times to have two
names.[427] Joel is Vashni.[428] Abimelech is Achish.[429] Kirjath-jearim
is Baalah.[430] In a double play, Maacah the daughter of Absalom
and Micaiahu the daughter of Uriel are considered to be one and the
same on the assumption that "both she and her father had two
names."[431] On the other hand, if Achish is called Abimelech, it is
possible that Abimelech was a general title of Philistine kings as
Pharaoh was of Egyptian kings.[432] Or if Othniel ben Kenaz and
Caleb ben Jephuneh are brothers, Kenaz was probably a family
name.[433] There is no special difficulty either if a father-son relationship becomes a grandfather-grandson relationship: Zerubbabel
may be the son of Pedaiah in one place[434] and the son of Shealtiel
elsewhere[435] because "sons of sons are considered as sons at many
places in the Bible."[436]

Radak preferred the "double-name theory" to what he considered amateurish philological solutions. At I Samuel 8:2 Samuel's
first born is said to be Joel while at I Chronicles 6:13 *Vashni*
appears instead. Radak rejects the ingenious solution that makes
Vashni ve-ha-sheni (and the second) so that the verse reads: *The
sons of Samuel are the first born and the second born Abiah.*[437]
Incensed over the gross disregard of grammatical subleties involved,
he demands to know "what led them to this quandary?"[438]

In coming to terms with these problems, Radak generally avoided
entering into discussions of etymologies, a basic starting point for
aggadic speculations. He was aware, of course, that some of these
changes were patently etiological in nature: "Achar is Achan but
he is called Achar contemptuously because he troubled (*'akhar*)
Israel."[439] All the names recorded as ending with -*boshet* (shame)
are derogatory substitutions for names originally ending with
-*ba'al*.[440] Indeed, at times, his left hand would introduce some of
those contraband *'aggadot* which his right hand barred.[441] Yet his
official posture is one of implacability toward the rabbinic midrashim:

There are many *derashot* on these names. Were we to expound them all, no book could contain them. We know only that which is written, for all these names are related to things known to [the ancients]. This is indicated with some of these names and we are not to seek those for which we have no information.[442]

The rabbis themselves are cited for testimony that excessive speculation on etymologies may prove futile.

Our rabbis said: "The name and its interpretation are not related. Either it should say *Noah will relieve us* (*Noah yanihenu*) or *Nahman will console us* (*Nahman yenahamenu*) [and not *Noah will console us* (*Noah yenahamenu,* Genesis 5:29)]."[443] This is true but respite from sorrow is consolation and the two are closely related. The holy tongue is not too strict concerning this. Similarly, Samuel should have been called Saul according to its interpretation.[444]

For Radak it is sufficient that "it is customary for the holy tongue to add or remove a letter in names derived from verbs . . . or to metathesize."[445]

Radak's insistence on the futility of name-etymologies is especially illuminating for, as elsewhere, his anti-midrashic stance seems to be masking other considerations. If one examines anti-Jewish polemical literature of this period, one finds that Christian theologians were themselves using midrashic techniques as an element in the *verus Israel* debate. In the endless argument as to who was the legitimate heir of biblical Israel, the question of the identification of the true bearers of such names as Israel, Judah, and Ephraim came into play. Some authorities of the Church might deny that such names had ever properly belonged to the Jewish people. Eusebius distinguished between the biblical Hebrews, the proto-Christians, and the Jews, while Augustine identified the Jews with the scriptural Edomites.[446] This thinking was supported by such "midrashim" as those found in the *Sefer Nizzahon Yashan.* This twelfth-century source tells us that Christians "are called *Yehudim* (Jews) because they recognize (*modim*) and confess (*mitvaddim*) before the priest . . ." and that "they are Ephraim since they have multiplied (*paru*) and increased."[447] Jewish sources expressed awareness of these manipulations. Indeed, the extant portion of Joseph Kimhi's *Book of the Covenant* breaks off with just such a discussion.[448] Radak himself does not reply to these etymologies directly. For the sake of consistency, only rarely will he offer a counter-etymology: "Jeshurun is known to be Israel and they are so called because they are upright (*yashar*) among the nations."[449] Yet we find Radak frequently stressing the congruency of all these names. "When Scripture speaks of the seed of Abraham, it refers to the seed of Israel";[450] "what was given to Abraham and Isaac was for the sake of the seed of Jacob";[451] the kings of Judah are called the kings of Israel because "Judah is included in Israel."[452] Radak carried out this debate elsewhere on other, more significant, levels. It would therefore seem likely that his anti-etymologizing tendency betrayed at its root a reluctance to give aid and comfort to the enemy.

Paralleling the "midrashic" type of name changes, there was yet another class which might be termed "masoretic." Such were the pairs Dodanim and Rodanim (Genesis 10:4, I Chronicles 1:7), Deuel and Reuel (Numbers 1:13, 2:14), Diblathah and Riblathah (Ezekiel 6:14, Numbers 2:14). Radak's predecessors treated these variations as the result of an assumed phonetic correspondence between *d* and *r* or with the double-name theory.[453] Radak does not start from either of these two positions but presents a new and strikingly different approach. Drawing on his methodology in the analysis of *ketiv* and *qere*,[454] Radak posits a confusion, not in the masoretic text itself, but in the *pre*biblical records upon which the biblical authors based their genealogies.[455] This confusion is based upon the *orthographical* similarity between *dalet* and *resh* or *vav* and *yod*.[456]

> Among the genealogists in ancient times were those who read Rodanim with a *dalet* (i.e., Dodanim) and those who read it with a *resh*. The names continued to be pronounced[457] with [both] *dalet* and *resh*. Therefore it was written in Genesis with one reading and written in this book (Chronicles) with the other in order to indicate that they are really the same name, though one is read with *dalet* and the other with *resh*. Similar are *Riblathah* with *resh* and *Diblathah* with *dalet*; *Reuel* with *resh* and *Deuel* with *dalet*. Similarly *vav* and *yod* may alternate since their written forms resemble each other.[458]

Fortunately, one cannot speak of error in the biblical texts since we are dealing here with "prebiblical" sources. Yet Radak's solution does provoke the question: which was the *original* form of the name? To preserve the honor of the Torah and Moses, he observes concerning Dodanim that "Moses read it with *dalet* since the holy spirit came to him, while Ezra wrote it with *resh* to make it known that it is the same word read differently."[459] This is of no assistance in instances of contradictions between books other than the Torah. Yet since these "errors" were purposely preserved, it does not seem to matter which had priority.

Second only to Radak's concern with names is his concern for numbers. Radak often attempted to unravel complicated chronological knots[460] where others considered the attempt hardly worth the effort.[461] Contradictions between parallel passages which involved numbers challenged his ingenuity[462] and it was his way to find a compromise solution. If Chronicles has the Levites serving from the age of twenty[463] while the Torah initiates their service at thirty,[464] it is because David lowered the age limit since they no longer had to perform heavy physical labor.[465] In Chronicles, the amount of money brought to Solomon from Hiram is less than that reported in Kings. Radak remarks that in Kings the travel expenses of the bearers were taken into account.[466] When a year is "lost" in a chronological list, Radak's explanation implies that royal chronologies are reckoned in terms of throne and not calendar years.

> *In the eighteenth year of King Jeroboam Abijah began to reign over Judah* (II Chronicles 13:1). We do not know why he was detained a year from ruling, for Rehoboam only reigned seventeen years and Jeroboam and Rehoboam began their reigns in the same year. One might explain that Rehoboam entered his eighteenth year but that it was not counted since he did not complete it. It was, however, counted with Jeroboam as usual.[467]

Contradictions of fact are similarly harmonized. In Chronicles,[468] Hiram is said to have given cities to Solomon rather than the opposite as stated in Kings.[469] As if he were reconciling a *ketiv* and *qere*, Radak explains that both statements are correct: they exchanged cities to "strengthen the alliance between them."[470] If Chronicles assigns the land of Bashan to Gad[471] and Deuteronomy assigns it to the half-tribe of Manasseh, Radak "partitions" the territory between them.[472]

Through such reconciliations, Radak can take a generally relaxed attitude to the internal midrash in the Book of Chronicles that amplifies or alters the material in the Torah or Former Prophets. He speaks, to be sure, of editorial involvement,[473] but it would be too much to expect him to speak of editorial bias. Rather, he takes it as natural that "what was not mentioned previously was mentioned here."[474] If *Hammolecheth* "was not mentioned in the Torah and in the Prophets, they knew it through tradition."[475] The Book of Samuel does not explain why David was not deemed worthy of building the Temple. The Chronicler rationalized David's failure to build a Temple to the Lord by placing the following words in his mouth: *"The word of the Lord came to me: you have shed much blood, and have made great wars; you shall not build a house to My name, because you have shed much blood upon the earth in My sight"* (I Chronicles 22:8). Radak remarks: "We have not found that God said this to him but rather David said it to himself . . . and even though it did not appear in the Book of Samuel, there are many similar occurrences."[476] It is possible that in some instances the new introduction of material is only apparent. If the second coronation of Solomon was not mentioned in the Book of Kings, it has its parallel, according to Radak, in the promise of David to Bathsheba that her son would reign.[477] The obviously tendentious statement that Saul did not seek the Lord is taken to mean that his use of black magic was equivalent to an abandonment of God.[478]

Radak seems, then, to have made up his mind that if Scripture was not one massive web of consistency, its inconsistencies were only apparent. Irregularities in factual data, like irregularities in grammar, were capable of arranging themselves in remarkable patterns of regularity.

Radak generally leaves the traditional rabbinic ascriptions of authorship of biblical books unchallenged. On the basis of I Samuel 9:9, Radak's northern French colleague Joseph Kara would conclude that "this book was not written in the days of Samuel."[479] Radak's solution:

> *Previously in Israel, when a man went to inquire of God, he said: "Come and let us go to the seer"; for he that is now called a prophet was previously called a seer.* The rabbis had the tradition that Samuel wrote the book bearing his name. This incident occurred at the end of his days, for Samuel

died in the lifetime of Saul, who only ruled two years. If so,
what is meant by the expression *previously* and *now*? One
might explain that the former custom of calling a prophet a
seer was common in Samuel's time also. Thus *previously* does
not imply that the practice ceased but that Saul and his servant were still using the old term "seer" . . . But in the days
of Samuel when prophecy became common, they also called
the seer a prophet . . . Thus in the time of Samuel there were
those who said "seer" as in olden times and those who said
"prophet."[480]

Yet Radak, with his mind ever on manuscripts, saw the traditional authors as editors who worked from older sources. Thus
while the rabbis state that Ezra wrote Chronicles,[481] Radak implies
that the basic material is older and that Ezra, with the aid of
Haggai, Malachi, and Zechariah, placed it in the Writings.[482]
As we have seen in the Dodanim-Rodanim discussion, Radak saw
Moses as working from older written sources.[483] David was the
redactor of the Book of Psalms but the author only of those psalms
beginning with "of David" (*le-David*) or with no attribution at
all.[484] Others, such as "the prayer of Moses" (Psalm 90), he
"found" and placed in the collection.[485] Thus the historical statements in the Bible that betray the traditional dates and authorship
of the texts, which so concerned Ibn Ezra, did not seem to trouble
Radak very much. He evades the problem of Genesis 12:7—*The
Canaanite and the Perizzite lived in the land then*—by taking *then*
as an emphatic particle rather than an adverb of time.[486] *The
Jebusites lived with the children of Judah at Jerusalem* (Joshua
15:63) are the words of Joshua "for he wrote his book according
to tradition. In his time he did not expel them from Jerusalem.
Even in the days of David we have found that they were there."[487]
The apparently anachronistic reference to a king of Israel in
Genesis is not treated as problematic. As elsewhere,[488] the word
king is used as a synonym for *judge.*[489]
Yet some inconsistencies would not be put off that easily.
When a place is cited under the name by which it was known only
long after the traditional date of composition, Radak applies the
principle of "by its future name."[490] Thus the city of Dan was
referred to "by its future name, for when Moses wrote this it was
called Leshem and when the Danites conquered it they called it
Dan after their father."[491] Yet at I Samuel 4:1, a safe distance

from the revered Torah itself, Radak notes that "the writing of Eben-Ezra here is the expression of the scribe and likewise *he pursued as far as Dan* (Genesis 14:14)." Thus in addition to proto-author and author-redactor, he distinguishes a later stage: the editor who prepared the work in its final form.[492]

Radak seemed to be generally satisfied with the work of these editors. Rashi had assigned the closing chapters of Judges[493] to the time of an early Judge, Othniel ben Kenaz.[494] Radak, on the other hand, maintains that they are in proper chronological order: the phrase *There was no King in Israel* (Judges 18:1) suggests an absence of leadership characteristic of the period between the sons of Samson and Eli.[495] This is all the more noteworthy since Radak is thus forced to follow the midrash in establishing Phineas' age as three hundred years.[496] He does not follow Rashi either in seeing chapter six of Isaiah as the prophet's first prophecy. Rather, he rationalizes the difficulties involved so that it might keep its assigned place.

> It has been said that Isaiah's prophetic mission began in the year in which Uzziah, king of Judah, was afflicted, since it says *"In the year of the death of King Uzziah"* (Isaiah 6:1) and *Whom shall I send?* (Isaiah 6:8), and *Here am I, send me* (Isaiah 6:9). Therefore, [they say] this chapter should have been the first prophecy, for the Torah does not necessarily follow chronological order.
>
> It is possible, [however, that Isaiah's] prophecy began during the beginning of Uzziah's reign, since it says in Chronicles (II Chronicles 26:22) *the rest of the acts of Uzziah, first and last, did Isaiah, the prophet, the son of Amoz, write.* It seems then that he had prophesied earlier. He saw that great vision, however, the likes of which he had not seen previously, in the year in which Uzziah died, and was consequently frightened by that vision. As for His saying *whom shall I send?* there were other prophets in [Isaiah's] time, such as Amos, Zechariah . . . and Hosea, the son of Beeri. He said *Whom shall I send?* so that [the prophet] would know that he must reprove [the people] for God sent them prophets who were of no avail. Isaiah therefore said, *Here am I, Send me,* that is, "I am still here. Send me, for if I have been of no use up to now, perhaps I may still be of benefit."[497]

Radak's justification of the context of these passages is consistent with his demands as an exegete that context be a prime consideration in interpretation. To this we now turn.

Context

Abraham Ibn Ezra's historico-methodological introduction to his Torah commentary is constructed upon the motif of the point-within-a-circle.[498] The center of the circle represents the method of Ibn Ezra himself, which he considered *peshaṭ*. Those who took a different approach were positioned at a distance from the center of the circle in proportion to the degree and nature of their error. All were charted on a graph: the geonic commentators who expatiated on all sorts of irrelevant matters; the Christians; the *darshanim;* and the Karaites, who saw themselves as having liberated Scripture from the *darshanim*. The locus of each school on this graph was plotted with two coordinates. The first was grammar, the "balance," the crucial first step. Yet this was *only* the first step. The true *pashṭan* would have regard not only for morphology and syntax but for the second coordinate, the context of a passage itself. To ignore the *'inyan,* to take a passage out of context, was to turn one's back on *peshaṭ*. For Ibn Ezra as for Radak, this was the basic failing of both Jewish midrash and Christian exegesis.[499]

It was, of course, precisely the liberties that the *darshan* took with the context that enabled him to pour new wine into old scriptural bottles. Thus he could, for example, overcome the barriers set by the Book of Leviticus,

> the hardest and "driest" from the point of view of its principal themes: by and large, the *minutiae* of laws and sacrifice and ritual purity. He who accepted the challenge of compiling an aggadic midrash on this book had to find a way to free it from consecutive passage by passage and chapter by chapter exegesis of the entire book.[500]

The leeway thus acquired by the *darshan* would allow him

> to base a sermon on the topic of "Moses and his prophecy" on the first chapter of Leviticus . . . without any consideration for the continuity of the chapter, which deals in its entirety with the details of fire-offerings, or . . . to construct an entire sermon on slander on chapter fourteen of Leviticus, which deals with the leper—on the basis of a play on *meẓura'* (leper) and *moẓi ra'* (slanderer) with no regard for the context and true subject of the passage.[501]

The *pashṭan* could be cognizant of the artistry and intent of the *darshan*. The latter had his place; but *derash* was not to be confused with *peshaṭ*. Radak, for example, watches with interest the rabbinizations of biblical heroes. David's chief warrior was named Adino because his study of Torah adorned (*me'adden*) him.[502]

> *Benaiah ben Johiada . . . slew a lion in the midst of a pit in time of snow* (II Samuel 23:20). Some say that this indicates that he broke blocks of ice and went down and bathed [in order to purify himself]; others say that he went through the Sifra of the School of Rav on a winter's day.[503]

Radak does not deny the scholarship of Adino or Benaiah; he simply says that this is not exegesis: "All these things are far from the *peshaṭ*. Scripture tells of their valiant deeds—*not* their learning or piety."[504]

As far as Christian violations of context, the rabbis had learned long ago that contextual evidence serves as the best refutation of a christological interpretation: "Whenever the *minim* (heretics) declare a heretical interpretation, the refutation is at its side."[505] Radak found this a sound methodology.

> As for those in error who say that *because they sell the righteous for silver* (Amos 2:6) refers to Jesus, answer them: The subject of the passage is the evil deeds that they would do every day—that is the subject of the chapter. Further why did he speak of the *transgressions of Israel* (*ibid.*)? He should have said the *transgressions of Judah,* for it was they who sold him, according to them. In the time of the second Temple, the ten tribes were not in existence.[506]

How, asks Radak, can the Christians refer Psalms 87:5 to the "spiritual" Jerusalem when they themselves admit that the context of the psalm refers to the terrestrial world?[507] How can they refer *the gate* [*which*] *shall be shut and not be opened* (Ezekiel 44:2) to Mary's virginity, when "it is clear that it speaks of the Temple and its gates, not of a woman. All the verses before it and after it refute them as any intelligent person can see. I need not therefore take up time refuting them."[508] For the Christians, Isaiah spoke to Ahaz of Jesus.[509] Radak objects:

The context refutes their words explicitly for Ahaz was afraid that these two kings, [Rezin and Pekah ben Remaliah], might take Jerusalem.

God therefore gave him a sign so that he might have faith that they would not do so. If this sign was Jesus as they say, what meaning did this have for Ahaz? How could he be encouraged by something which did not happen in his own time and was not to come for another four hundred years?[510]

For Radak, such substantiations of theological dogmas were sheer inventions. The best reply to them, however, was not an *ad hoc* refutation of each christological interpretation but consistency in the Jewish position. The Christian must not be allowed the advantage of claiming that the Jew too ignores the context.

Allegorization

Radak's insistence on contextuality came as a response not only to such christological interpretations but to a far more serious affront of Christian exegesis. This was the allegorization of Scripture and in particular of the Torah; the turning of a book of "precepts and statutes" into one of "riddles and parables."[511] Here we have not the uprooting of a particular passage from its context but the rejection of context in its entirety.

> *Remember the Torah of Moses My servant as I commanded him at Horeb* (Malachi 3:22). Not as the Christian heretics who say that it was given literally for a limited time. Then Jesus the Nazarene came and explained it spiritually.[512]

> *Your testimonies are wonders* (Psalms 119:129). One may ask: Moses . . . said: *This commandment which I command you today is no wonder to you* (Deuteronomy 30:18). How then could David have said, *Your testimonies are wonders?* The answer: *It is no wonder to you* means that the commandments were not expressed allegorically so that you might wonder how to understand the allegory. *The word is very near to you, in your mouth, and in your heart, so that you may do it* (Deuteronomy 30:14). Thus just as you learn it with your mouth, so do you understand it with your heart and so do you do it. For the commandment is not allegory. This is an answer to the Christians who say that the Torah is allegory.[513]

Yet the problem was not so simply settled. It was not simply a question of Jewish preservation of the "letter" in the face of Christian spiritualization. Even Joseph Kimhi explains:

> Know that the fact is that the Torah is not [to be taken] altogether literally or altogether figuratively. If one says to his servant, "Take the horse and ride it on the sea," we must try to interpret this figuratively . . . There is no need for figurative interpretation if he says to him, "Board the ship and go on the sea in it." Some commandments may be understood both literally and figuratively. *Circumcise yourselves to the Lord and take away the foreskins of your heart* (Jeremiah 4:4) is to be taken figuratively, but *at the age of eight days, every male among you shall be circumcised* (Genesis 17:12) is to be taken literally. Both the circumcision of the flesh, i.e., the flesh of the foreskin and of the heart, are obligatory.[514]

Yet these commonsense "departures" from the letter of Scripture could hardly be categorized as allegory. Joseph Kimhi tells us only half the story. The fact is that the Spanish exegetes in this period did recognize the legitimacy of philosophically oriented allegorical interpretation. No sooner, for example, does Ibn Ezra berate the Christians for their "spiritualization" of the Torah than he admits that legitimate allegory is indeed possible.[515] Indeed, in some cases, such as the Garden of Eden story, it might even be preferable. Nonetheless, Ibn Ezra advocated that allegory may be resorted to only when the *peshaṭ* presented exceptional difficulties. Even then *peshaṭ* was not to be ruled out entirely; both exoteric and esoteric senses were to be granted equal status.[516]

De jure, Maimonides seemed to allow a broader base for allegory. In his classic statement, he expounds the verse *a word fitly spoken is like apples of gold in vessels of silver* (Proverbs 25:11):

> In every word which has a double sense, a literal and a figurative one, the plain meaning must be as valuable as silver and the hidden meaning still more precious . . . The figures employed by prophets, taken literally . . . contain wisdom useful for many purposes, among others for the amelioration of the condition of society . . . Their hidden meaning, however, is profound wisdom, conducive to the recognition of real truth.[517]

Yet, *de facto,* he too exercised stringent economy in his own reve-
lation of the esoteric. Only selected passages—such as the story of
creation and the Chariot vision of Ezekiel—are allegorized.[518] Yet
despite the reticence of Maimonides, many of his contemporaries
and successors understood his words as a general license for indulgence in allegorization, and this question became a central issue
in the controversy over his writings. On the one hand, he was
damned by his opponents for placing "the Scriptures like a thief in
the underground passage of allegory";[519] on the other, he was
praised by his partisans for revealing that there are "certain things
meant for the Sages which are beyond the level of the masses";
that "Moses had to write those things with a double meaning, one
obscuring the other . . . the exoteric for the masses, the esoteric
for the Sages."[520] Among the circle of intellectuals that formed
the Provençal "school" of Maimonides, allegory became quite the
fashion.[521] In time, any and all parts of Scripture would be allegorized with as much verve and intensity as the rabbis had devoted
to midrashic interpretation. Yet those in the vanguard proceeded
with caution. Samuel Ibn Tibbon, who was himself responsible for
introducing the *Guide for the Perplexed* to Provence, stressed that
Maimonides' apparent opinion was that the true intent of the entire
Torah or, let us say, the principal part of it is to "provide the sages
with allusions to true reality by means of esoteric meanings and
secrets," and he insisted that the "intention of the Torah is to
benefit the masses."[522] Whether this was only a disclaimer to ward
off criticism or a sincere expression of belief in the limitations of
allegory, Ibn Tibbon provided esoteric explanations of the
Hexaemeron, the Chariot vision and other passages, although these
efforts appear rather modest when compared with later writings in
this genre.[523]

In Radak's circle, then, allegory was *de rigueur.* Ibn Ezra,
Radak's guide on "the way of *peshaṭ*"; Maimonides, his master;
Ibn Tibbon, his friend—all stirred the brew which was proffered to
Radak. The latter knew of the bill of prohibition passed on this
beverage by many of his contemporaries.[524] The arguments they
would level against philosophical exegesis would sound strikingly
similar to those with which he himself would counter the Christians.[525]

... How can it occur to anyone that what was said concerning the one who was gathering sticks in the wilderness on the Sabbath day—*all the congregation shall stone him with stones* (Numbers 15:35)—was said allegorically. For this will the Torah languish and its judgment will not see light. For it has seen Gentiles entering its sanctuary and Greeks defiling its holy temple.[526]

Yet Radak drank of the forbidden libations with zest, a zest which comes to expression in the amount of detail and elucidation he lavished on his philosophical commentaries. Of these there were two; the commentary on the Hexaemeron and that on the Chariot vision. These are short and occupy only several folios in manuscript. Yet whereas Radak's general commentaries display discretion and restraint despite their length, in these tracts he allows himself free rein. In the Hexaemeron commentary, for example, we learn that the Garden of Eden represents the active intellect and the Tree of Life the human intellect, while the Tree of Knowledge of Good and Evil symbolizes the material intellect. The human intellect is all virtue and strives toward the active intellect by pursuing the divine sciences, while the material intellect is tainted because of its material lusts. With these *dramatis personae,* Radak knits a web of allusion and parable. Of the three sons of Adam, we learn that Cain was a farmer and devoid of intellectual accomplishments. He was, after all, concerned principally with the acquisition[527] of the necessities of life. Abel was occupied with silver and gold, the superfluities and vanities[528] of life. He was rather better endowed with material intellect but owing to his lack of resistance to physical passions he had practically no human intellect. The third son, Seth, ate from the Tree of Life and was created in the image of Adam. It was he who shared, with Adam, the human intellect. Indeed, Seth was born of another woman, for Eve had returned to her source, the earth. Seth was therefore "good seed" and the true founder of mankind.[529] In this fashion Radak continues verse after verse in his elucidation of the secrets of creation.

The commentary to Ezekiel 1 is even more elaborate. It is clearly Maimonidean in tone: the explanations of the creatures, the wheels, the four faces, the rider, and so forth, have their roots

in the *Guide for the Perplexed.*[530] Yet where Maimonides gave
"a short explanation of plain things" and relied on the reader to
"obtain a perfect and clear insight into all that has been clear and
intelligible" to him,[531] Radak takes nothing for granted. His
exposition of the number "four," only touched upon by Maimonides,[532] is heroic in its attempt to be exhaustive. It is perhaps one
of the most thorough treatments of the virtues of this number in
the entire medieval-Pythagorean tradition.

> . . . the four elements from which the lower world was formed
> and the world is of four species: mineral, vegetable, animal,
> and rational. The great luminaries which direct the lower
> worlds move in fours, for the sun moves in its course through
> four seasons of the year and the moon in four phases in a
> month. The day is divided into four periods against the four
> elements. Similarly the animal and vegetable kingdoms are in
> fours . . . In a like fashion, the government of the microcosm
> is related to the number four for the governors of the human
> body are four: the nutritive, the sensitive, the imaginative,
> and the appetitive. The nutritive is divided into four faculties:
> the ingestive, the retentive, the digestive, and the eliminative,
> with the four qualities: heat, cold, dryness, and humidity.
> Item, the four humors through which the body is maintained:
> blood, white gall, red gall, and black gall. Item, the four prime
> problems: existence, what, how, and why . . . and four is the
> first perfect square. Again, $1+2+3+4$ is equal to ten . . .[533]

In the general commentaries, Radak makes no secret of the
esoteric commentaries and alludes to them freely.[534] "The exoteric
sense of this passage," he tells us concerning the speaking of the
serpent, "is very garbled but it is clear according to the esoteric
sense."[535] "Ezekiel saw an obscure vision and heard an incomprehensible utterance."[536] Yet allegory is never allowed to invade the
domain of the *peshaṭ* commentary itself. Even if allegory might on
occasion lend greater clarity to a passage than the contextual
peshaṭ, the line of demarcation between the two must remain firm.
Of course, the segregation of the esoteric from the exoteric was
encouraged by the need to avoid the potential danger implicit in
the exposure of the general public to philosophical interpretation.
Since rabbinic times, public discussion of Ezekiel 1 had been
interdicted.[537]

Now since our rabbis forbade expounding the Chariot, I am not at liberty to record in this commentary those interpretations which have occurred to me. If I do so, I shall be as one who expounds it in public since this commentary is available to any student. I have therefore written the commentary on the Chariot as a separate tract which is safely stored in my files so that I may not forget it and so that it might benefit any scholar who is worthy of having the secrets of Torah revealed to him.[538]

Yet over and above the need to withhold the esoteric sense from the uninitiated, an even more compelling principle seems to have been operative: that of contextuality. Nowhere is this made clearer for us than in the least known of Radak's commentaries, that on Proverbs. The Book of Proverbs, revolving as it does on the axis of "wisdom," was an ideal subject for the craftsmanship of the allegorist. Radak observed:

When I considered the various biblical commentaries and I examined all that my wise predecessors expounded . . . I found that everyone had his own opinions concerning the Book of Proverbs and that this confused the mass of people. Some of the exegetes say that Solomon likened the Torah to a beautiful wise woman and idolatry to a wicked foreign woman. Some explained that he likened matter to the harlot and the intellectual form to the good and wise woman. They all bring proofs to confirm their words.[539]

Radak believed that Solomon indeed wrote the book with "two intents,"[540] one philosophical and the other practical. Yet ultimately it is the latter and *only* the latter with which his commentary will deal. No promise was ever kept more faithfully. Although at times he may admit that "there is another meaning to this parable, we shall explain the matter according to the *peshaṭ*."[541] Wisdom is consistently understood as practical or traditional wisdom and not philosophy.

To receive the discipline of wisdom (Proverbs 1:2). Discipline means punishment, that is, that which comes upon man from stupidity, which is the opposite of wisdom.[542]

The foolish shall be servant to the wise of heart (Proverbs

11:29). It will be the fate of the lazy servant to be the servant
of the wise of heart for [the latter] will seek out and earn his
livelihood and have enough to eat while the fool will go
begging bread at his door.[543]

If Radak feels that the primary intent of a passage in Proverbs is
moral guidance, he does not intellectualize it. "Rabbi Jonah[544]
explained it [Proverbs 5:19] allegorically as referring to wisdom,"
he tells us. "It is possible that the author of the book wrote it with
two intents in mind but it is probable that he spoke [only] about
the woman."[545] He does not even comment on the mildly rationalistic observations in his father's commentary.[546] So firm is Radak
in his determination to remain true to the context that a verse is
never allowed to hint even remotely at a philosophical meaning.
Thus in the commentary on Psalms, where Radak restricts himself
less, he cites the epistemological discourse based on the interpretation of his father[547] on the parable of the seven pillars of wisdom.[548] Yet in the Proverbs commentary there is no trace of such
interpretations. Similarly, where *the beginning of wisdom* (Psalms
112:10) in the Psalms commentary is taken to refer to the "science
of true investigation, the knowledge of creation," similar expressions in Proverbs are allowed no such connotation.[549]

Radak proceeds in this fashion elsewhere in the commentaries.
Thus it may be granted that Jeremiah 17:12 has esoteric implications in remarks made in the Psalms commentary.[550] Yet *ad locum:*

> *The throne of glory, on high from the beginning, the place
> of our sanctuary* (Jeremiah 17:12). The rabbis referred this
> to the Temple and said: "Seven things were created before
> the world was created.[551] One of them was the place of the
> Temple as it is said, *the throne of glory, on high from the
> beginning, the place of our sanctuary. From the beginning*
> [means] before the world was created." They said too that
> the Temple faces the Throne of Glory.[552] The commentators
> have followed this approach. In the *Book of Creation* it
> says . . . "the holy sanctuary is set in the middle"[553] . . . I
> have dealt with this matter at length in my commentary to
> Psalms. *It is good but it is not connected to the preceding or
> following verses.*

Elsewhere, in Jeremiah, Radak cites Maimonides' ingenious
explanation of verse 9:23, which comes at the close of the *Guide*

for the Perplexed.[554] He finds it "fitting but not related to the context." His own function is clear: "I have clearly explained these two verses for you according to the subject of the chapter in relation to the context."[555]

Radak's rejection of allegory in his Proverbs commentary and his aloofness from esoteric interpretation elsewhere teach an important lesson concerning his exegetical enterprise. He grants that a passage *may* be taken out of context for a particular purpose. Yet the exegete, when explaining the passage *in situ,* has not the license to do so. In another age, Radak would have been the university instructor who lavishes praise upon a student's paper for its insight while awarding it a C+ for its irrelevance to the topic.

A Coincidence of Opposites

These then were the technical criteria for Radak's critique of midrash: observance of the rules of grammar and stylistic principles and suitability to the context. These formal and technical principles, however, were only aids in determining the *peshaṭ*. Recourse to the grammar book or dictionary alone would not suffice. *Peshaṭ* was not necessarily the "letter," the *mashma'*.[556] A literal interpretation, as we have seen,[557] could be most unreasonable; indeed, it could be the foundation of *derash* itself.

> *Is not this a brand plucked from the fire?* (Zechariah 3:2). Like a firebrand which is drawn from the fire so that it will burn no longer, [Joshua the priest] would be plucked from the fire of exile to come to Jerusalem, build the Temple, and officiate in it. The rabbis expounded this[558] according to the letter (*dareshu bo ke-mashma'o*): [Joshua] was with Zedekiah and Ahab whom the King of Babylon consigned to burning. They were burned but he was saved.[559]

Conversely, we have found Radak's statement that he will "cite some *derashot* for those who are fond of *derash*"[560] not quite accurate. Somehow—as we have seen[561]—the murmur of the ambiguous partitive *"some"* becomes muffled by the rushing cataract of midrash and *'aggadah* that courses the commentaries. As the expression "for those who are fond of *derash*" would suggest, a fair proportion of this material does appear to be ornamental or diversionary.[562] Much of it did indeed serve to illustrate to the reader what *peshaṭ* was *not* in order to reinforce the conception of what *peshaṭ was*.[563] Yet even all this barely scratches the surface. The reader need not go far in the commentaries before he becomes aware of the fact that rabbinic exegesis is doing far more than passively waiting for censure. In Radak, midrash does not content itself with the *pashṭan*'s pious attempt at appeasement: "They who said it knew what they said for they had greater breadth of knowledge than we."[564] Rabbinic exegesis begins to assert itself, now subtly and discreetly, now openly and vociferously. If *pashṭanim* could stumble onto the "way of *derash*," midrash could find the way of *peshaṭ*. Radak's argument was with specific interpretations and not with a body of literature. Indeed, the phrase "midrashic" (*derekh derash*) became for Radak, as for Ibn Ezra,[565] an expression of dissatisfaction with any interpretation regardless of source[566] —to the extent that an interpretation of Ibn Ezra could itself be labeled *"derash."*[567]

The legitimacy of an interpretation was not to be determined by its origin but by its compatibility with Radak's conception of *peshaṭ,* a conception which was a fusion of all those sides of Radak to which we have been exposed: the grammarian and literary critic, the rationalist, the social observer, the preacher and pedagogue. In this framework, there is much room for midrash. *'Aggadot* need not be rejected out of hand. Rather, they are measured on a scale according to their suitability to the context: implausible, more plausible, plausible indeed.

> *They covered him with clothes, but he could get no heat* (I Kings 1:1). There is a *derash:* Whoever does not treat garments with respect is destined to have no benefit from them. Since David cut the hem of Saul's coat, he had no benefit from [his] garments in his old age.[568] There is another *derash* which is *more plausible* than this: when David saw the angel with his sword drawn . . . *he was terrified* and caught a chill as it is written, *he was terrified because of the sword of the angel of the Lord* (I Chronicles 21:30).[569]

Thus the *'aggadah* which accounts for David's chill on the basis of textual evidence is more plausible than one that is capricious and unsubstantiated.

Indeed, even the introduction of apparently extraneous and fabulous elements do not prevent a *derash* from serving as legitimate exegesis. If such a *derash* can explain the sequence of Judges 6:11-14, all the better:

> *The angel of the Lord came and sat under the terebinth* (Judges 6:11). In the *derash:* He waited there until he found some merit in him and then appeared to him. They said: His father Joash was threshing grain. Gideon said: My father, you are old. Go home and I will thresh. If the Midianites come, you will not have the strength to flee. The angel said: You have fulfilled the commandment of honoring [your father] and you are worthy of delivering my sons. Immediately, *the angel of the Lord appeared to him, etc.* (v. 12). Gideon said to him *Is the Lord with us?* (v. 13). Last night we read the Hallel and my father had me read *when Israel went out of Egypt* (Psalms 114:1).[570] If our forefathers were righteous, do this for our sake. If they were wicked, perform a miracle for us as you performed one for them.
>
> The Holy One, blessed be He, said, By your life, you have championed the cause of My sons. You are worthy of having Me speak to you. Immediately, *the Lord turned to him and said: Go in this your might* (v. 14), in the might of your having championed the cause of My sons. *This derash is correct because it gave a reason for the hesitation of the angel and [explained] why it says* He turned to him (*ibid.*).[571]

Plausibility is not, however, ascertained only by *literary* context. Radak as political observer preferred a midrashic passage concerning Shimei's betrayal of David not only because it left a verse intact but because it exemplified a demonstration of political astuteness.

> Shimei says to David: *Your servant knows I have sinned. Therefore I am the first of all the house of Joseph to go down to meet my lord the King* (II Samuel 19:21). There is a *derash:* Shimei said to David: Joseph's brothers dealt him evil while he requited them with good. This is my case. I have dealt you evil. Requite me with good.[572]
>
> There is another *derash* more plausible than this. All of Israel are called Joseph as it is written, *The Lord . . . may be gracious to the remnant of Joseph* (Amos 5:15) . . . Shimei said to David: All Israel have dealt you evil and I more than any. All Israel are sitting and waiting to see what you will do with me. If you accept me, all Israel will come to you and be reconciled to you.[573]

Elsewhere, Radak accepts what would otherwise seem to be a forced association of passages because it reflects the reality of his own time—the forced conversion:

> *Absalom the son of Maacah* (II Samuel 3:3). They expounded a midrash: Since he was the son of a beautiful woman that David captured in war, Absalom was a stubborn and rebellious son. It is for such a reason that the passage concerning a stubborn and rebellious son (Deuteronomy 21:18–21) was juxtaposed [to the passage concerning the treatment of a] captive woman (Deuteronomy 21:10–14)[574] *... This midrash is correct.* Since she is a captive, she is compelled to convert to Judaism although her heart is not in it. The seedling thus grows as the root directs.[575]

For Radak then, the corpus of rabbinic exegesis was hardly a monolith, and he knew how to distinguish among the various kinds of rabbinic interpretations. In more formal terms, he informs us in his introduction to Joshua: "I shall also bring the words of the rabbis at those places where we need their interpretation (*perush*) and tradition (*qabbalah*). I shall also bring some *derashot* for those who are fond of *derash*." Radak speaks then of three categories: *derash per se,* interpretation and tradition. As for the last, it is clear that this is not an exegetical category at all. Rather we are dealing here with a series of historical traditions felt to be absolutely reliable. Even though the text itself might point in another direction, "if the words of the rabbis follow a tradition, we are obligated to accept them."[576]

> ... Our rabbis said that Moses died on the seventh of Adar.[577] They derived this from the verses following a tradition ... Yet if it were not for the tradition, one could say that Moses died in Shevat or in Adar before the seventh. We have indeed found such an opinion in rabbinic literature[578] even though the discussion in the Talmud states that Moses died on the seventh ... [Yet] the tradition appears to be correct.[579]

Between the traditions, which are decisive for Radak in exegesis, and the *derash,* which is not, lies the third category: interpretation. "Interpretation" is, of course, a neutral word. It is not charged with the connotation of either *peshaṭ* or *derash*. The phrase "the rabbis interpreted" is ambiguous in this regard, for we never know quite what to expect.[580] Note, however, the following confrontation.

> *Joshua the son of Nun sent two spies out of Shittim secretly* (*heresh*) (Joshua 2:1). In the *derash: heresh* (secretly) is like *heres* (pottery).[581] He equipped them with pots so that they would appear to be potters and not be noticed. Some said they had carpenter's tools as it says: *with the work of an engraver* (*harash*) *in stone* (Exodus 28:11).
> Some of them explained (*pereshu*) it according to its apparent sense (*mashma'o*) and its *peshat*. Joshua said to them, "Remain silent and maintain secrecy."[582]

Here *derash* is contrasted with a *perush*, an interpretation, of a different sort: one that conforms to *peshat*. Often such explanations provide the sole commentary on a passage. It may be a question of a definition of a word: "*He worships it* (*va-yishtahu*) (Isaiah 44:15). With the feet extended as the rabbis interpreted";[583] or of a very penetrating *peshat* interpretation:

> *When they say* [*to you*]: *Where shall we go? Then tell them: Thus says the Lord: such as are for death, to death; and such as are for sword, to the sword; and such as are for famine, to the famine; and such as are for captivity, to the captivity* (Jeremiah 15:2). The rabbis said: "Each punishment mentioned in this verse is more severe than the one before. The sword is worse than death. This I can demonstrate either from Scripture or from observation. The proof from observation is that the sword deforms but death does not deform; the proof from Scripture is in the verse *Precious in the eyes of the Lord is the death of his saints* (Psalms 116:15). Famine again is harder than the sword; this again can be demonstrated either by observation, the proof being that the one causes [prolonged] suffering but the other not, or if you prefer, from the Scripture, from the verse *They that be slain with the sword are better than they that be slain with hunger* (Lamentations 4:9). Captivity is harder than all, because it includes the sufferings of all."[584]

At other times, midrash is apparently brought as supportive material for Radak's own view, as when he explains why Jacob spaced the droves of sheep he brought as a gift to Esau:

The reason he set each drove apart was in order to make the gift appear that much grander and more impressive. His brother would be impressed by such a splendid gift.

Similarly in Genesis Rabbah:[585] Why did he not bring them to him all at once? In order to overwhelm that wicked one. When [the procession] was about to finish, [Jacob] said: Take more![586]

Or an aside may be used in interpreting:

> They buried him in the ascent of the sepulchres of the sons of David (II Chronicles 32:33). In the distinguished of them, that is, the most prominent. Thus the rabbis said: near the most distinguished in the family, namely, David and Solomon.[587]

I say "*apparently* brought as supportive material" because in such instances one can no longer really say who supports whom, where the rabbis end and where Radak begins.

"In many asides of which he may not be fully aware," S. Baron tells us, "he showed himself deeply steeped in the local aggadic heritage transmitted by the hermeneutic school of Moses the Preacher."[588] One suspects that precisely because of the sifting and winnowing of midrash undertaken by Radak, he was keenly conscious of the introduction of these "asides." In any event, there is no question that Radak and midrash frequently speak with one voice. Although unacknowledged, the sources of these interpretations are readily recognizable:

> *Reuben spoke to his father: Slay my two sons if I do not bring him to you* (Genesis 42:37). Reuben spoke foolishly [by saying] that Jacob could kill his sons. Jacob said to him: Foolish first-born! Are not your sons mine?[589]

> *. . . The famine was heavy in the land* (Genesis 43:1). Judah said to his brothers: Leave the old man alone until there is no grain left in the house. Then he will agree to send his son with us![590]

> [*The messengers returned to Jacob and said: we came*] *to your brother Esau* (Genesis 32:7). They said *Esau* after they said *your brother,* that is to say, he is the same Esau he was when he hated you.[591]

Often one encounters the unexpected: methodologically these interpretations may be very far removed from that which one normally encounters in Radak. Without support of "scientific philology," we find the use of *noṭariqon*:[592] "*Hiddekel* (*ḥiddeqel*) (Genesis 2:14) . . . It is called *ḥiddeqel* because its waters are sharp (*ḥad*) and swift (*qal*)";[593] and the apparent acceptance of etymology bordering on *'al tiqre*:[594] *the cherubim of image work* (*za'aẓu'im*) (II Chronicles 3:10) are "like children (*ẓe'eẓa'im*) as our rabbis said: 'cherub' (*keruv*) is related to the Aramaic *ke-ravya* (like a child) for they had faces of children."[595] Indeed it would appear that methodology is itself only of secondary importance. Radak is prepared to interpret a word as if the vowels were to be read differently as long as context is not betrayed.[596] It was one thing for Radak to wonder how the rabbis expected one to "believe that Shem was alive" in the time of Rebekka.[597] Yet he had no difficulty in accepting the rabbinic identification of Phinehas and Elijah[598] when it supported his view concerning a text-critical question.[599]

Yet even this strong current of midrashic *peshaṭ*, as it were, is not the most intriguing aspect of Radak's employment of rabbinic literature. In many places where Radak clearly cites a midrash *outside* the framework of *peshaṭ*, a curious phenomenon occurs. One finds that Radak does not limit himself to merely citing the midrash and thereby fulfilling his obligations to the "lovers of *derash*." Rather, there unfolds an exegesis of midrash alongside the exegesis of Scripture, a sort of literary lagniappe unanticipated by the reader. These expressions vary in complexity. Some are philological and explain a Greek or Aramaic word in the rabbinic text.[600] Some explain the methodology of the midrash: "the rabbis said this taking special notice of the word . . ."[601] Often Radak indicates the textual basis of a midrash: "This [verse] supports the *derash* we have written";[602] "there is a support for the opinion of the rabbis";[603] "this substantiates the *derash* we wrote above."[604]

There gradually emerges an apologetic even for midrashim of the "irrational" variety. On the basis of *Abraham was the father of Isaac* (Genesis 25:19), the midrash derives a physical resemblance between the two.[605] Radak observes that the midrash has a resemblance of action in mind.[606] The rabbis take *This land on which you are lying I will give to your descendants* (Genesis 28:13) literally and learn from it that God rolled up the entire Land of

Israel under Jacob's head.[607] Radak succinctly and elegantly explains: "*as if* He folded it up."[608] The rabbis provide two traditions as to when Abraham recognized his Creator. One has it at the age of three; the other at the age of forty.[609] Radak argues that the latter is more rational and plausible.[610]

Indeed, lest midrashim be considered irrational, Radak seizes the tools of the rationalists themselves and claims that the rabbis were expressing themselves in poetic imagery. Like Abraham ben Isaac, Radak too harked back to the Geonim.

> We expound the *haggadot* as is proper and correct, for they are permeated with reason and reflect science as our predecessors the Geonim, such as R. Sherira, R. Hai, R. Isaac Alfasi, and the other pillars of the universe and rocks of the earth taught us. We live according to their word and rely on them in questions of *haggadah* and on no one else.[611]

It would be natural for Radak to refer back to as early a source as possible in order to establish a lengthy tradition of rationalistic interpretation of the midrash. Yet geonic interpretations of 'aggadot themselves were cited very rarely in the commentaries and not even these were fully accepted.[612] Radak's actual "rationalistic" interpretations are cast in the mold of those of his master Maimonides in the *Guide for the Perplexed.* These approaches were varied. At times, Maimonides would allude to the esoteric character of a midrashic passage without stating the "inner meaning" explicitly. In this way, he observed: "You must know that their words which I am about to quote are most perfect, most accurate and clear for those for whom they were said. I will therefore not add long explanations, lest I make their statements plain, and I might thus become a revealer of secrets."[613] Yet this principle of reticence was not consistently observed even by Maimonides. Consequently, one finds him elaborating on what he feels is the true esoteric meaning of a midrashic text[614] or even using a midrash as a proof text in a philosophical discussion.[615] Radak follows this procedure. The rabbis explained that seven things were created before the creation of the world: Paradise, the Torah, the Righteous, Israel, the Throne of Glory, Jerusalem, and the Messiah.[616] Radak observes that "the meaning of the *derash* is not as most students understand it. It means that they were created *in potentia* before the creation of the world for these things are the purpose of the world."[617] The rabbinic statement that "the upper world and the lower world were created simultaneously—the upper alive and the lower dead"[618] teaches that "the four elements are dead bodies with no will or choice but just the nature with which they were endowed. If one of them leaves its natural place under compulsion, it will return to its place in a straight line when the compelling force is removed."[619] The more fantastic a midrash, the more wonderful its meaning: "How excellent is this for those who understand";[620] "How excellent is their parable . . . This is firmly established for him who understands."[621]

Again following the lead of Maimonides, Radak allows a midrash to justify a philosophical interpretation as well as the reverse. So were midrashim employed to illustrate the preordained nature of miracles,[622] the intellectual superiority of Adam[623] and the fact that the three angels who came to Abraham existed only in a prophetic vision.[624]

Such active and enthusiastic solicitation of the support of midrash would suggest that if Radak cited midrashim for "the lovers of *derash*," he must be numbered among them. Midrash courses through the commentaries in many streams, ostensibly at cross-currents. There is first of all the thoroughgoing critique, both patent and latent, of much of midrashic exegesis. Over against this is the acceptance and even defense of midrash as *peshat* or as a manifestation of a profound philosophical truth. Finally, there is the use of midrash as a supplement to the *peshat* which accounts for the lion's share of aggadic material in the commentaries.

It is clear, however, that all these facets of Radak's relationship to midrash are complementary. First, Radak demonstrates that much of so called "midrash" is to be considered *peshat*. Second, even where midrash can not be so considered, Radak does not reject it as such, for in its own framework, it is quite valid. He insists, rather, that midrash not take the place of *peshat* where it does not fulfill the criteria of *peshat*. In this way, Radak's "undermining" of midrash is in reality a buttressing. By clearly defining the boundary between scriptural exegesis (*peshat*) and midrashic homiletics, Radak refutes those, both Jewish and Christian, who criticize the latter for not being the former. By "freeing" Scripture from midrash, midrash is itself freed to play its own role—the role

that it played in the academies of Babylonia and the Land of
Israel and the role that it played in the academy of Moses the
Preacher. Wherever Radak himself preached, midrash was at his
side.[625] Where Scripture spoke of consolation and the redemption
of Israel, midrash was there to reinforce it and reconfirm it—in as
unpashtanic a manner as it might be expressed.[626] Where Radak's
hands are tied exegetically, midrash comes to loosen the bonds.[627]

Radak the rationalist saw Micaiah's report of the heavenly vision
in which he sees the Lord seek an angel to lead Ahab astray as "a
figure of speech. This was merely Micaiah's style of presentation.
Micaiah did not see or hear these things for the spirit of prophecy
[conveys] only truth in the name of God. *Nevertheless,* I shall
write the midrashic version . . ."[628]

Nevertheless! The more Radak became the lord of *peshaṭ,* the
more was he the vassal of midrash.

IV   "Let Come the Morn"

*Then my enemy shall see it and shame
shall cover her* (Micah 7:10) . . . [When]
my enemy sees God take me into the
light, she will be ashamed that she said
to me in exile: "Where is your God?"[1]

Radak's literary enterprise was permeated with the consciousness of Israel's exile and the longing for her redemption. For
Radak, as for so many medievals, both punishment and reward
were predicated upon the principle of measure for measure.[2] In all
contexts—*peshaṭ,* sermon, midrash[3]—one finds that the consequence is always of the same nature as the cause: Jacob halted
after his encounter with the angel because of his halting belief in
God's promises.[4] All of Joseph's tribulations ironically correspond
in some way to his slanderous behavior against his brothers.[5]
Samson's eyes were gouged out because he allowed them to lead
him into error.[6] As for the nation as a whole:

> *Because of all the idols of your abominations and as the
> blood of your children that you gave them* (Ezekiel 16:36).
> [*As the blood*] with the prefix *as* (*kaf*). You have received
> punishment measure for measure in accordance with the sin.
> You had no compassion on the blood of your children when
> you slaughtered them to the idols. I have no compassion on
> your blood either and bring the vengeful sword . . . upon
> you.[7]

Yet the principle of measure for measure could be positive as
well as negative. Israel's rewards in the future would counter-
balance, if not outweigh, her tribulations in the past. But just as
the exile was of this world, so must the redemption be of this
world, of flesh and blood, of "wood and stones."[8] Radak knew of
a spiritual Jerusalem, of the supernal Sanctuary for the immortal
intellect[9]—but this was quite a different matter.

> *The soul that sins shall die* (Ezekiel 18:4). R. Saadia Gaon
> wrote that the life and death referred to here are of the next
> world. I say that this is true, for reward and punishment is
> mainly a matter of the next world. However, what is discussed
> *here* is *not* a matter of the next world. For this is a reply to
> those of that generation who said that the son bears the sins
> of the father, when they saw the great afflictions of the sons

while the fathers had sinned and were no longer. They were
not perturbed about the next world—*for they did not know
what it is*—but about what they saw with their own eyes. The
answer has to fit the question . . .![10]

No, the redemption of Israel must be a concrete redemption. The
Messiah of Israel must redeem in a real, not a ghostly, sense. What
Christianity was trying to perpetrate, Radak could not fathom:

> *Yea, he says: It is too light a thing that you should be My
> servant to raise up the tribes of Jacob, and to restore the off-
> spring of Israel. I will also make you a light of the nations
> that My salvation may be unto the end of earth* (Isaiah 49:6).
> The Christians refer these verses to the Nazarene, saying that
> he illuminated the eyes of the nations to the end of the earth.
> How did he illuminate the eyes of the Gentiles? By faith in
> him to the end of the earth? Most of the nations do not
> believe in him for Israel and Ishmael do not . . . They say that
> God has become his strength (v. 5) to save him from his
> enemies. He was not saved nor protected from his enemies
> who sought his soul and harmed him.[11]

Can it be Jesus that *will be exalted and lifted up and shall be
very high* (Isaiah 52:13)? The only place "he was lifted up and
exalted was the tree on which they hanged him!"[12] Can the "ruler
of Israel" of Micah 5:1 refer to Jesus? "He did not govern Israel
but they governed him!"[13] The Messiah will not be poor, as they
say. The biblical expression refers to humility.[14] If he is to ride on
a donkey, it is not for want. All the world is under his rule! He
rides it to demonstrate that Israel will have no more need of horses
and chariots.[15]

Yet even granting this notion of a spiritual Messiah, Radak con-
tends that the Christians cannot maintain their case consistently.
They "halt between two opinions."[16] As had Joseph Kimhi, David
set forth Christianity as a web of inconsistencies.

> The very verse which they bring as a proof-text and a support
> for their error is their own stumbling block: *The Lord said to
> me, "You are My son"* (Psalms 2:7).
> When they tell you that he was the son of God, tell them
> that it is impossible to say that the horse is the son of Reu-
> ben. If so, he to whom God says *You are My son* must be of
> His nature and divine like Him. Scripture says further *I have*

begotten you this day (*ibid.*) and the procreated is of the same species as the procreator.

Tell them that there can be no father and son in the Divinity, for the Divinity is indivisible and is one in every aspect of unity, unlike matter, which is divisible.

Tell them further that a father precedes a son in time and a son is born through the agency of a father. Now even though each of the terms "father" and "son" implies the other . . . he who is called the father must undoubtedly be prior in time. Therefore, with reference to this God whom you call Father, Son, and Holy Spirit, that part which you call Father must be prior to that which you call Son, for if they were always coexistent, they would have to be called twin brothers . . .[17]

This alleged inconsistency is nowhere more evident than in the Christians' Messiah concept.

He asked life of You (Psalms 21:5). If it is to refer to [Jesus'] humanity, he cannot be said to have had a life. If to his divinity, why did Scripture say *You gave it to him* (*ibid.*)? It says further, *His glory is great through Your salvation* (v. 6). If so, he is not divine. If it refers to his humanity, [he had no glory] for he was belittled and scorned.

For the king trusts in the Lord (v. 8). If it refers to his divinity, he should have no need to trust in another. Nor should he have need for the Most High that *he shall not be moved* (*ibid.*). If it refers to his humanity, he was certainly moved—in downfall.[18]

How can Christians claim that Jesus established Jerusalem? Since he accomplished nothing in the terrestrial Jerusalem, Radak concludes, they must be thinking of the spiritual Jerusalem. Yet this cannot be, as long as they took the context of their proof-text literally.[19] No matter which path they took, they came to an impasse.

God must be taken at His word. If His promises have not yet been fulfilled, we have every right to expect them to be realized in the future.

I will turn their captivity, the captivity of Sodom and her daughters (Ezekiel 16:53). This verse is a reply to the Christian heretics who say that the future consolations have already been fulfilled. Sodom is still overturned as it was and is still unsettled.[20]

And what of Israel? Radak does "not know the mind" of Jonathan, whose translation of a prophecy seems to imply a reference to the second commonwealth.[21] The Lord has *not* yet gone before Israel in redemption: the remnant of the flock has *not* yet been gathered;[22] the Temple as envisioned by Ezekiel has *not* yet been built;[23] the children of Judah and the children of Israel have *not* yet been united.[24] The continued absence of Israel was Radak's trump card. The Church may refer the redemption of Judah to itself but the promise to Israel still remains to be fulfilled.

> *I will afflict the seed of David for this but not forever* (I Kings 11:39). Here is an answer to those who say that we wait in vain for the days of the King Messiah . . . The prophet says, *but not forever.* Since the kingdom of David was divided in the time of Rehoboam, it was never reunited . . . When [the Jews of the] exile returned, the tribes did not return—only . . . Judah and Benjamin.[25]

Christianity claimed that the ten tribes of Israel had been given a *bill of divorce* (Jeremiah 3:8); that *the daughter of Israel has fallen and is to rise no more* (Hosea 5:2). Not quite, replies Radak. "It is *as if* He had given them a bill of divorce."[26] "She is not to rise again—*for a long time.*"[27] But in the time of the redemption, *all the house of Israel* (Ezekiel 11:15) will be included.[28] They will all be restored to their former tribes[29] and their former status. Joseph Kimhi was conservative with respect to the passage: *They shall bring all your brethren from all nations . . . and some of them I shall take for priests and for Levites* (Isaiah 66:20). He understood the *for* quite literally, "for the assistance (*le-ẓorekh*) of the priests."[30] Radak, however, claims that those who were originally of priestly or levitical descent would be restored to their function even though "they were immersed among the Gentiles on distant islands to the point of oblivion . . . and it is possible that they have deviated somewhat from Judaism (*shanu qeẓat min ha-dat*)."[31]

The possible deviations from orthodoxy to which Radak alludes were not necessarily a cause for distress. The fact that one is running a fever is at least proof that he is still alive. The patient was Eldad, the famous "emissary" of the Danites, who had appeared in Europe and made public his *halakhot,* or "laws," which were at variance with rabbinic tradition.[32] Radak knew of Eldad[33] and no doubt of his laws. For him, they would be further evidence that the Danites and the others were there—across the river Sambation in the land northeast of Babylon;[34] that they were waiting there to join Judah and Benjamin and proceed to the Land of Israel.[35] Radak's great ally in establishing the futurity of biblical passages was *peshaṭ*. Context determined the reference of a passage. Credibility was based on the fact that exegetical considerations preceded polemical concerns.

> *I have aroused up one from the north* (Isaiah 41:25). The exegetes have interpreted this verse with reference to Cyrus, king of Persia, for his country is northeast of Babylonia . . . My father . . . interpreted this passage with reference to the Messiah since it says *I have roused up* and it does not say whom until it says *Behold, My servant, whom I uphold* (Isaiah 42:1). This is correct.[36]

> First I will explain this passage according to those who interpret it as referring to the past even though I did not find that any of them had a complete interpretation . . . Then I shall explain it according to what I find.[37]

This credibility was enhanced by Radak's readiness, where necessary, to refer a passage to the past;[38] to admit his uncertainty;[39] or to give a verse a double reference.[40] Yet if there is hesitation as to whether a particular passage refers to the future, there is no hesitation as to the redemption itself.

> *From afar the Lord appeared to me: I have loved you with an everlasting love, therefore with affection have I drawn you* (Jeremiah 31:3). It appears to me that the verse consists of a statement and a response. The Congregation of Israel in exile says: God's statement that [*Israel*] *has found grace in the wilderness* (Jeremiah 31:2) is true for *from afar the Lord appeared to me* but now He has hidden His face from me in exile. God answers her: *I have loved you with an everlasting love* (Jeremiah 31:3). My love for you was not transient . . . but permanent. *Therefore, with affection have I drawn you* (*ibid.*) . . . Even though I have left you in exile many years, *I will build you again and you shall be built* (Jeremiah 31:4).[41]

Despite the length of time that is to elapse, there is always a sense of presence about the redemption. In speaking of the future, the prophet says *now* because "even if it is far off, it is as if it were in their own time."[42]

> *For [the day of the Lord] is near* (Obadiah 15). Even though it is far from the day of prophecy, it is as if it were near. If God said it would take place, it is possible to think of it as having [already] taken place.[43]

For this reason, future prophecies are often phrased in the past tense: "Past instead of future, and there are many instances of this. It is frequent in prophecy. Even though the prophecy refers to the future, it is as if it were already fulfilled."[44] "Past instead of future . . . for the word of the prophet is as certain as if it had already been fulfilled."[45]

As had his father,[46] Radak insists that the *Glory of Israel will not lie* (I Samuel 15:29); that man may regret a promise but that God does not. Even if its fulfillment is delayed because of man's sins, the covenant remains in effect.[47] The Christians speak of a "new covenant" which Jesus innovated. Radak corrects them:

> *Behold the days come, says the Lord, that I will make a new covenant with the house of Israel and with the house of Judah* (Jeremiah 31:30). *A new (hadashah) covenant.* [This refers to] its renewal (*hiddushah*). It will be permanent and not interrupted as was the covenant which He struck with the children of Israel at Mount Sinai.
> The erring Gentiles say that the prophet prophesied concerning a new Torah which is destined to [be] revealed . . . that is, the new Torah which Jesus the Nazarene . . . innovated. The answer to them: Was He not quite explicit concerning [precisely] what this is: *not like the covenant [that I made with their fathers]* (v. 32), which they violated . . . They will *not* violate this covenant for I shall place My Torah in their hearts and write it upon their hearts that it never be forgotten . . . The renewal of the covenant means the *preservation* of the covenant. Malachi, the last of the prophets, closes his words with *Remember the law of Moses My servant which I commanded him at Horeb for all Israel, statutes and ordinances* (Malachi 3:22). That passage refers to the future . . . Here you see that there will never be a new Torah. [The only Torah] is that which was given at Mount Sinai as it says, *which I commanded at Horeb* (Malachi 3:22).[48]

As there is no "new covenant," there is no "new Israel." The Jews remain God's elect: a special people among the nations;[49] the foundation of the world;[50] the fruit of the olive tree where the nations are the chaff and the wood.[51] Israel's enemies are God's enemies.[52] She remains favored above all: Amos' famous utterance is read: *I have brought up Israel out of the Land of Egypt!* [*But Have I up brought up*] *Philistines from Caphtor and Aram from Kir?* (Amos 9:7).[53]

Israel unto the flesh and Israel unto the spirit are one. According to the flesh:

> *I lifted my hand unto the seed of house of Jacob* (Ezekiel 20:5) . . . for that which He gave to Abraham . . . was for the sake of Jacob.[54]

According to the spirit, the issue is simply decided. Israel is known by her fruits. Radak describes the moral uprightness of the Provençal communities.

> We are the ones who maintain religion, following without hypocrisy the words of the rabbis. We attend the House of God at dawn and even, standing in fear and trembling as befitting an Israelite. We are meticulous in the observance of religious law . . .
>
> We have inherited the legacy of our father Abraham of which God testified *to the end that he may command his children and his household after him* (Genesis 18:19). Our houses are open wide to every passer-by and to all who seek rest. We weary ourselves day and night over the Torah and secretly support the poor. We do justice at every opportunity. Among us are those who provide books for the poor who have none and who give stipends for the study of Bible and Talmud.[55]

Echoing the more extensive social critiques of his father,[56] Radak contrasts this way of life with that of the Christians. The Jews behave honorably toward the Gentiles[57] although the latter oppress them.[58] "Foul language is customary among the nations of the world";[59] but the refinement of Jews is seen in the modesty of their young ladies.[60] Of the celibate priesthood, on which the Christians prided themselves,[61] Radak insinuates "the priests . . . have no *known* family."[62]

If Christianity insisted on being identified with ancient Israel, though, perhaps Radak could meet the Christians half way. Do they not persist in the same sins that brought about the exile? Are they not the heirs of the ancient idolators?

I will cut off the names of the idols (Zechariah 13:2) . . . the idols that the Gentiles serve *today*.[63]

The Christians are to be considered idolators for they bow down to worship the image of Jesus of Nazareth[64] . . . [along with] the cross of gold.[65]

For Radak, idolatry was not a phenomenon of antiquity alone but of the present as well. In expounding Isaiah's taunt of the idol-makers, the immediacy of the description is evident. He expands and dilates on every verse: "*Who fashions a god* (Isaiah 44:10). Who would do such a nonsensical thing—exerting oneself for nothing and investing one's money in nonsense! Is there anything so insane?"[66]

Israel, on the other hand, has rejected the idols. Even through-out most of the pre-exilic period, the Israelites were faithful—"all the days of Joshua and in the days of the Judges . . . and of Samuel . . . David and Solomon . . . and the rest of the kings who were good. No other people ever served the Lord together."[67] Certainly in the post-exilic period, there is no question that Israel eschewed idolatry[68] —despite the fact that the Jews were surrounded by idolators:[69] "*I will make you stop playing the harlot* (Ezekiel 16:41) . . . From the day that Jerusalem was destroyed, Israel has not worshipped other gods."[70]

The respective attitudes of Judaism and Christianity to the commandment of monotheism is paralleled by their attitudes to others. As part of their arraignment of Judaism, Christians charged that the commandments had been abrogated, "that the law of Moses in which are found six hundred and thirteen commandments was given for a temporary cause."[71] The axes of this discussion were the commandments of Sabbath and circumcision, precepts of the flesh which had been transmuted into the more spiritualized Sunday and baptism. As evidence, contemporary Christian apologists vied with each other in finding ways to prove that various biblical figures—even God Himself—broke the Sabbath.[72] In this context, Radak's rather prolix excursuses on such incidents take on special relevance.[73] In one long digression, he carefully proves that King David did not travel on the Sabbath and that the showbread was not baked on that day despite the apparent meaning of the text.[74] He finds the same problem with respect to circumcision. According to the report in Joshua, Joshua had to circumcise all the adult males that had been born in the wilderness.[75] The Christian interpreters took this as evidence that circumcision was not really mandatory; otherwise, the Israelites would not have been allowed to wander uncircumcised for forty years in the wilderness.[76] An apostate of Radak's time claimed that the only reason that Joshua circumcised his men was so that they might be distinguishable from the Canaanites if they fell on the battlefield.[77] To elucidate this problem Radak uses the same technique as that employed in the explanation of David's Sabbath observance. On the basis of rabbinic literature and his own ingenuity, he proves that this was only a temporary "dispensation" of circumcision in accordance with divine will.[78]

More subtle, however, was the objection raised by Christianity that contemporary Jews broke the Sabbath quite regularly. In a simple—and to the Jewish mind simplistic—illustration, an anonymous apostate claims: "If your son fell into a well, would you extricate him or not? If not, you are false and a homicide; if you extricate him, you break the Sabbath."[79] Radak replies with a discourse on the verse *Your navel string was not cut, nor were you washed with water to cleanse you, nor rubbed with salt nor swabbed with bands* (Ezekiel 16:4). Each of these particulars is carefully explained. Implicit in the mass of detail, however, is the fact that "if these things are not done to the newborn, he is in danger of death. Therefore [the rabbis] permitted doing them on the Sabbath."[80] Thus Radak shows the absurdity of the Christian charge that the Jews break the Sabbath: the Sabbath cannot be considered desecrated as long as there is a question of the preservation of life.

Yet Radak knew that all these considerations of Israel's faithfulness to the covenant skirted the main issue. In the eyes of Christianity, the Jews were deluding themselves by maintaining a "covenant" that God had long since abandoned. As the apostate would put it: "O Hebrew! Are you incredulous? Do you not believe that *I* have the name of Israel? Do you not see that *I* am blessed on earth by the God of heaven, amen? . . . *ergo,* I am Israel."[81] The decisive proof was the rejection of Israel in the *present*. The Jews could speak of future promises but these are belied by reality. Peter Alphonse, the twelfth-century apostate, triumphantly describes this reality: Jews are slaughtered, burnt, sold into captivity—thirty for one piece of silver; they are loaded onto ships which are set afloat at sea without a helmsman; they are dejected and suffer intolerable laws; they cannot study their law or teach their children. If they do so, they are burnt or combed with iron combs. They are not allowed to celebrate the Sabbath or Passover or to circumcise their sons. They must suffer the humiliation of the *jus primae noctis* exercised by the local prince.[82]

Of course, Peter, drawing on early post-destruction midrashic literature,[83] may overstate the case. Yet for him, the more gruesome the description, the better. He contrasts the first exile with the second. The Babylonian captivity came in the wake of countless and egregious sins.[84] Yet it lasted only seventy years. Relying again on Jewish sources, he stresses that the Jews of the second commonwealth were virtually free of these same sins. Yet this exile has lasted over a thousand years! More striking is the fact that God has gone beyond his declared standards of justice: *The fathers shall not be put to death for the children, nor shall the children be put to death for the fathers, every man shall be put to death for his own sin* (Deuteronomy 24:16) and *the soul that sins shall die* (Ezekiel 18:4).

"Moyses," Peter's Jewish interlocutor, maintains the standard position. He agrees that the Jews are indeed suffering for the sins of their fathers but denies that God has imposed greater severity than His own word requires. Is it not written: *I the Lord your God am a jealous God, visiting the iniquity of the fathers upon the children unto the third and fourth generation of them that hate Me* (Exodus 20:5); *Our fathers have sinned and are not and we have borne their iniquities* (Lamentations 5:7)?

Peter skillfully borrows a leaf from the rabbis[85] in reconciling these passages. The sons do not bear the sins of the fathers as long as they do not practice the sins of the fathers. When the sons do bear these sins, it is because they have followed in their fathers' footsteps.[86] The sin that would be responsible for an endless and intolerable exile must fit two conditions: it must be of unprecedented villainy and it must have been perpetrated by both fathers and sons. Clearly, the sin is the fact that

> You killed Christ the son of God saying that He was a sorcerer and born of a whore and that He led the entire people into error . . .

Your being under the tribulation of damnation is no doubt
derived from the fact that you have persisted in the will and
the faith of the fathers.[87]

On the background of such thinking, we see Radak's reply take
form. Although Radak has stressed the righteousness of contemporary Israel, it is still they, the generations of the present exile, that
are responsible for their fate.

> *They shall bear their shame* (Ezekiel 39:26). They shall bear
> [it] with their own mouths and remember their own shame in
> exile and their betrayal of Me. For they suffer the reproach
> of the Gentiles as a punishment for their sins today . . .[88]

Radak admits that the sins of the fathers are a contributing
factor in the length of the exile.[89] In his Proverbs commentary,
where no theological subtlety is attempted, he assumes that if one
who is wicked "is not punished, his posterity will be punished."[90]
But when he is faced with a biblical account involving a son's suffering the consequences of his father's deed, Radak's agitation is
evident. As is his wont, he lapses into a long excursus rationalizing
the difficulty: Gehazi's sons are cursed only because they were
party to their father's deeds;[91] Absalom's nature was sinful and he
was not forced to sin, as the text implies, as a punishment for
David;[92] Saul's sons were executed only because they themselves
were party to the slaying of the Gibeonites.[93] Radak even wonders
how Hannah's vow, made before Samuel's birth, could have been
binding upon him. He expresses surprise that the rabbis never
discussed this.[94]

Radak's central treatment of this problem is found in his discussion of the first verses of Ezekiel 18 cited above.[95] In a way,
this passage seems to form a centerpiece in Radak's commentaries.
It contains a syntactic peculiarity which is rather common in
biblical style: the substitution of the preposition *'el* for *'al*. For
this reason, one seems to be constantly encountering the phrase
"as in *he does not eat upon ('el) the mountains*" (Ezekiel 18:6)
throughout the commentaries.[96]

Whether the choice of this particular instance of this phenomenon was deliberate or not, one is constantly referred to it. In the
lengthy commentary which accompanies this verse, Radak insists

that all of Israel are free of the cardinal sin of idolatry and that *most* of Israel are free of other sins. As for the fathers:

> In saying that the son will not bear the iniquity of the father, it refers to a son who has attained his majority and is subject to reward and punishment in his own right . . . [On the other hand], wicked sons . . . have no benefit of the merit of their fathers. Likewise, the righteous are not affected by the sins of their fathers, as it says in the Torah *Who visits the sins of the fathers upon the sons* [*to the third and fourth generation*] (Exodus 20:5) adding *of them that hate Me* (*ibid.*).
>   Yet concerning reward, He said *Who keeps covenant and mercy* [*with them that love Him and keep His commandments for a thousand generations*] (Deuteronomy 7:6), for reward is more far-reaching than punishment. The merit of the fathers preserves the sons and benefits them . . . to a thousand or several thousand generations, as He has kept the covenant of our fathers Abraham, Isaac, and Jacob to this day . . . [But] the sins of fathers are kept for the wicked sons . . . for four generations *and no more*.[97]

In other words, whether the length of Israel's present exile is due to present sins and failure to repent[98] or to God's own deliberate purpose,[99] any connection with the happenings of antiquity is denied. On the contrary, not only is Israel not being punished for the sins of the fathers, she is being preserved by the *merit* of the fathers. Only this could account for Israel's survival.

> *O Lord, I have heard the report of You and am afraid* (Habakkuk 3:2). I have heard the voice of prophecy tell me of the long exile which Israel will undergo in the future; I feared that Israel could not survive the years among their enemies. I therefore pray that You *keep him alive* (*ibid.*). Keep Israel alive throughout the long years they will be in exile that they not perish among their enemies.[100]

By rights, Israel should have disappeared long ago. The very fact of her physical survival is remarkable.[101] That she has received a much lighter punishment than she deserves provokes wonder.[102] But the conclusive evidence lies in the fact that Israel has remained a distinct nation. It would have been natural, under the circumstances, to expect a mass apostasy and assimilation. Yet God tells the Israelites: "If you want to cease serving Me, *I will not let you.*

Even if you are in exile among the nations a long time, you will
not cease to be a nation. Even if a few of you leave the fold, most
of you will be a nation before Me forever."[103]

It would be simple for a free people in their own land to maintain their promises to their God. That they have done so under conditions of exile is proof that

> *He* has kept the covenant of our fathers Abraham, Isaac, and
> Jacob with us until today for we love Him and keep His com-
> mandments. Even though there are wicked ones among us, all
> Israel today are innocent of the sin of idolatry. Of . . . other
> sins most of Israel are innocent . . . He promised our fathers
> of this . . . [and of the preservation of the covenant for
> Abraham's] sons as He said, *I will remember My covenant*
> *with Jacob and also My covenant with Isaac and also My*
> *covenant with Abraham will I remember* . . . (Leviticus
> 26:42) . . . The covenant is established for the seed of Abra-
> ham, Isaac, and Jacob, who will not cease to be a nation
> before God.[104]

The fact of the permanence of the covenant is established by the
failure of the Gentiles to disprove it.

> *Your commandments make me wiser than* [literally: from]
> *my enemies* (Psalms 119:98). My master, my father, inter-
> preted literally: *From* my enemies, You have made me wise
> and taught me Your commandments. When I see that *they*
> *cannot remove Your Torah* from my mouth, for Your Torah
> is a "covenant of salt" . . . I grow wise of the fact that it is
> Your will. . . .[105]

In this way has God's word been fulfilled:

> Israel are dispersed throughout the exile at the four corners
> of heaven and are one nation cleaving to their Torah and
> belief. All of them—east or west—believe in the same Torah.
> They did not change their religion in the stress of the exile
> and the persecutions which came upon them incessantly.[106]

The identity of Israel is thus well established. Yet the prophets
speak not of Israel alone. They speak of other nations whose roles
were decisive in antiquity, are still so in the present, and will continue to be so at the end of days. In order to fit the mosaic of the

redemption together, it would be necessary to establish the identification of the other nations as well. As to the present, Radak
follows the rabbis in declaring that

> the nations are indistinguishable today except for Israel, who
> are distinguished by their Torah and who did not assimilate
> . . . The other nations intermingled and are divided between
> the religion of the Ishmaelites and that of the Christians [so
> that] when [Scripture] mentions Edom, Moab, and the
> Amorites, it means their lands and those who dwell in
> them . . .[107]

Radak lists, in addition to the biblical lands, those closer to home:

> the lands of Rome: Alemania, Ascalonia, França, which is
> Zarephath, and the lands of Sepharad that they call Spania.[108]
> It is a tradition that those of Alemania are Canaanites; When
> the Canaanites fled Joshua . . . they went to Alemania and
> Asclavonia, which they call Ashkenaz. To this day, they call
> them Canaanites.[109]

Yet if the nations of antiquity have lost their individuality and
occupy—as does Israel—a new world, two nations remain dominant
Edom and Ishmael. The former is Rome and Christianity,[110] the
latter Islam. These nations together with Israel make up Radak's
world. He knows of the existence of other nations beyond the
horizon[111] but they are not of great consequence. "For most of
the Gentiles are divided between the Kingdom of Edom and the
Kingdom of Ishmael."[112] It is these with which Israel must con-
tend.

> *The bear out of the wood ravages it, that which moves in the*
> *field feeds on it* (Psalms 80:14). The boar and that which
> moves refer to the nations of the world who devour Israel
> with relish . . . The boar out of the wood refers to Esau and
> that which moves in the field refers to Ishmael for these two
> nations rule over Israel . . .[113]

These two nations together are the fourth Kingdom of Daniel.[114]
The prophet referred to this kingdom as grizzled and bay (*'amuẓ-*
zim)—grizzled because Rome has grizzled the Torah; *bay* (*'amuẓ-*
zim) because "they rise up (*mit'ammeẓim*) to seek conquest

wherever it lay."[115] Israel has been immersed in their impurity; to live among them is to be defiled.[116] They strike a righteous pose but their uncleanness is patent.

> *They that sanctify themselves and purify themselves to go unto the gardens behind one in the midst, eating swine's flesh, and the detestable thing and the mouse, shall be consumed together, says the Lord* (Isaiah 66:17). Most of the commentators refer this to the Christians, who *sanctify themselves* with the sign of the cross. They call this worthless sign *santiguar* in the vernacular. Those that *purify themselves* are the Ishmaelites, who constantly purify their bodies and wash themselves. They are impure and polluted in their evil deeds although they put on a display of being pure . . . Those who *eat swine's flesh* are the Christians for the Ishmaelites do not eat swine. The *detestable thing and the mouse* refer to the Ishmaelites, who eat the detestable thing and the mouse.[117]

Though Radak's feelings toward Ishmael were less than positive, his main offensive was waged against Edom–Rome.[118] He repeatedly stresses the punishment that awaits Rome as a consequence of its persecution of Israel.[119] "*Measure for measure, to the islands He will pay recompense* (Isaiah 59:18). As He wreaked vengeance on Pharaoh and Sennacherib and the other persecutors of Israel, so will He wreak vengeance when He delivers them from their exile . . . He stated this twice for further emphasis . . ."[120] Just as "Babylonia fell into the hands of Persia, Persia in the hands of Greece, and Greece in the hands of Rome, so shall Rome fall in the hands of Israel."[121] Radak stresses that "the nation of Edom will fall *wherever* they are."[122] In the fall of Rome, he sees the rise of Israel.[123] Radak sees little mercy for Edom. Where even Ammon and Moab will return to their historic homeland at the end of days,[124] the biblical land of Esau will become the territory of Israel.[125] The prophecy of the destruction of Edom is yet to be fulfilled.[126] Radak can not come to terms with the traditional understanding of Joel 4:21: *I will hold as innocent their blood which I have not held as innocent.* Realigning the syntax of the verse, Radak reads:

> *I will hold as innocent* the silver and gold that [the Gentiles] took from Israel, for Israel too will take [spoil] from them in the future . . . but *I shall not hold them innocent of the blood they spilt.* [It shall be] life for life.[127]

In the wars of Gog and Magog, a multitude of the Gentiles—essentially the sinful among them[128]—will perish.[129] Edom shall indeed be *small among the nations* (Obadiah 2), not in size, but in status, for it shall be "mean and low so that the nations will not notice you if you perish."[130]

Radak's stress on the retribution to be poured out on the Gentiles is of course a countermeasure to the sufferings inflicted by them on the Jews. To be sure, the Jews were exiled because of their sins and were not destined for an era of comfort and tranquillity. Yet the Gentiles "transgressed [all] conventions and laws in their oppression of Israel."[131] They went further than they had any right to.

Yet there is another element which makes their crime even more severe. Who, after all, are these Romans—Christians?

> Most of Rome consists of Edomites who embrace the religion of the Nazarene. Even though many nations mingled among them (as happened with the kingdom of the Ishmaelites), they are named after the root-stock. King Caesar was an Edomite as were all the kings of Rome after him. These two nations did evil to the tribes of Judah and Benjamin who were exiled among them and spilled their blood like water in their land. Edom, which is the Kingdom of Rome, destroyed the second Temple by the hand of the wicked Titus.[132]

Despite the intermingling of the nations, Christianity and Edom are one and the same. Technically then, there is blood kinship, fraternal status, between Jew and Christian. Now the Church, where it was convenient, had been for some time stressing this point in connection with the question of taking interest on loans. Since the Torah forbids the taking of interest from one's brother,[133] the Church argued that the Christian should be exempted from the payment of interest on loans from Jews.[134] Most Jewish polemicists rejected this claim of kinship outright.[135]

Radak, however, hand accepted it unconditionally. *My brethren* (Psalms 22:23) refers to "the Edomites among whom we are in exile and also the Ishmaelites and the Keturites for they are all the sons of Abraham our father."[136] Yet it is precisely the anti-fraternal behavior of the Christians which annuls their fraternal rights:

The foregoing of the collection of interest is an act of special kindness incumbent only upon those who reciprocate. The Jew is not required to lend [Gentiles] money for nothing, for in general they hate Israel. [Only] if a Gentile acts with goodness and kindness toward the Israelite must the Jew act with kindness toward him.[137]

This, then, is the paradox of Israel's relationship with the Gentiles: the persecution of brother by brother. It is this which renders the nations all the more liable to severe punishment at the time of judgment.[138] The relationship of Jacob and Esau was always ambiguous but it shall be so no more.

> *The elder shall serve the younger* (Genesis 25:23). [The syntax of the verse is such that it is difficult to know which is the subject and which the object]. This was so . . . since sometimes the elder serves the younger as in the days of David and sometimes the younger serves the elder as it is today. The word order would seem to indicate though that the elder would serve the younger most of the time. So it shall be after the return of the exile.[139]

Radak does not envision an enslavement of the Gentiles by the Jews or a treatment similar to that dealt out by the former to the latter during the exile. The submission to the "government of Israel"[140] will entail only a temporary subservience in order that the Gentiles acquire a sense of humility.[141] After this—with the exception of Edom—the nations shall return to their homelands.[142] The Gentiles will live at peace not only with Israel but with one another.[143] Some of the Gentiles will convert to Judaism: "*He will speak to His people and to His saints* (Psalms 85:9). To the exemplary Gentiles who will convert to the religion of Israel."[144] To be judaized are the territories adjacent to the Land of Israel—presumably those of Edom.[145] All territories, however, will observe the seven commandments of the sons of Noah[146] and will join Israel in sacrificing to God at the Temple.[147]

The "neutralization" of the Gentiles and their return to their original lands is tantamount to the necessary precondition of redemption: the restoration of the Land of Israel. The restoration of the land represents a return to the natural order of things, to God's original intention. Even though the Land today is closed to

Israel,[148] its reopening is guaranteed, "for since He gave it to Abraham and his sons, His truth is to maintain that gift . . . for He is a God of truth and His good word will not be turned back."[149] From the very beginning the Land was reserved for Israel. The Canaanites were placed there only to prepare it.[150] When Abraham appeared, they did not lift a finger against him for God placed His fear upon them.[151]

Like Rashi in the remark which opens his Torah commentary,[152] Radak stressed that "the earth is the Lord's . . . He takes from one and gives to the other."[153] For a millennium now, the Lord had been taking from one and giving to the other. The interchange between Edom and Ishmael was incessant.

> *The uncircumcised and the unclean* (Isaiah 52:1). *The uncircumcised* are the Kingdom of Edom . . . and the *unclean* are the Kingdom of Ishmael who affect purity by washing their bodies but are . . . impure in their evil deeds. These two kingdoms have held Jerusalem from the day of the destruction. They fight over it endlessly and one conquers it from the other. But from the day of the redemption, they will no longer pass through it.[154]

Their attempts to gain effective control of Jerusalem are in vain. Their building is no building: *"Our holy . . . house . . . is burned with fire* (Isaiah 64:10). The place of the Temple was never built by the Gentiles."[155]

> *Your holy cities have become a wilderness. Zion is a wilderness, Jerusalem a desolation* (Isaiah 64:9). Even though the Gentiles came and built it after its destruction, it is desolate and devoid of . . . inhabitants because Israel is not there . . . The Edomites take it from the Ishmaelites and destroy it . . . It was like this since the day Israel was exiled from it.[156]

The association of the Land of Israel with the Gentiles is ludicrous: it is like the marriage of an old man with a maiden or of a young man with a matron.[157] The Land of Israel is "allergic" to foreigners, it spews them out.

> *He planted it in a field of seed* (Ezekiel 17:5). In a field which is suitable for seed and makes that which is sown there flourish. Thus good men of integrity, the servants of God, should

be in Jerusalem. Their opposite are people alien to the land, as it says *alien gods of the land* (Deuteronomy 36:16), *that the land not vomit you out as it vomited out the nation that was before you* (Leviticus 18:28).[158]

Thus shall the restoration begin with a purification of Jerusalem.

> *They shall come there and take away all the detestable things* (Ezekiel 11:18). The detestable things and the abominations which the Christians made: the detestable things of the crucified one—for it will be in their hands when the redemption comes. They will find the detestable thing in it— which is the pit (the sepulchre) of the crucified one, of which it says *to make the detestable thing desolate* (Daniel 12:11).[159]

Jerusalem shall henceforth be the home of the righteous only. While this probably includes the righteous Gentile as well as the righteous Jew,[160] "it is possible that strangers will not enter Jerusalem at all because its sanctity will increase in the future. Just as no one, not even a priest, can enter the sanctuary, thus will the city be holy and no strangers from among the nations will enter it."[161]

Thus, in "retaliation" for Israel's exile, Edom is to undergo herself a double exile—one from her own land, the Land of Esau, and one from Jerusalem, which she sought to dominate. On the other hand, Israel will undergo a double redemption. The exodus itself will startle the world. "When will God's praise be great? At the ingathering of the exiles when the whole world sees the wonders He accomplishes with Israel."[162] It is not only that "He will take a nation out of the midst of many nations, [for] they were engulfed in exile so many years that all the nations thought that they would never escape their control . . . But He will bring them to the Land of Israel with great honor *upon horses and in chariots and litters* (Isaiah 66:20)."[163]

In return for their impoverishment in the exile, they will leave the exile with silver and gold and the spoil of the Gentiles.[164] Their dominion will of course be securely established.[165] They shall return to their former rank and be above the nations.[166] The fears of the exile will cease. They will never again have to climb the walls and close the gates in the face of the enemy.[167] They will never again have overseers above them.[168] Since there will be no ruler but the Messiah, they shall not have to pay taxes to foreigners.[169]

Yet glorious as this is in itself, Radak's dreams go farther than a mere political restoration. No longer the measure-for-measure moralist, he is now the proletarian who aspires to the bourgeoisie. Israel is not only to be compensated but compensated on a Jobian scale. A new era in the history of the world will be inaugurated. So great will be the grace of God that the interminable exile will appear as but an instant.[170]

> *For as the earth brings forth her growth and as the garden causes the things that are sown in it to spring forth, so the Lord God will cause victory and glory to spring forth before all the nations* (Isaiah 61:11). He likened the salvation of Israel to a land which brings forth her growth. The seed in the ground was rotted and decayed but then it blossomed, revived, and recovered, and was better and finer [than ever] . . . This is Israel. For a long time, they were rotting and decaying in exile with their hope almost lost. Yet at the time of redemption, they shall blossom and grow and multiply and increase in number and glory and greatness many times over what they were . . . [Also], since plants do not bloom at the same time but each in its own time, so one good thing will happen to Israel after another.[171]

As we have seen, everything will be on a greater scale. The Land of Israel will be greater than it was.[172] The dimensions of the rebuilt Temple will be increased.[173] It will be of unprecedented beauty.[174] It will have (as do the cathedrals) stained-glass windows.[175] The young men of Israel, like the Gentile aristocracy, will tour the world in their finery.[176] But more than this. Nature herself will be forced to abdicate her authority in this world. When the Temple is built, it will be built not through human labor but through the power and will of God![177] Abundance will stand in readiness without human exertion or effort as if the mountains were themselves dripping with sweet wine and the hills flowing with milk.[178] "*Every tree for food whose leaf shall not wither nor shall its fruit fail . . . miraculously.*"[179]

Yet these miracles stop at the borders of the Land of Israel. The world's one disadvantaged nation now becomes the one that is advantaged. Radak objects to Ibn Ezra's interpretation of *for I create new heavens and a new earth* (Isaiah 65:17) because it implies that all mankind will benefit from increased longevity. "If it is as he interprets it," argues Radak, "it would apply to all nations, while Scripture says *for as the days of a tree shall be the days of My people* (Isaiah 65:22), not other peoples."[180] Thus the people who felt themselves dying before their time because they died without seeing the Messiah[181] receive their lives now. This extraordinary longevity is mentioned often;[182] three to five hundred year lifespans will not be unusual.[183] People will live so long that it will no longer be felt necessary to weep for the dead.[184]

As the life of the individual shall be extended several hundred years, so shall the life of the nation be extended indefinitely. Israel need never fear that the third Temple will go the way of the first and second. Man's wicked inclinations will be miraculously transformed.[185] Since sin will be abolished, there is no danger of another destruction.[186] As Israel remembers her ways and is ashamed of them, so does God promise to maintain the covenant for ever.[187] Never again will Israel know shame for *this* time the Jews shall suffer no troubles upon their return. Never again shall the walls of Jerusalem fall, for "*I have set watchmen* (divine providence) *upon them day and night. They shall never hold their peace* (Isaiah 62:6)."[188]

Radak portrays his millennium of light to his readers, but its date of inception remains shrouded in darkness. It was fashionable in that age to discourage such predictions but equally fashionable, in the same breath, to predict.[189] Radak does not seem to care to: it will come "in its own time."[190] This does not mean that he was not desperately curious:

> *So teach us to number our days* (Psalms 90:12). This may . . . refer to the end of the exile. This was not revealed because the words of Daniel are obscure, and the angel told him that he would confound whatever he did understand of it. He said: Teach us when the end will be and how long the exile will last. When will the prophet come to Israel?[191]

Yet Radak was too occupied exploring other avenues. Radak's conception of exile was multifaceted. We recall the image of the circle, a circle composed of an infinity of sides. Alongside the exile of a nation is the exile of its God: "*His own arm brought Him salvation* (Isaiah 59:16). The master is obliged to save His servant from those who hold and oppress him as do the nations of the world today. Through the redemption of the servant, the master is redeemed."[192] Alongside the exile of Israel in strange lands is man in a strange world: "Man in this world is like a stranger in a land which is not his, for man has no certainty of his status in this world. He is ever in the process of leaving it for he does not know when his time will come."[193]

The first exile, the arch-exile, was that of Adam from Eden. The Bible is explicit concerning Adam's task in Eden, man's task in the world: *The Lord God took the man and placed him in the Garden of Eden to work it and keep it* (Genesis 2:15). As is his custom, Radak paraphrases: "He placed him in it to work the ground by weeding, hoeing, and tending plants for his food and to keep it as well as he could from animals."[194] Yet he adds: "Our rabbis explained this figuratively: "*To work it* refers to study; *to keep it* refers to commandments."[195] In this precise form, this passage does not appear to be extant in rabbinic literature today.[196] Whether Radak had such a text before him or whether he "remembered" it in hindsight, the direction in which he is moving is clear. This is made even clearer in his philosophical commentary on Genesis: "*To work it* refers to study; *to keep it* refers to guarding one's mind against those who are rebellious and corrupt so that [God] be remembered and kept in mind constantly."[197] Each level of interpretation is a lens which refines the focus. The guardian of the physical world becomes the guardian of man's soul; first through study and practice of the Torah and then through study and contemplation alone. This is the task of man in the world, a task of which not all are aware.

> The world is constructed like a house: the heavens are the roof on the house; the stars are . . . the candles placed in the house; the plants of the earth are . . . the table that has been laid in the house. The master and builder of the house is God . . .
>
> Man in the world is like a steward in the house who has been entrusted with all affairs of the house. He has never seen the master of the house with his own eyes. Yet he grew up in the house, was told that his father was an overseer in that house, and that he would follow in his footsteps.
>
> Now if the overseer is intelligent, he will seek out the master of the house . . . so that he may always stand in His presence and not be remiss in his stewardship. He knows that sooner or later he will come to a reckoning with [the master]

over his stewardship. He takes cognizance of the fact that He is above him always and observes him and his actions. If he has done his deeds intelligently, he will please the master of the house. Should [the master] find him unworthy, He will remove him from his stewardship, punish him, and strike him.

The foolish steward does not do this. Seeing himself steward, he does as he pleases and fancies and does not concern himself with the identity of the master of the house. He says to himself: "Since I do not see with my own eyes that this house has a master, who'll make me think that it has a master? So I'll eat and drink whatever I find in this house and I'll do as I please as long as I find it. I don't care if the house has a master or not."

When the master of the house learns of this, he angrily evicts him from the house and imprisons him . . . God is Lord of the world and He made man steward in this world. It is proper to fear Him as the servant fears his master. If he sees intellectually that the world could not exist without One Who governs, manages, and orders, then he will please the Lord. But if he is a fool, he will encounter the reverse . . . By saying to himself "I don't care if there is a Lord or not, I'll follow my own inclination and manage as I see fit," God banishes him from the world and renders him powerless and ineffective . . . Thus does it say, *Who brings princes [to nothing]* (Isaiah 40:23). He shows then that there is a Lord in the world Who makes poor and makes rich, humbles and exalts.[198]

The duty of stewardship is discharged by man's fulfillment of himself as a rational being. Rationality, "the supernal soul," is the defining characteristic of man. "*He remembers that we are dust* (Psalms 103:14) . . . The bestial and corporeal lusts . . . are dust but man's superiority lies in his supernal soul, which is of angelic nature."[199] Only by virtue of this soul is man man. Following the imagery of Ezekiel's four creatures, Radak explains that "when a man follows [his] supernal soul, his face is that of a lion or an ox or an eagle."[200] The supernal soul, if freed from bestiality and given free rein, instinctively follows the path to knowledge.

The rational soul longs for science even though there is no [material] reward in attaining it . . . It is the nature of the soul to desire science just as it is the nature of the appetitive soul [to desire] fine food. Thus do the sages engage in Torah and science by nature even though there is no reward for this.[201]

With his rational soul, man struggles to "consider [God] in his heart, to understand through philosophical proof as science instructs him."[202] Yet the road to perfect knowledge is so long that man can traverse only a small portion of it in this world. In the normal lifespan, all that can be attained is the knowledge of God's name.[203] Enoch strived so hard to attain ultimate knowledge that his body was shattered and God took him.[204] How long is the journey? The rabbis communicated this in a midrashic parable:

> "The tree of life extends over an area of five hundred years' journey, and it is from beneath it that all the waters of the creation sprang forth," and they added the explanation that this measure referred to the thickness of its trunk, and not to the extent of its branches, for they continue thus, "Not the extent of the branches thereof, but the stem thereof has a thickness of five hundred years' journey."[205] . . . That is to say, the distance from the earth to heaven is [a] five hundred years' [journey] as the rabbis said and as the scientists have said. It is the intent of the parable in this passage to say that the trunk refers to the attainment of natural science, which is terrestrial, by the human mind. The foliage refers to what is above the heavens, including a knowledge of astronomy and of the intelligences.[206]

The figure of five hundred years has a familiar ring. This was the lifespan predicted for Israel by Radak for the era of redemption.[207] The need for such a lifespan now becomes apparent.

Until that time, however, only in the afterlife, "the world to come," is this perfect knowledge attained. Only then does the soul "delight in the supreme glory"[208] and attain the vision of God.[209]

> *They are abundantly satisfied with the fatness of Your house* (Psalms 36:9). All this refers to the world to come which is the world of the souls and angels . . . *the house of God, the Temple of God, His holy mountain, the mountain of the Lord, and the pleasantness of the Lord.* The fatness and pleasure is the attainment of the knowledge of God . . . This is the good after which there is no evil and the satiety after which there is no hunger or thirst, the life after which there is no death, the light after which there is no darkness.[210]

The soul in this world is not in its true home. It, like Israel, is in exile. The resolution of Israel's exile is the return to Jerusalem; to the holy Temple "in which the ark was kept, the habitation of Your house,"[211] to "Your holy sanctuary,"[212] to "the house of God,"[213] to "Your holy Temple,"[214] to "Your holy mountain."[215] The resolution of the soul's exile is the return to the heavenly Jerusalem, to *"His Temple* (Psalms 18:17) . . . the heavens."[216]

> *O Lord, who shall sojourn in Your tabernacle and who shall dwell upon Your holy mountain* (Psalms 15:1). *Who will sojourn* and *who will dwell* refer to the supernal soul . . . which will dwell in the place of glory after one's death.[217]

Exile is joined to exile as Temple is joined to Temple. The earthly Temple is the "gate of heaven" for it faces the throne of Glory.[218] To dwell in the earthly Temple leads to dwelling in the heavenly Temple.

> *To dwell in the House of the Lord* (Psalms 27:4). The house which contains the ark; [in which were] the prophets and the righteous, the priests and the Levites . . . who engage in the service of God and the tasks of the soul. *To behold the graciousness of the Lord and to visit in His Temple (ibid.)* . . . to engage in the tasks of the soul.[219]

Here is the root of David's longing for freedom from exile and tribulations;[220] for freedom to remain "in seclusion to know Your ways."[221] In one Temple could David aspire to the other: *"Who shall sojourn in Your tabernacle and who shall dwell upon Your holy mountain* (Psalms 15:1). *Your tabernacle* . . . is the heavens; *Your holy mountain* is Mount Moriah, the place of the Temple . . . the most noble place on earth."[222]

As the Jews are preserved in their exile by a covenant,[223] the soul is preserved by its covenant.

> *The counsel of the Lord is with them that fear Him; and His covenant to make them know it* (Psalms 25:14). The covenant is that which He established with the soul to enlighten it and to gather it to its glory when it separates from the body. He called this the covenant in speaking to Moses: *Behold I make a covenant; before all the people I will do marvels* (Exodus 34:10). The covenant is that He has endowed one with the light of intellect and that one's soul cleaves to the upper world.[224]

Ultimately, however, both covenants are one: *"My heart is stead-fast, O God, I will sing . . . praise with my glory* (Psalms 108:2). Even though I have been in exile many years, I have not despaired of redemption . . . My soul itself sings with *intellectual contemplation."*[225]

Maimonides had taught that divine providence is a function of intellectual development.[226] For the animals—devoid of intellect—providence implies only preservation of the species. Radak concurs in this:

> *Your loving kindness, O Lord, is in the heavens; Your faith-fulness reaches the skies* (Psalms 36:6). [God's] faithfulness is the preservation of the species from destruction, for although the individuals . . . perish the species survives forever . . . Loving kindness refers to the preparation for the mainten-ance of the world. He prepares each animal's food in the form most convenient for it . . . for that which is most necessary for the maintenance of the world is most common. Liquids are more necessary for the maintenance of life than [solid] foods, therefore, water is more abundant than food and [involves] no work of preparation.[227]

An entire species will be eradicated only if it is totally corrupt. Barring this, God is faithful in maintaining it.[228]

The principle of preservation of the species applies to the human race as well. With respect to the "multitude," Maimonides "con-sidered [them] according to their true worth; some of them are undoubtedly like domesticated cattle and others like wild beasts."[229] Radak thus defines the man who is devoid of intellec-tual activity (and, he adds, religious practice) as one who eats with his ox in the same manger.[230] Individual providence is bestowed only upon the true intellectual. If one who has not fulfilled himself intellectually as a "true man" benefits from divine care, it is only by virtue of his membership in the species.

> I say that the loving kindness which You bestow on the wicked who deny You is like the loving kindness You bestow upon the beast which is incognizant of it . . .
> This is the meaning of *You preserve man and beast, O Lord* (Psalms 36:7). The wicked and the fool is a beast in the form of a man . . .[231]

Who though are these "masses" and who are the intellectuals? Clearly all human beings are potential candidates for intellectual perfection.[232] If all of God's "creatures are His glory . . . then this is certainly true of the human species, as it is written, *Whom I have created for My glory* (Isaiah 43:7)."[233] Yet, as one surveys the human species, one sees few signs of such perfection. Most of humanity is steeped in the epitome of the irrational: idolatry. True, among the nations there are some sages who are too sophisticated to believe in the efficacy of the idols.[234] Yet they are rare indeed. In an ironic turn of Psalms 87:4, understood christologically by the Church,[235] Radak observes: "*This one was born there,* if there be a sage among all those great nations, it will occur so rarely that they will say in praise, 'This sage was born there.' "[236]

Thus, although those "*whom I have created for My glory* (Isaiah 43:7)" refer "to the human species [in general], as it is written *I have formed him, yea, I have made him* (*ibid.*), since Israel recognizes the glory of God more than do the rest of mankind, except for the sages among them, *the verse is said with reference to Israel.*"[237] It is clear therefore that Israel is a *nation* of sages who

recognize and know that God created them and created the world and are witnesses, for they recognize the glory of God and confess [His existence]. They meditate on the creation of man and how his limbs were formed in wisdom and how his sustenance is provided from the day he was born. This wisdom brings man to recognize God and to praise Him and give thanks to His name, for this is the glory of God. Therefore, He said "Israel, *whom I have created for My glory,* is he who meditated on My deeds and confessed My unity."[238]

To be sure, not all are equal in intellectual fulfillment. To assume this would be absurd.[239] Yet the Jews, by their actions, have proved that they have grasped the basic conception of God's divinity and have thereby proved their humanity.

You my sheep, the sheep of My pasture are men . . . (Ezekiel 34:31) . . . I shall pasture them on knowledge, understanding, and insight. *Then* shall you be called men—not sheep and cattle. Man and beast are one in the material sphere: he and his ass eat from the same manger . . . Yet when we are concerned with matters intellectual, our humanity is discernible and we are distinguishable from the beast and those people who resemble it . . . Our rabbis said: "You are called *men* (*ibid.*). The nations of the world are not called men."[240]

This is the glory of Israel.

> *Let him that glories glory in this, that he understands and knows Me . . .* (Jeremiah 9:23). Understanding God is understanding that He is one, eternal and noncorporeal, that He creates all and supervises all; that He manages the upper and lower worlds in wisdom. The knowledge of God is walking in His ways, performing mercy, justice, and righteousness, as He performs with them . . . He who walks in His ways knows Him, as it says: *Did not your father eat and drink and do justice and righteousness? Then it was well with him. He judged the cause of the poor and the needy; then it was well. Is not this to know Me? says the Lord* (Jeremiah 22:16f).[241]

The covenant which has preserved Israel in the Exile is the covenant of reason. Until the light of redemption breaks through, the flame of the intellect illumines the way.

Appendix

Abbreviations of Works Cited
Manuscripts Cited
Bibliographic Note

Notes

Index of Biblical Citations
General Index

Appendix
The Acrostic Ascribed to Radak
in Ms. Vat. Ebr. 320

Since the pointing in the manuscript is rather faulty, I have repointed it completely. Lexical, but not orthographic, emendations have been noted in the apparatus.

תְּפִלָּה מָעֲלָה בְּכָל בֹּקֶר

לְרַב דָּוִד קִמְחִי זצ"ל

שִׁיר לַמַּעֲלוֹת

שָׂמַחְתִּי בְּאוֹמְרִים לִי בֵּית יְיָ נֵלֵךְ

שָׂשׂ אָנֹכִי עַל אִמְרָתָךְ כְּמוֹצֵא שָׁלָל רָב   5

אָמְרַי הַאֲזִינָה יְיָ בִּינָה הֲגִיגִי

הַקְשִׁיבָה לְקוֹל שַׁוְעִי מַלְכִּי וֵאלֹהָי כִּי אֵלֶיךָ אֶתְפַּלָּל

יְיָ בֹּקֶר תִּשְׁמַע קוֹלִי בֹּקֶר אֶעֱרָךְ לְךָ וַאֲצַפֶּה

אֶקְרָא לְךָ חָנֵּנִי בֹּקֶר

לֵב וּכְלָיוֹת הַכֹּל סוֹקֵר   10

הַרְחִיקֵנִי מִדְּבַר שָׁקֶר

יְיָ תִּשְׁמַע קוֹלִי בֹּקֶר

בֹּקֶר אֶעֱרָךְ לְךָ וַאֲצַפֶּה

צַדִּיק אַתָּה הַכֹּל צוֹפֶה

קָרְבֵנִי בַּל אֶהְיֶה נִסְפֶּה   15

עִם מוֹרְדִים לֹא רָאה בֹּקֶר

165

בֹּקֶר בִּינָה קוֹל רַחֲשִׁי

חַלְצֵנִי וְהַעֲבֵר מוֹקְשִׁי

מִסִּבְכֵי אֵל בְּכֹל נַפְשִׁי

לָאֵל מְשׁוֹמְרִים לַבֹּקֶר   20

בֹּקֶר צַלֵּה לַדְּפְזָרִים

שַׁלַּח אַבּוֹר הַאֲאֲסָרִים

מַיִם אֵין פֹּו הֵנָּה אוֹמְרִים

לָעֶרֶב מִי יָתֵּן בֹּקֶר

בֹּקֶר דְּרוֹשׁ נִמְפַּר מְשָׁנֶה   25

אֵיךָ בַּפְשׁוֹ לָב מְקָנֶה

זָעַק לָב מֵאֵין עוֹנֶה

הֵנֵּה לוֹ פֵלָהָה בְּטֶרֶם בֹּקֶר

בֹּקֶר הַיּוֹם אֲהָאנוּ

צַדִּיק אַתָּה מוֹשִׁיעֵנוּ   30

לָךָ נָשָׂאנוּ אֶת עֵינֵינוּ

וְחָפִינוּ עַד אוֹר הַבֹּקֶר

בֹּקֶר וְעַד נָא אֵל צֵירוֹם

הַמְצֵא לָאֲסוּרִים פִּדְיוֹם

יָגִילָה יְשִׁישׂוּ פֵּיוֹם הַשְּׁלִישִׁי   35

בִּהְיוֹת הַבֹּקֶר

בֹּקֶר זְכוֹר בְּזִפוֹר רַחֲמִים

לְעַם לַחֲסָדֶיךָ הֵנָּם הוֹמִים

נָא צוּרִי הַשְּׁמִיעֵם מִמְּרוֹמִים

נַעֲלֶה הֶעָנָן בַּבֹּקֶר   40

בֹּקֶר חָנָה אֶת רַעְיָתֶךָ
וְאִם עָלֶיהָ עֲבַרְתֶּךָ
סָמְכָה פִּי זֹאת מִדָּתֶךָ
וַיְהִי עֶרֶב וַיְהִי בֹקֶר

בֹּקֶר טַהֵר עַם לְךָ הוֹמֶם   45
שָׂפָה נוֹפֶלֶת בָּא קוֹמֵם
זֵדִים קָמִים הָאֲשִׁימֵם
יֵרְדוּ עַם יְשָׁרִים לַבֹּקֶר

בֹּקֶר לְשַׁמִּיעֲךָ אֶת קוֹלוֹ
בֶּנֶךָ בְּכוֹרְךָ מִפַּדָּה אֵלוֹ   50
מְעִי יָם הוֹמֶה לְמוֹ
פִּי לֹא הָנִיחָה אוֹתוֹ עַד בֹּקֶר

בֹּקֶר פָּעִיר מֶלֶךְ נֶאֱמָן
הָאִירָה אֵל יֵרֹשֶׁב אֲשְׁמָן
הַרְאֵה צִנְצֶנֶת הַמָּן   55
לְמִשְׁמֶרֶת עַד בֹּקֶר

בֹּקֶר לִלְקוֹט הָמָּה יָצְאוּ
בָּרָאוּ פֶּן אֲנִי יָרָאוּ
אֶחָד אֶחָד הַמָּה מָצְאוּ
אוֹתוֹ בַּבֹּקֶר   60

בֹּקֶר מַעֲלֶה מַיִם יָחֲשֶׂה
מִמַּיִם רַפִּים עַם יַמְשֶׂה
כַּאֲשֶׁר הוֹלִיךְ לִימִין מֹשֶׂה
וַיְהִי בְּאַשְׁמֹרֶת הַבֹּקֶר

בֹּקֶר נֶאֱמַן רוֹעֶה הַפֶּה   65

יָמוֹן שָׁמוֹ נִקְרָא מְשֻׁפֶּה

לְעוּף הַבָּר יַעֲנֶה

יָעִיר פַּבֹּקֶר פַּבֹּקֶר

בֹּקֶר סַלְעִי שִׂיחִי יִנְעַם

לָךְ הִשָּׁפוֹךְ עַל צוּרְבְרִי זַעַם   70

פַּבְמוֹף מוֹפְתֶיךָ עַל הַיָּם

הַסֶּבֶשׁ הָאֶחָד תַּעֲשֶׂה פַּבֹּקֶר

בֹּקֶר עֶזְרָה מְצַר הֲבָה

וּשְׁשׂוֹן יִשְׁעַב הָשִׁיבָה

לָנוּ גָּאֳלָתָךְ קָרְבָה   75

לְהַגִּיד חַסְדְּךָ פַּבֹּקֶר

בֹּקֶר פְּנֵה אֵלַי תִּפְנֶה

אָכְתּוֹב עַם צַדִּיקִים פִּי נֶפֶשׁ וְנַעֲנֶה

הָקֵם חֶזְיוֹן נָבִיא הַפֶּה

אָמַר שׁוֹמֵר אָתָא פֹּקֶר   80

בֹּקֶר צוּרֵנוּ עַצְמָח

קֶרֶן פַּלְכוּת מֶלֶךְ הַפָּשִׁיחַ

אוֹר שֶׁבְעָתַיִם יַזְרִיחַ

הִבְאוֹר הַשֶּׁמֶשׁ יִזְרַח פֹּקֶר

בֹּקֶר קוֹמֵם פֵּית הָעֲטֶרֶת   85

שָׁמָּה יַעֲמוֹד אִישׁ הַפְּשָׁרֶת

עַל מִזְפַּחֲךָ יַקְטִיר קְטֹרֶת

סַמִּים הַקָּה פַּבֹּקֶר פַּבֹּקֶר

בֹּקֶר רוֹמֵם נָא בִּשְׁמֶךָ

90 קַרְנֶנּוּ בִּגְאוֹן שַׁחַר עֲנָנֶיךָ

יִקְרָא מֵעַל מְתָקוֹ מֵמִיר

חַסְדְּכֶם פַּעֲנַן בֹּקֶר

תְּקָר שָׁמַיִם עָדֶיךָ

נֶאֱמָנִים כִּי אֵין בִּלְעָדֶיךָ

95 תָּמִיד מְסַפְּרִים כָּבוֹדֶךָ

מוֹצָאֵי עֶרֶב וָבֹקֶר

בֹּקֶר תַּעֲרֹךְ לָךְ נִשְׁמָתִי

שֶׁבַח מֵיטַב תְּהִלָּתִי

וָאֶרְגַּן לָךְ רְצָתִי

100 עֶרֶן יַחַד פּוֹכְבֵי בֹּקֶר

תם

הערות

17 בצד ימין: ס"א אל קול לחשי.   18   בצד שמאל:

חנני אל.   25   בצד שמאל: ס"א נָשָׁנָה.   26-27   במקור:

זעק איך נפשו לך מקנה לך מאין עונה.   29   בצד שמאל:

לך.   33   בצד ימין: יועד.   34   במקור: הַצָּא.

48 בצד שמאל: יָרְהוּ בם כמו וירד מים עד ים | תהלים

עב ח| זה משיח.   פרש' בלק כך פי' רש"י |במדבר כד

יט|.   בתחתית העמוד: וירד מים עד ים ולא יהיה שריד

לבית עשו.   וירד מיעקב והאביד שריד מעיר |במדבר כד

יט| בתשלום דברי הימים פסוק וכנרת להם ישובו וירדו

בהם וגו' |נחמיה ט כח| בפרש' בו וביום עשרים וד'

לחדש |שם ט א|.   51   בצד שמאל: מְצַר הומה.

57 בצד שמאל: מנאצים כראו כן יראו.   בצד ימין:

אזי ראו כן מופת יראו.   67   בצד ימין: יעוף.   אולי

יש לגרוס לָעָיֵף.   65-68   בתחתית העמוד: בקר נס אל

שרש ישי/ יעמוד יובילו שרים ישי |צ"ל שי/ מַצְבָּי מָהַּ

|ישעיה יג יד| ממקדשי/ נותר ממנו עד בקר.   75   בצד

שמאל: ס"א לי.   80   בצד ימין: ישעיה רגם לילה.

84 בצד ימין: שמואל בסוף וכאור בקר יזרח שמש בקר

לא עבות מנגה ממטר דשא מארץ.   100   בצד ימין: איוב

מן הסערה.   בתחתית העמוד: ברון יחד פי' הם שרים

שברקיע יריעו כל בני אלהים |איוב לח ז| והם המלאכים

המשולחים בארץ בשליחות שרים העליונים כמו בני

הנביאים תלמידיהם כן בני אלהים שלוחים.

‫4 תהלים קכב א. 5 שם קיט קסב. 6 שם ה ב.‬

‫7 שם שם ג. 8 שם שם ד. 11 ע"פ שמות כג ז.‬

‫13 תהלים ה ד. 19 שם קיט קטז. 20 שם קל ו.‬

‫24 ע"פ דברים כח סז. 25 נמכר משנה| הוגלה‬

‫פעמים. 35 ע"פ הושע ו ב. 44 בראשית א ה.‬

‫46 עמוס ט יא. 47 ע"פ תהלים פו יד. 50 ע"פ‬

‫שמות ד כב. 54 אשמן| חושך. עיין רש"י על‬

‫ישעיה נט י. 55 ע"פ שמות טז לז. 56 ע"פ‬

‫שמות טז כב. 57-60 עיין שם טז יד ואילך.‬

‫61 ע"פ ישעיה סו יא. 62 ע"פ שמואל ב כב יז‬

‫(תהלים יח יז). 63 ע"פ ישעיה סג יב.‬

‫64 שמות יד כד. 66 תהלים עב יז. 67 מוף|‬

‫כינוי למצרים ע"פ הושע ט ו. 72 שמות כט לט.‬

‫76 ע"פ תהלים צב ג. 78 ע"פ ישעיה נג ז.‬

‫80 ע"פ ישעיה כא יב. 83 ע"פ ישעיה ל כו.‬

‫84 ע"פ שמואל ב כג ד. 86 איש המשרת| כאן‬

‫הכוהן הגדול. השוה ישעיה סא ו. 87-88 ע"פ‬

‫ריקרא טז יב. 92 ע"פ הושע ו ד. 95 ע"פ‬

‫תהלים יט ב. 100 איוב לח יז.‬

Abbreviations of Works Cited

Abrahams	I. Abrahams, *Hebrew Ethical Wills,* 2 vols. (Philadelphia: Jewish Publication Society, 1948)
Abulafia	Meir ben Todros Halevi Abulafia, *Masoret Seyag la-Torah* (Florence, 1750)
Alfakhar 1	First letter of Judah Alfakhar to David Kimhi, *Qovez,* III, 1c–3b
Alfakhar 2	Second letter of Judah Alfakhar to David Kimhi, *Qovez,* III, 4a–b
Alfakhar 3	Third letter of Judah Alfakhar to David Kimhi, *Qovez,* III, 4c–d
Algazi	Samuel ben Isaac Algazi, *Toledot 'Adam,* ed. A. Habermann (Jerusalem: Bamberger and Wahrmann, 1943–44)
Altmann	A. Altmann, ed., *Book of Doctrines and Beliefs* (Oxford: East and West Library, 1945)
Aptowitzer	A. Aptowitzer, "Deux Problèmes d'Histoire Littéraire," *REJ,* LV (1908), 84–92
'Arukh	Nathan ben Jehiel, *Aruch Completum,* ed. A. Kohut (Vienna: Brög, 1926)
Asher	A. Asher, *Itinerary of Rabbi Benjamin of Tudela,* 2 vols. (New York: Hakesheth, n.d.)
Assaf	S. Assaf, *Meqorot le-Toledot ha-Ḥinnukh,* 4 vols. (Tel-Aviv: Dvir, 1930)

Bacher, "Einleitung"

W. Bacher, "Abraham ibn Esras Einleitung zu seinem Pentateuch Kommentar," *Sitzungsberichte der Wiener Akademie, Philosophisch-historische Klass,* LXXXI (1875), 362–444

Bacher, *'Erke*

W. Bacher, *'Erke Midrash* (Tel-Aviv, 1922–23)

Bacher, *Ibn Esra*

W. Bacher, *Ibn Esra als Grammatiker* (Budapest, 1881)

Baer

Y. F. Baer, *A History of the Jews in Christian Spain,* 2 vols. (Philadelphia: Jewish Publication Society, 1961)

Bahya

Bahya Ibn Paquda, *Duties of the Heart,* ed. M. Hyamson, 5 vols. (New York: Bloch Publishing Co., 1925)

Barol

M. Barol, *Menahem ben Simon aus Posquieres und sein Kommentar zu Jeremia und Ezechiel* (Berlin, 1907)

Baron

S. W. Baron, *A Social and Religious History of the Jews,* 12 vols. (Philadelphia: Jewish Publication Society, 1952–1960)

Bass

S. Bass, *Sifte Yeshenim* (Zolkiew, 1806)

Benjamin

Benjamin ben Jonah of Tudela, *Itinerary of Benjamin of Tudela,* ed. M. N. Adler (London: H. Frowde, 1907)

Ben Yehudah

E. Ben Yehudah, *Millon ha-Lashon ha-'Ivrit,* 16 vols. (Berlin: Langenscheidt; Jerusalem: Ben Yehudah; New York: T. Yoseleff, 1908–1959)

Bereshit Rabbati

Ch. Albeck, ed., *Midrash Bereshit Rabbati* (Jerusalem: Mekiẓe Nirdamim, 1940)

Berman

L. V. Berman, "Greek into Hebrew: Samuel ben Judah of Marseilles,

	Fourteenth Century Translator and Philosopher," in *Jewish Medieval and Renaissance Studies,* ed. A. Altmann (Cambridge, Mass.: Harvard University Press, 1967)
Bet Yosef	Joseph Karo, *Bet Yosef;* standard editions of *Ṭurim*
Blumenkranz	B. Blumenkranz, *Juifs et Chrétiens dans le Monde Occidentale* (Paris: Mouton, 1960)
Brown	P. R. L. Brown, *Augustine of Hippo* (London: Faber, 1967)
Brüll	N. Brüll, "Die Polemik für und gegen Maimuni in 13ten Jahrhunderte," *Jahrbücher für Jüdische Geschichte und Literatur,* IV (1879), 1–35
B. T.	Babylonian Talmud
Cassuto	U. Cassuto, *Codices Vaticani Hebraici* (Rome: Biblioteca Apostolica Vaticana, 1956)
Chomsky	W. Chomsky, *David Kimchi's Hebrew Grammar* (*Mikhlol*) (Philadelphia: Dropsie College, 1952)
Cohen	H. Cohen, *The Commentary of Rabbi David Kimhi on Hosea* (New York: Columbia University Press, 1929)
Covenant	Joseph Kimhi, *Book of the Covenant,* ed. F. Talmage (Toronto: Pontifical Institute of Medieval Studies, 1972)
Darmesteter	A. Darmesteter and D. S. Blondheim, *Les Gloses Françaises dans les Commentaires Talmudiques de Raschi* (Paris, 1929)
David Ibn Yahya, *Leshon*	David Ibn Yahya, *Leshon Limmudim* (Constantinople, 1542)
David Ibn Yahya, *Qav*	David Ibn Yahya, *Qav ve-Naqi* (Constantinople, 1492)
De Lattes	Isaac de Lattes, *Sha'are Ẕiyyon,* ed. S. Buber (Jerusalem, 1835)

Derenbourg	Jonah Ibn Janah, *Opuscules et Traités,* ed. J. and H. Derenbourg (Paris, 1880)
Dupont	André Dupont, *Les Cités de la Narbonnaise Première* (Nimes, 1942)
Duran	Simon ben Zemah Duran, *Qeshet u-Magen,* ed. S. Steinschneider (Berlin, 1881)
EI	*Enẓiqlopediyah 'Ivrit* (Jerusalem, 1949—)
Eissfeldt	O. Eissfeldt, *The Old Testament: An Introduction* (Oxford: Blackwell, 1966)
EJ	*Encyclopedia Judaica,* 9 vols. (Berlin, 1928–1934)
Eliezer of Beaugency	S. Poznanski, ed., *Perush 'al Yeḥezqe'el u-Tere 'Asar le-Rabbi 'Eli'ezer mi-Belgenẓi* (Warsaw: Eppelberg, 1913)
Epstein	A. Epstein, "Rabbi Mosheh ha-Darshan mi-Narbonah," in *Kitve Rabbi 'Avraham 'Epstein* (Jerusalem: Mosad Harav Kuk, 1949–50), I, 215–244
'Eshkol	Abraham ben Isaac, *Sefer ha-'Eshkol,* ed. B. H. Auerbach, 2 vols. (Halberstadt, 1868)
ET	*Enẓiqlopediyah Talmudit* (Jerusalem, 1955—)
'Eṭ Sofer	David Kimhi, *'Eṭ Sofer* (Lyck, 1864)
Ezovi	Joseph Ezovi, "The Silver Bowl," trans. I. Freedman, *JQR,* VIII (1896), 534–540
Finkelstein	L. Finkelstein, *The Commentary of David Kimhi on Isaiah* (New York: Columbia University Press, 1926)
Fleischer	J. L. Fleischer, "Maddu'a yaza rabbenu 'Avraham 'Ibn 'Ezra mi-Sefarad?" *Mizraḥ u-Ma'arav,* III (1929), 325–335
Friedlander	M. Friedlander, *Essays on the Writings of Ibn Ezra* (London, n.d.)

Galui	Joseph Kimhi, *Sefer ha-Galui,* ed. H. W. Mathews (Berlin, 1887)
Geiger	A. Geiger, *Qevuẓat Ma'amarim* (Berlin, 1877)
Geiger-Poznanski	A. Geiger, *Qevuẓat Ma'amarim,* ed. S. Poznanski (Warsaw: Tushiyah, 1910)
Ginsberg	H. Ginsberg, "New Trends in Bible Criticism," *Commentary,* X (1950), 276–284
Ginsburg	C. D. Ginsburg, *Introduction to the Massoretico-Critical Edition of the Hebrew Bible* (New York: Ktav, 1966)
Ginzberg	L. Ginzberg, *Legends of the Jews,* 7 vols. (Philadelphia: Jewish Publication Society, 1929)
Ginze	*Ginze Nistarot,* 4 vols. in 3 (Bamberg, 1868–1878)
Goitein	S. D. Goitein, "Mikhtav 'el Rabbenu Yehudah ha-Levi 'al 'asefat shirav ve-ha-biqqoret she-nimteḥah 'alehem," *Tarbiẓ,* XXVIII (1958–59), 343–361
Goldberg	N. Goldberg, "Commentary of Rabbi David Kimhi on the Book of Joshua," unpub. Ph.D. diss., Columbia University, 1961 (University Microfilms, Ann Arbor)
Goshen-Gottstein	M. Goshen-Gottstein, "The Authenticity of the Aleppo Codex," *Textus,* I (1960), 17–58
Graetz	H. Graetz, *History of the Jews,* 6 vols. (Philadelphia, 1894)
Gross	H. Gross, *Gallia Judaica* (Paris, 1897)
Guide	Moses Maimonides, *Guide for the Perplexed,* trans. M. Friedlander (London: G. Routledge, 1904)
Halkin	A. S. Halkin, "Le-toledot ha-shemad bi-yeme el-muvaḥidun," *Joshua Starr Memorial Volume* (New York: Con-

	ference on Jewish Relations, 1953), pp. 101–110
Heinemann	I. Heinemann, *Darke ha-'Aggadah* (Jerusalem: Magnes Press, 1970)
Hell	V. Hell and H. Hell, *The Great Pilgrimage of the Middle Ages* (London: Barrie and Rockliff, 1966)
Heschel	A. Heschel, "The Quest for Certainty in Saadya's Philosophy," *JQR*, XXXIII (1942–43), 265–313
Hirsch	S. A. Hirsch, *A Book of Essays* (London: Macmillan, 1905)
Hirschfeld	H. Hirschfeld, *Literary History of Hebrew Grammarians and Lexicographers* (London: Oxford University Press, 1926)
Hopper	V. F. Hopper, *Medieval Number Symbolism: Its Sources, Meaning, and Influence on Thought and Expression* (New York: Columbia University Press, 1938)
HUCA	*Hebrew Union College Annual*
Ḥuqqah	Joseph Kimhi, *Sefer Ḥuqqah* (Commentary on Proverbs), ed. B. Dubrowo (Breslau, 1861)
Ibn Daud	Abraham Ibn Daud, *'Emunah Ramah,* ed. S. Weil (Frankfurt, 1852)
Ibn Ezra, *Moznayim*	Abraham Ibn Ezra, *Mozne Leshon ha-Qodesh* (Offenbach, 1791)
Ibn Ezra, *Yesod*	Abraham Ibn Ezra, *Yesod Mora ve-Sod Torah* (Jerusalem: Ḥokhmat Yisra'el, 1930–31)
Ibn Gabirol	Solomon Ibn Gabirol, *Improvement of the Moral Qualities,* ed. S. S. Wise (New York: Columbia University Press, 1902)
Ibn Janah	Jonah Ibn Janah, *Sefer ha-Riqmah,* ed. M. Wilensky (Berlin: Akademie-Verlag, 1928–1930)

Ibn Janah, *Roots*	Jonah Ibn Janah, *Sefer ha-Shorashim,* ed. W. Bacher (Berlin, 1896)
'Iggeret	Moses Maimonides, *'Iggeret Teman,* ed. A. Halkin (New York: American Academy for Jewish Research, 1952)
JE	*Jewish Encyclopedia*
J. Heinemann	Joseph Heinemann, *Derashot ba-Zibbur bi-Tequfat ha-Talmud* (Jerusalem: Mosad Bialik, 1970–71)
JJGL	*Jahrbücher für Jüdische Geschichte und Literatur*
JQR	*Jewish Quarterly Review*
Judah Ibn Tibbon	Introduction to *Duties of the Heart,* printed in Bahya
Kimhi 1	First letter of David Kimhi to Judah Alfakhar, *Qovez,* III, 1c
Kimhi 2	Second letter of David Kimhi to Judah Alfakhar, *Qovez,* III, 4b–c
Kimhi 3	Third letter of David Kimhi to Judah Alfakhar, *Qovez,* III, 3b–4a
Kirchheim	R. Kirchheim, ed., *Ein Commentar zur Chronik aus dem 10then Jahrhundert* (Frankfurt, 1874)
Kuzari	Judah Halevi, *Kuzari,* trans. H. Hirschfeld (New York: Schocken, 1968)
Levy, *Contribution*	R. Levy, *Contribution à la Lexicographie Française selon d'Anciens Textes d'Origine Juive* (Syracuse: Syracuse University Press, 1960)
Lipschütz	E. M. Lipschütz, *Rabbi Shelomoh Yizhaqi* (Warsaw: Tushiyah, 1914)
Llamas	José Llamas, "Los Manuscritos Hebreos de la Real Biblioteca de San Lorenzo de El Escorial," *Sefarad,* I (1941), 7–43
Martini	R. Martini, *Pugio Fidei* (Leipzig, 1687)
Marx	A. Marx, "Gabirol's Authorship of the *Choice of Pearls* and the Two Versions of J. Kimhi's *Shekel ha-*

	Kodesh," *HUCA,* IV (1927), 438–448
Merchavia	Ch. Merchavia, *Ha-Talmud bi-Re'i ha-Naẓrut* (Jerusalem: Mosad Bialik, 1970)
Mevaqqesh	Shem Tov ben Joseph Ibn Falaquera, *Sefer ha-Mevaqqesh* (Warsaw: Traklin, 1924)
MGWJ	*Monatsschrift für Geschichte und Wissenschaft des Judenthums*
Midrash ha-Gadol	*Midrash ha-Gadol,* ed. S. Schechter (Cambridge: Cambridge University Press, 1902)
Midrash Samuel	*Midrash Samuel,* ed. S. Buber (Lemberg, 1893)
Midrash Tehillim	*Midrash Tehillim,* ed. S. Buber (Vilna, 1891)
Mikhlol	David Kimhi, *Mikhlol* (Lyck, 1862)
Mikhlol Yofi	Solomon Ibn Melekh, *Mikhlol Yofi* (Vienna, 1818)
Millás-Vallicrosa	J. M. Millás-Vallicrosa, "Un Tratado Anónimo de Polémica contra los Judíos," *Sefarad,* XIII (1953), 3–34
Minḥat Shai	J. S. Norzi, *Minḥat Shai;* various editions of the rabbinic Bible
Miẓvot	Moses Maimonides, *Sefer ha-Miẓvot,* ed. M. Sachs (Jerusalem: Mosad Harav Kuk, 1957–58)
MJC	A. Neubauer, ed., *Medieval Jewish Chronicles and Chronological Notices,* 2 vols. (Oxford, 1887–1895)
Morag	S. Morag, "Reshit ha-millona'ut ha-'ivrit ve-ha-'aravit," *Molad,* XXVI (1970), 575–582
M. Simon	M. Simon, *Verus Israel* (Paris: E. de Boccard, 1948)
M.T.	Moses Maimonides, *Mishneh Torah;* standard editions

MWJ	*Magazin für die Wissenschaft des Judentums*
NEJ	*Encyclopedia Judaica,* 16 vols. (Jerusalem: Keter, 1971)
Neubauer	A. Neubauer, *Catalogue of the Hebrew Manuscripts of the Bodleian Library* (Oxford, 1886)
Newman	L. I. Newman, *Jewish Influence on Christian Reform Movements* (New York: Columbia University Press, 1925)
Niẓẓaḥon	*Sefer Niẓẓaḥon Yashan,* in W. C. Wagenseil, *Tela Ignea Satanae* (Altdorf, 1681)
Nutt	J. W. Nutt, *Three Treatises of . . . Ibn Janah* (London, 1870)
Ortuto y Murgoito	F. J. Ortuto y Murgoito, *Moisés Kimchi y su obra Sekel Tob* (Madrid, 1920)
Picquet	Louis Picquet, "L'Histoire de Narbonne—Tirée des Auteurs Anciens et modernes et des monumes, marbres, inscriptions, qui se voient dans cette ville." Ms. Bibl. Narbonne 26
Pirqe	*Pirke de Rabbi Eliezer,* trans. G. Friedlander (London, 1917)
PL	J. P. Migne, *Patrologiae Cursus Completus, Series Latina* (Paris, 1857–66)
P.T.	Palestinian Talmud
Qoveẓ	*Qoveẓ Teshuvot ha-RaMBaM ve-'Iggerotav,* ed. A. Lichtenberg (Leipzig, 1859)
Rabad	Abraham ben David, *Hassagot;* standard editions of *Mishneh Torah*
Rabinowitz	A. S. Rabinowitz, *Perush le-Khitve ha-Qodesh le-Rabbi Yonah 'Ibn Janaḥ* (Tel-Aviv, 1936)

Ramban   Moses ben Nahman, *Kitve ha-RaMBaN,*
                        ed. D. Chevel (Jerusalem: Mosad
                        Harav Kuk, 1952–53)
Rankin   O. S. Rankin, *Jewish Religious Polemic*
                        (Edinburgh: Edinburgh University
                        Press, 1956)
Rashbam   Samuel ben Meir, *Perush la-Torah,* ed.
                        D. Rosin (Breslau, 1881)
Rashi   Commentary of Solomon ben Isaac;
                        standard editions of the rabbinic
                        Bible
Regné   J. Regné; "Étude sur la Condition des
                        Juifs de Narbonne du Ve au XIVe
                        Siècle," *REJ,* LVII (1908), 1–36,
                        221–243; LVIII (1909), 75–105,
                        200–225; LIX (1910), 59–89; LXI
                        (1911), 228–254; LXII (1911), 1–27,
                        248–266; LXIII (1912), 75–99
REJ   *Revue des Études Juives*
Roots   David Kimhi, *Sefer ha-Shorashim,* ed.
                        J. Biesenthal and F. Lebrecht (Ber-
                        lin, 1847)
Rosenthal   J. Rosenthal, "Ra'yon Biṭṭul ha-Miẓvot
                        ba-ʾEskaṭologiyah ha-Yehudit,"
                        Meyer Waxman Jubilee Volume
                        (Jerusalem, 1966)
Samau'al   Samau'al al-Maghribi, *Ifḥām al-Yahūd,*
                        ed. M. Perlmann, *Proceedings of the
                        American Academy for Jewish
                        Research,* XXXII (1964)
Samuel Ibn Tibbon   Samuel Ibn Tibbon, *Ma'amar Yiqqavu
                        ha-Mayim* (Pressburg, 1837)
Sarachek   J. Sarachek, *Faith and Reason* (Wil-
                        liamsport, Pa.: Bayard, 1935)
Sarna   N. M. Sarna, "Hebrew and Bible Stud-
                        ies in Medieval Spain," in R. D.
                        Barnett, *The Sephardi Heritage*
                        (London: Valentine, Mitchell, 1971),
                        pp. 323–366

Scholem	G. Scholem, *On the Kabbalah and Its Symbolism* (New York: Schocken, 1965)
Seder 'Olam	*Seder 'Olam*, ed. B. Ratner (Vilna, 1894)
Segal	M. H. Segal, *Parshanut ha-Miqra* (Jerusalem: University Press, 1943)
Shatzmiller	J. Shatzmiller, "Li-temunat ha-maḥloqet ha-rishonah 'al kitve ha-RaMBaM," *Zion*, XXXIV (1969), 126–144
Shirat	Moses Ibn Ezra, *Shirat Yisra'el,* trans. B. Halper (Leipzig: Stybel, 1933–34)
Silver	D. J. Silver, *Maimonidean Criticism and the Maimonidean Controversy, 1180–1240* (Leiden: Brill, 1965)
Simon	"RABA' ve-RaDaQ: Shte Gishot li-She'elat Mehemanut Nusaḥ ha-Miqra," *Shenaton Bar 'Ilan,* VI (1967–68), 191–236
Smalley	B. Smalley, *Study of the Bible in the Middle Ages* (Oxford: Oxford University Press, 1952)
Soloweitschik	M. Soloweitschik and S. Rubasheff, *Toledot Biqqoret ha-Miqra* (Berlin: Dwir-Mikra, 1924–25)
Sonc.	Soncino English translation of the Babylonian Talmud, 35 vols. (London, 1935–1952) and translation of Midrash Rabbah, 13 vols. in 10 (London, 1939)
Southern	R. W. Southern, *Western Society and the Church in the Middle Ages* (London: Pelican, 1970)
Stein	S. Stein, "A Disputation on Moneylending between Jews and Gentiles in Meir ben Simeon's *Milḥemeth Miṣwah* (Narbonne, 13th c.)," *Jour-*

	nal of Jewish Studies, X (1959), 45–61
Stein, "Disputations"	S. Stein, "Jewish-Christian Disputations in Thirteenth Century Narbonne," (London: University of London, 1969)
Talmage, "Polemicist"	F. Talmage, "R. David Kimhi as Polemicist," *HUCA,* XXXVIII (1967), 213–235
Talmage, "Rationalist"	F. Talmage, "David Kimhi and the Rationalist Tradition," *HUCA,* XXXIX (1968), 177–218
Talmage, "Sources"	F. Talmage, "David Kimhi and the Rationalist Tradition II: Literary Sources," in C. Berlin, ed., *Studies in Jewish Bibliography, History, and Literature in Honor of I. Edward Kiev* (New York: Ktav, 1972), pp. 453–478
Tanḥuma	*Midrash Tanḥuma* (Vilna, 1833)
Tanḥuma, Buber	*Midrash Tanḥuma,* ed. S. Buber (Vilna, 1885)
Tauber	J. Tauber, *Standpunkt und Leistung des R. David Kimchi als Grammatiker* (Breslau, 1867)
Tiqvat	A. Schwarz, ed., *Tiqvat Enosh* (Berlin, 1868)
Toati	C. Toati, "Les Idées Philosophiques et Théologiques de Gersonides (1288–1344) dans ses Commentaires Bibliques," *Revue des Sciences Religieuses,* XXVIII (1950), 335–367
Twersky, "Aspects"	I. Twersky, "Aspects of the Social and Cultural History of Provençal Jewry," *Journal of World History,* XI (1968), 185–207
Twersky, "Criticism"	I. Twersky, "The Beginnings of Mishneh Torah Criticism," in A. Altmann, ed., *Biblical and Other Studies* (Cam-

	bridge, Mass.: Harvard University Press, 1963), pp. 161–182
Twersky, *Rabad*	I. Twersky, *Rabad of Posquières* (Cambridge, Mass.: Harvard University Press, 1962)
Twersky, *Sefer*	I. Twersky, *Sefer Mishneh Torah la-RaMBaM, Divre ha-'Aqademiyah ha-Le'umit ha-Yisre'elit le-Madda'im,* V (Jerusalem, 1971–72)
Urbach	E. E. Urbach, *Ba'ale ha-Tosafot* (Jerusalem: Mosad Bialik, 1955–56)
Vajda	G. Vajda, "Samuel b. Judah Ibn Tibbon's Ma'amar Yiqqawu ha-Mayim," *Journal of Jewish Studies,* X (1959), 137–149
Williams	A. L. Williams, *Adversus Judaeos* (Cambridge: Cambridge University Press, 1935)
Yesodot	Isaac Israeli, *Sefer ha-Yesodot,* ed. S. Fried (Drohobycz: Zupnik, 1900)
Zacut	Abraham ben Samuel Zacut, *Sefer ha-Yuḥasin* (Frankfurt: Wahrmann, 1924)
ZDMG	*Zeitschrift der Deutschen Morgenländischen Gesellschaft*
Zuckerman	A. J. Zuckerman, *A Jewish Princedom in Feudal France, 768–900* (New York: Columbia University Press, 1972)

Manuscripts Cited

Writings of Radak

Escorial

Biblioteca del Monasterio de San Lorenzo el Real, G–I–5. Commentary on Psalms. Fols. 2r–89v.

Biblioteca del Monasterio de San Lorenzo el Real, G–II–6. Commentary on Chronicles. Fols. 41r–80v.

London

British Library, Add. 27179. Philosophical Commentary on Ezekiel. Fols. 61v–70v.

British Library, Add. Or. 27046. Commentary on Latter Prophets.

Madrid

Biblioteca Nacional, 5457. Commentary on Psalms.

Oxford

Bodleian Library, Bodl. Or. 143. Commentary on Jeremiah, Ezekiel, and Isaiah 50:9–51:6.

Bodleian Library, Bodl. Or. 147. Commentary on Isaiah and Jeremiah.

Bodleian Library, Can. Or. 52. Commentary on Former Prophets.

Bodleian Library, Can. Or. 53. Commentary on Isaiah.

Bodleian Library, Can. Or. 68. Commentary on Psalms.

Bodleian Library, Huntington 300. Commentary on Former Prophets.

Bodleian Library, Huntington Don. 24. Commentary on Ezekiel and Minor Prophets.

Bodleian Library, Kennicott 5. Commentary on Former Prophets.

Bodleian Library, Mich. 381. Commentary on Psalms.

Bodleian Library, Opp. 757. Replies against the Christians.
Bodleian Library, Opp. Add. fol. 37. Commentary on Prophets.

Parma
Biblioteca Palatina, 2550. Commentary on Samuel and Kings.

Rome
Biblioteca Angelica, Or. 72. Commentary on Former Prophets and Psalms.
Biblioteca Apostolica Vaticana, Ebr. 73. Commentary on Samuel.
Biblioteca Apostolica Vaticana, Ebr. 89. Commentary on Proverbs. Fols. 2r–62v.
Biblioteca Apostolica Vaticana, Ebr. 320. Liturgical Poem. Fols. 23r–24v.
Biblioteca Apostolica Vaticana, Ross. Ebr. 533. Commentary on Prophets.
Biblioteca Apostolica Vaticana, Urb. Ebr. 13. Commentary on Kings and Isaiah.
Biblioteca Apostolica Vaticana, Urb. Ebr. 14. Commentary on Isaiah, Jeremiah, and Minor Prophets.
Biblioteca Apostolica Vaticana, Urb. Ebr. 16. Commentary on Psalms.

Valladolid
Biblioteca Universitaria, 355. Commentary on Former Prophets.

Works Incorrectly Ascribed to Radak

Hamburg
Staats- und Universitätsbibliothek, Levy 152. Commentary on "Hilkhot Shehiṭah" of Maimonides. Fols. 45v–90v.

Parma
Biblioteca Palatina, 2348. Commentary on Proverbs. Fols. 2v–3v.

Other Manuscripts

Narbonne
Bibliothèque de la Ville de Narbonne, 26. L. Picquet, "L'Histoire

de Narbonne—Tirée des Auteurs Anciens et modernes et des
monumes, marbres, inscriptions, qui se voient dans cette ville."

Parma
Biblioteca Palatina, 2749. Meir ben Simeon ha-Me'ili, "Milḥemet
Miẓvah."

Bibliographic Note

Radak's writings were among the first Hebrew books to be printed, the earliest being the Psalms commentary (Bologna, 1477), which itself contained the first printed biblical text in Hebrew (Ginsburg, p. 780). His commentary on the Latter Prophets was printed at Guadalajara in 1482, three years before the biblical text itself (Soncino, 1485). It was in this latter edition that the commentary on the Former Prophets was first printed. The commentary on Chronicles first appeared in print in the Venice Rabbinic Bible (1547). The commentaries on Genesis and the Hexaemeron were published only in modern times; the former by A. Ginzburg (Pressburg, 1842) and the latter in Finkelstein, pp. liii–lxxiv. Radak's remarks on the four latter books of the Pentateuch were collected from his grammatical writings in M. Kamelhar's edition of *Perushe Rabbi David Qimhi 'al ha-Torah* (Jerusalem: Mosad Harav Kuk, 1970), pp. 211–288, and his remarks on Job in *Tiqvat,* pp. 129–145. A commentary on Ruth ascribed to Radak was printed at Paris by J. Mercer in 1553, but it shows no evidence of being his work. The only one of Radak's commentaries that remains unpublished is that on Proverbs (Ms. Vat. Ebr. 89).

Several of Radak's commentaries were reprinted many times in various editions of the Rabbinic Bible, often with decreasing reliability. Baron observes: "More fortunate than most of his fellow commentators, David Qimhi and his works were subjected to closer examination by modern scholars" (Baron, VI, 467, n. 60). The following editions exist: The first forty chapters of the Isaiah commentary were critically edited by L. Finkelstein: *The Commentary of David Kimhi on Isaiah* (New York: Columbia University Press, 1926); and the Hosea commentary by H. Cohen: *The Commentary of Rabbi David Kimhi on Hosea* (New York: Columbia University Press, 1929). The commentaries on Joshua and Amos have been critically edited in two unpublished doctoral dissertations:

N. Goldberg, "The Commentary of Rabbi David Kimhi on the Book of Joshua" (Columbia University, 1961–62); S. Berkowitz, "Critical Edition of the Book of Amos" (Cambridge University, 1939). An edition of the Judges commentary is presently being prepared by M. Celniker as a Ph.D. dissertation at the University of Toronto.

The Genesis commentary was republished by Kamelhar, as cited above. For the Hexaemeron commentary see above. See also R. Livnat, "Haggahot ve-he'arot be-ferush RaDaQ le-sefer bereshit," *Sinai,* LII (1962), 36f.

Portions of the Book of Psalms have been edited with various degrees of competence by S. M. Schiller Szinnesy, *The First Book of the Psalms* (1–41) (Cambridge, 1883); S. I. Esterson, *The Commentary of Rabbi David Kimhi on Psalms* (42–72) (Cincinnati, 1935), printed also in *HUCA,* X (1937–38), 309–443; J. Bosniak, *The Commentary of Rabbi David Kimhi on the Fifth Book of the Psalms* (107–150) (New York: Bloch Publishing Co., 1951); J. Baker and E. W. Nicholson, *The Commentary of Rabbi David Kimhi on Psalms CXX–CL* (Cambridge: Cambridge University Press, 1973), has recently appeared. The Psalms commentary was reprinted by I. Brickenstein (Tel-Aviv, 1946) and A. Darom (Jerusalem: Mosad Harav Kuk 1971). See also E. Z. Melamed, "Perush RaDaQ li-Tehillim," *'Areshet,* II (1960), 35–69.

Despite the editions, serious research on Radak cannot be undertaken without the consultation of manuscripts. First, the lion's share of his commentaries remain unedited. Second, those editions that do exist are of very uneven quality. Fortunately, manuscripts are abundant. A fine collection exists at the Jewish Theological Seminary in New York and others at various libraries in Jerusalem. Italy leads Europe, and indeed the world, as a storehouse for Radak manuscripts. They are found in abundance from the libraries of Rome and the Vatican as far north as Milan, with much valuable material in Parma and the remarkable De Rossi collection. Other major concentrations of manuscripts are to be found in England, especially at Oxford and Cambridge.

My own interest in the manuscripts stemmed from a search for polemical material which might have been expunged by the censors. Radak's commentaries were subjected to the censor's mark beginning with the act of the Mantua commission of 1581 which expurgated "the commentaries of R. Solomon and Chimi and

Rabbi Hierosolymitani to the Old Testament . . . in these works are contained things contrary to our faith, especially in regard to the prophets" (Newman, p. 327). I found not just a few stray anti-Christian remarks but fully as much unknown and unpublished material as was known previously (see Talmage, "Polemicist").

Above and beyond this, however, a manuscript has many a time clarified an obscurity in the printed edition. Scribal prejudices (see n. 211 to Chap. I) and Radak's own ambiguities (see n. 322 to Chap. I) lead to divergences in the manuscript traditions which can only be resolved by study of a large sampling of the texts. One may indeed occasionally find the exact opposite of the reading of the editions (although the reading of the manuscript is not always to be preferred). It is a long way from "sin is the stumbling-block of this world and repentance removes it" (Isa. 57:13, ed. Soncino) to "this world is a stumbling block" (Ms. Brit. Lib. Add. 27046, fol. 38v; Ms. Bodl. Can. Or. 53, fol. 105v, omits the passage altogether). In questions of masorah and the history of the biblical text in the Middle Ages, there is much of value as well. Harmonization of Radak's commentary with a variant biblical manuscript tradition is not uncommon (see n. 284 to Chap. III).

Unfortunately, even edited texts do not always alleviate the situation. Important readings may be neglected because an insufficient number of manuscripts were consulted (see n. 276 to Chap. III). Editions utilizing all or most of the manuscript evidence are very much to be desired.

Some of Radak's commentaries have been translated into European languages. The Nahum commentary was published with a German translation by W. Windführ, *Der Kommentar des David Qimchi zum Propheten Nahum* (Giessen: Töpelmann, 1927), while that on Joel was published in German by G. Widmer, *Die Kommentare von Raschi, Ibn Esra, Radaq, zu Joel* (Basel: Volksdruckerei, 1945). An English translation of the Zechariah commentary was done by A. M'Caul, London, 1837. A partial translation of the Psalms commentary can be found in R. G. Finch, *The Longer Commentary of Rabbi David Kimchi on the First Book of Psalms* (New York: Macmillan, 1919). See also G. Calò, "Una Traduzione Italiana del Commenta di R.D.Q. ai Salmi," in *Miscellanea di Studi Ebraica in Memoria di H. P. Chajes*, ed. E. S. Artom (Florence, 1930), pp. 10–18.

Of Radak's grammatical writings, the *Roots* was first published

in Naples 1479, while the grammatical portion of the *Mikhlol*
(*ḥeleq ha-diqduq*) was printed in Constantinople in 1525. The
most commonly used edition of the *Mikhlol* is that published in
Lyck, in 1862; the most commonly used edition of the *Roots*
(ed. J. Biesenthal and F. Lebrecht) was published in Berlin in 1847.
W. Chomsky's English version of the *Mikhlol* consists of a coherent
rearrangement of the material with many learned and informative
notes. An additional grammatical treatise, the *Petaḥ Devarai,* was
attributed to Kimhi by Abraham de Balmes in his *Miqneh 'Avraham*
(Venice, 1523), chaps. *ba-ḥaluqqat ha-pe'alim* and *binyan hitpa'el,*
but this was rejected by W. Bacher in "Un Abregé de Grammaire
Hebraïque de Benjamin ben Juda de Rome et le Petaḥ Devarai,"
REJ, X (1885), 133f.

Radak's masoretic treatise, the *'Et Sofer,* was printed at Lyck in
1864.

Radak wrote no independent polemical treatises, although some
have been ascribed to him. See A. Marmorstein, "David Kimḥi,
Apologiste," *REJ,* LXVI (1931), 246–251; N. Porges, *REJ,* LXVII
(1932), 128–131; D. Camerini, *REJ,* LXVII (1932), 292–294;
F. Talmage, "An Hebrew Polemical Treatise," *Harvard Theological
Review,* LX (1967), 323–348. The *Replies of Rabbi David Kimhi
to the Christians* (*Teshuvot ha-RaDaQ la-Noẓerim*), first printed
with Yom Tov Lippmann Müllhausen's *Sefer ha-Niẓẓaḥon* (Altdorf,
1644), is a collection of remarks culled from Radak's Psalms commentary. See now F. Talmage, ed., *Sefer ha-Berit u-Vikkuḥe ha-
RaDaQ* (Jerusalem, Mosad Bialik, 1974).

Concerning the halakhic writings, the *piṭṭum ha-qeṭoret* commentary was printed in *Qoveẓ Devarim Neḥmadim* (Husiatyn,
1902), pp. 59–63, and in Ch. M. Horowitz' *Toratan shel Rishonim,*
(Frankfurt, 1881), II, 60. The ascription of this commentary to
Radak has been generally denied by scholars. See Finkelstein,
p. xx, n. 3; A. Marx, *Zeitschrift für Hebräische Bibliographie,* IX
(1905), 97–104; *He-Ḥaluẓ,* XII (1887), pp. 103f.; Horowitz,
Jahrbuch für Jüdische Geschichte und Literatur, V (1883), 160.
It should be noted, however, that each of the printed editions is
based on a separate manuscript. That in *Qoveẓ Devarim Neḥmadim*
is taken from Ms. Parma 2785 (see I. B. De Rossi, *Mss. Codices
Hebraici,* Parma, 1803, pp. 181f.), while that in *Toratan shel
Rishonim* is taken from a fourteenth-century Roman *maḥzor* in
Ms. Montefiore 217, fol. 39v (see H. Hirschfeld, *Descriptive*

Catalogue of the Hebrew Mss. of the Montefiore Library, London,
1904, p. 69). While these texts differ considerably from each
other, there does appear to be material common to both, and both
end with similar ascriptions to Kimhi: *Qovez*, p. 63 (Parma manuscript): "Re'eh zeh maẓati 'amar David ben Qimḥi me-'asher
ḥippasti ve-ḥaqarti ba-yerushalmi u-va-bavli u-farsi [sic!] 'asher
maẓati 'al ha-tosefta ha-shenuyah la-'asher 'averu lefanai ve-higdalti
ve-hosafti ka-'asher hissigah yede maḥshavti ba-'asher H[a-shem]
'itti, Yishma' hakham ve-yosif leqaḥ." Ms. Montefiore 217, fol.
39v (ed. Horowitz): "Re'eh zeh maẓati 'amar David ben Qimḥi
Be-R[abbi] Yosef Qimḥi ZaL me-'asher ḥippasti ve-ḥaqarti
ba-yerushalmi u-va-bavli u-va-perush 'asher maẓati 'al ha-tosefta ha-
shenuyah la-'asher 'averu lefanai ve-higdalti ve-hosafti ka-'asher
hissigah yad maḥshavti ka-'asher H[a-shem] 'itti. Yishma' hakham
ve-yosif leqaḥ ve-navon taḥbulot yiqneh." One might be justified
in assuming then that both these commentaries drew on an original
work of Kimhi's.

It has been noted that the commentary in the Parma manuscript resembles one ascribed to Maimonides in Aaron ha-Cohen,
'Orḥot Ḥayyim (Florence, 1750), I, 67. (See Marx, cited above).
However, since Kimhi admittedly makes no claim to originality,
this would not seem to militate against his authorship.

The commentary on Maimonides' laws of slaughtering is found
in Ms. Hamburg Levy 152, fols. 45v–90v. The text is entitled
"Perush Sheḥiṭah le-R[abbi] David ben Yosef Qimḥi ZaL" but
from internal evidence little can be established. An "R. David" is
cited several times (fols. 46v, 55r, 61v, 62r, 63r, 64v, 66r) and
the *Mikhlol* (*Shorashim*) is cited once. The frequent use of Arabic
expressions and the reference to the "sages of Yemen and Aden"
(fol. 75v) might lead one to suspect an Oriental origin for this text.
Radak is in fact cited by Meir ben Simeon ha-Me'ili (*Sefer ha-
Me'orot* to Ḥullin, ed. M. Blau, New York, 1964, p. 158) in the
context of a discussion of laws of slaughtering, but the passage
cited is not found in the Hamburg manuscript. However, this additional evidence makes it appear likely that here too there existed
an original work of Kimhi's from which both the author of the
Hamburg text and Meir ben Simeon ha-Me'ili drew.

Notes

References to Radak's commentaries are by verse number. Thus Radak's commentary at Isaiah 2:11 is given simply as Isa. 2:11. References to other works are usually by an abbreviated form about which full bibliographic information may be found in the Abbreviations of Works Cited. All translations from the Hebrew are my own except where otherwise indicated.

Chapter I. NARBONA: VILLA JUZAYGA

1. Picquet, Ms. Bibl. Narbonne 26, p. 395. *L'Histoire de Narbonne* of the Minim Father Louis Picquet is a charming and highly chauvinistic account of the history of the city. It consists of two parts: a chronicle and a list of the *illustres* of Narbonne. In his zeal to demonstrate the glories of his birthplace, Fr. Picquet calls on anything and everything at his disposal, including those Jews of whom he has some knowledge.

2. See Halkin and bibliography listed there.

3. The major persecutions began in 1148 but the emigrations seem to have begun before this date. See Fleischer, pp. 325, 335. On Ibn Ezra's journeys, see Fleischer's articles listed in *Qiryat Sefer,* XXXIII (1957–58), 227–237.

4. Benedict, p. 100. On the Jews of Narbonne in the Middle Ages, see Regné.

5. Picquet, Ms. Bibl. Narbonne 26, p. 11.

6. *Ibid.,* pp. 11f.

7. "Charlemagne" in these texts is in reality Pepin the Short.

8. Benedict, p. 86; Regné, *REJ,* LVII (1908), 19ff. Zuckerman in *A Jewish Princedom* advances the theory that the Jews of the region enjoyed considerable autonomy and that the *Nasi* had sovereign powers.

9. Most authorities establish the beginning of Benjamin's travels in 1165 (Baron, VI, 435, n. 88) but see Asher, II, xi, 18.

10. Benjamin, p. 3 (translation mine).

11. Picquet, Ms. Bibl. Narbonne 26, p. 395.

12. *Ibid.*

13. Regné, *REJ,* LVIII (1909), 76.

14. Dupont, p. 433.

15. *Ibid.,* pp. 587f.; *NEJ,* XII, 827ff.

16. Richard of Devizes, quoted in Southern, p. 47.

17. Mic. 5:10.

18. *Covenant*, pp. 41f. Cf. Bahya, I:3, v. 1, pp. 35f.

19. *Galui*, p. 1.

20. See above, "Family and Career."

21. Such phrases as *"ve-gam ki mi-pi sefarim ve-soferim yesh li-lemod"* reoccur in the introduction to the *Galui*, p. 2.

22. Jer. 36:2.

23. See above, "Grammar and Masorah," Chap. III.

24. Jos., int.

25. Gen. 5:4.

26. Ps. 119, int.

27. Twersky, "Aspects," p. 195.

28. Twersky, *Rabad*, pp. 7–10.

29. Benedict, p. 100.

30. Among the "scholars of Narbonne" were Abraham ben Isaac, author of the *'Eshkol*, and Moses ben Joseph ben Merwan Halevi. Contemporaries of Radak were David ben Levi, author of *Sefer ha-Mikhtam*, and Meir ben Simeon ha-Me'ili, author of the *Sefer ha-Me'orot* and the *Milhemet Mizvah*. Many prominent Provençal and Catalonian talmudists studied in Narbonne, among them Abraham ben David of Posquières (himself born there), Meshullam ben Jacob of Lunel, and Zerahya Halevi; see Twersky, *Rabad*, pp. 1–19.

31. *Ibid.*, p. 93.

32. See Epstein.

33. For bibliography, see Baron, VI, 410f., n. 24.

34. Benedict, p. 91.

35. Rashbam, Exod. 25:33.

36. Northern French.

37. Benedict, p. 88, n. 32, p. 91. Joseph Tov-Elem (Bonfils), a northern French scholar whose exegesis has not survived, was a Narbonnese as well. See Jacob ben Meir Tam, *Sefer ha-Yashar* (Vienna, 1811), p. 74b.

38. On this and the following, see *Covenant*, pp. 9–25.

39. Judah Ibn Tibbon, p. 2; English citation from Twersky, "Aspects," p. 195.

40. The *Book of Remembrance* (*Sefer ha-Zikkaron*), published by W. Bacher, Berlin, 1887, and the *Open Book* (*Sefer ha-Galui*) published by H. W. Mathews. Berlin, 1888. The former is a systematic grammar in which Kimhi made several innovations in the presentation of the vowel system and in the theory of the verb which were widely accepted until modern times. The latter consists of a critique of Jacob Tam's (1100–1171) *Decisions* (*Hakhra'ot*) on the *Compendium* (*Mahberet*) of Menahem Ibn Saruq (910–970) and a compilation of Kimhi's own criticisms of points raised in the *Mahberet* left untouched by Tam. Both works contain prefaces which eloquently defend the importance of the study of grammar. For further references, see *Covenant*, p. 10.

41. A fragment of Kimhi's translation of Bahya was printed in the

Benjacob edition of Ibn Tibbon's translation (Leipzig, 1846) and reprinted in the Zifroni edition (Jerusalem, 1938). The adaptation of the *Choice of Pearls,* the *Sheqel ha-Qodesh,* is extant in two recensions. See Marx. On R. Joseph's failure as a translator, see *Covenant,* p. 12.

42. The Proverbs commentary was published under the title *Sefer Ḥuqqah* by B. Dubrowo, Breslau, 1861. The Job commentary was partly published by A. Schwarz in *Tiqvat 'Enosh,* Berlin, 1868, pp. 71–126. Citations from the Torah commentary were collected and published by H. Gad under the title *Sefer ha-Torah* in *Ḥamishah Me'orot Gedolim,* Johannesburg, 1952. A Song of Songs commentary, probably incorrectly attributed to J. Kimhi, is still in manuscript (Ms. Bodl. 63 [Uri 150]). See Geiger, p. 208; Neubauer, col. 69. A commentary to the prophets, *Sefer ha-Miqnah,* is no longer extant. See *Ḥuqqah,* p. 3; Geiger, pp. 201f.

43. Ibn Ezra, *Yesod,* p. 1; see Jonah Ibn Janah's defense of the study of grammar, *Riqmah* I, 11ff.

44. *Galui,* p. 2.

45. *Ibid.*

46. *Zikkaron,* p. 2.

47. *Galui,* p. 1; Ps. 119, int.

48. *Galui,* p. 1.

49. *Ḥuqqah,* p. 1.

50. Since the pioneering efforts of W. Bacher, little has been done in the way of a comprehensive or systematic treatment of medieval Jewish biblical exegesis. See Baron, VI, 234–313, and notes, M. H. Segal, *Parshanut ha-Miqra* (Jerusalem, 1943); *JE,* III, 164ff.

51. Barol, p. 3, n. 1.

52. See especially his comments to the first chapter of Ezekiel where speculation, esoteric or exoteric, is rejected and most of the discussion is grammatical; Ms. Brit. Lib. Add. 24896, no foliation. On Menahem in general, see Barol. A critical edition of his Jeremiah commentary has been prepared by E. Dessen as a Ph.D. dissertation at the University of Toronto.

53. Jud. 11:31.

54. See above, Chap. II.

55. Ps. 86:16.

56. B.T. 'Arakhin 16b, cited at Gen. 21:20.

57. The reference "my brother, my teacher," was rather unusual in Hebrew literature while "my master, my father," was commonplace.

58. See Geiger, pp. 220–230; *NEJ,* X, 1008.

59. Barol, p. xxxviii.

60. Geiger, p. 225.

61. I Sam. 20:29.

62. *Mahalakh Shevile ha-Da'at* (Pesaro, 1508). R. Moses' grammar, *Sekhel Tov,* was published by Castelli in *REJ,* XXVIII (1894), 212–227; XXIX (1894), 100–110. On R. Moses as a grammarian, see Ortuto y Murgoito.

63. Paris, 1520.

64. Geiger, p. 221.

65. Printed in the Rabbinic Bibles ascribed to Abraham Ibn Ezra.

66. Printed in *Tiqvat,* pp. 149–166.

67. *Ḥuqqah,* p. 34.

68. *Ḥuqqah,* p. 26.

69. Printed in Rabbinic Bibles ascribed to Abraham Ibn Ezra.

70. See above, "Obscurities and Discrepancies," in Chap. III.

71. Bass, p. 190; see Geiger, p. 229.

72. Referring to Moses and David, he notes " . . . on les a aussi dits natif [*sic*] d'Espagne, mais sans doute qu'on a voulû dire originaires." Picquet, p. 395.

73. See Finkelstein, pp. xviiif.

74. The interrelationship between northern Spain and Septimania can indeed be traced back several centuries prior to this period. See Zuckerman, pp. 9ff., and J. Shatzmiller, *Recherches sur la Communauté Juive de Manosque au Moyen Age* (Paris, 1973), pp. 13ff.

75. In his *Ma'amar Yiqqavu ha-Mayim.* See Vajda.

76. See below, "Allegorization," in Chap. III.

77. Twersky, "Aspects," p. 186, n. 3.

78. Twersky, "Aspects," p. 186.

79. *Galui,* p. 2.

80. Caspi's *Guide to Knowledge* in Abrahams, I, 51–92. Ezovi's *Qe'arat Kesef:* Hebrew version in *Musar Haskel le-Rav Hai Ga'on* (Berlin, 1860); English version in *JQR,* VIII (1896), 534–540.

81. Assaf, II, 29–32. Naturally all "anachronisms" (including the mention of David Kimhi himself) have been omitted. Since the *Mishneh Torah* of Maimonides was not in circulation before 1180, it too has been omitted, since Kimhi would have been at least twenty years of age at that time.

82. Assaf, II, 29.

83. *Mikhlol Yofi,* p. 2b.

84. Cohen, pp. xx–xxv; Chomsky, pp. xi *et seq.* The notes to Chomsky's translation of the *Mikhlol* are an important source study of the work. On the development of Hebrew grammatical studies in the Middle Ages, see Baron, VII, 3–61.

85. *Mikhlol,* p. 1a.

86. *Galui,* p. 2.

87. *Mevaqqesh,* p. 75.

88. Twersky, "Aspects," pp. 191f. and notes.

89. Ezovi, p. 537.

90. On the development of this trend, see Twersky, "Aspects," p. 194 and notes.

91. Assaf, II, 29f.

92. A.l.; cf. Ps. 119:100, 131:2.

93. Ps. 119:152; Prov. 1:4; Ms. Vat. Ebr. 89, fols. 3r, v.

94. Jos., int.; Ps. 111:10; cf. Jos. 1:8, Ps. 131:1.

95. I Sam. 3:7.

96. Mishnah, Avot 5:21; Assaf, II, 31f.

97. See Talmage, "Rationalist" and "Sources."

98. Ps. 4:1.

99. Assaf, II, 32f.

100. Ibn Aqnin in Assaf, II, 40.

101. On the use of acronyms in the Middle Ages, see *NEJ*, XII, 810f.

102. *NEJ*, X, 1007.

103. Gen. 2:18, 3:1; I Sam. 28:7.

104. Jer. 9:19.

105. I Sam. 16:6.

106. I Kings 1:6.

107. Gen. 29:18.

108. Int. to Avot, *MJC*, II, 227.

109. Ezovi, p. 537; cf. *Kuzari*, II:72; Moses Ibn Ezra, *Shirat*, p. 117; Joseph Ibn Aqnin's *Marpe ha-Nefashot* in Assaf, II, 40, and note; Alfakhar 1, *Qovez*, III, 1d.

110. *Qovez*, III, 3d.

111. Assaf, I, 130f.

112. Picquet, p. 15.

113. A.l., Ms. Vat. Ebr. 89, fol. 12r; cf. Prov. 9:2f. and Ms. Vat. Ebr. 89, fol. 29r.

114. Prov. 11:26; Ms. Vat. Ebr. 89, fol. 36r.

115. Prov. 10:19; Ms. Vat. Ebr. 89, fol. 32r; cf. I Sam. 9:13.

116. See above Chap. II and Chap. IV; Talmage, "Polemicist."

117. Ps. 101:2.

118. Moses Kimhi (Pseudo-Ibn Ezra) to Prov. 9:1.

119. I Chron. 2:52.

120. Ezek. 40:13, 42:5.

121. *Roots*, p. 420.

122. B. T. Keritot 6a.

123. See Bibliographic Note.

124. A.1. Cf. *Mizvot*, positive commandment 212; cf. Gen. 17:11 and *Mizvot*, positive commandment 215.

125. Zech. 8:19; *M. T.* Hil. Ta'aniyot 5:19; commentary to Mishnah, Rosh ha-Shanah 1:3; cf. Hos. 11:5 (on Deut. 17:16); *Mizvot*, negative commandment 46.

126. Gen. 32:33; I Sam. 9:13; Hos. 4:8, 9:4; Mal. 1:14.

127. Gen. 1:28.

128. Cf. Gen. 17:23, 25:1, 38:2, 38:24; Jos. 1:8; I Sam. 14:32; II Sam. 12:9, 12:20; I Kings 12:15; II Chron. 4:6.

129. A.1.; cf. *Roots, 'br.*

130. The Jewish "creed" consisting of the pentateuchal passages Deut. 6, 4-9, 11, 13-21, and Numbers 15, 37-41.

131. *Bet Yosef, 'Orah Hayyim*, 61.

132. *Mikhlol*, pp. 26f.

133. Baer, I, 250; cf. Twersky, *Rabad*, p. 24; Urbach, p. 71.

134. B.T. Shabbat 118b.

135. B.T. Shabbat 119b.

136. Jer. 17:21.

137. Isa. 56:6, 58:13; Ezek. 20:12.

138. Gen. 2:3, Isa. 58:13.

139. Zech. 9:11.

140. Gen. 17:11ff., 21:4; cf. Jos. 5:2.

141. See above, Chap. II and Chap. IV.

142. On Radak's knowledge of Moses the Preacher, see Albeck, *Bereshit Rabbati,* p. 32. R. Moses is cited at Prov. 5:19 (Ms. Vat. Ebr. 89, fol. 19v) but the citation is most probably taken from Rashi.

143. On the sermons of Rabad of Posquières, see Twersky, *Rabad,* p. 110.

144. *NEJ,* XIII, 215.

145. J. Heinemann, pp. 9f.

146. *M. T.* Hil. Teshuvah 4:2.

147. See especially *M.T.* Hil. De'ot 1:4.

148. Ps. 34:10, 49:11ff.

149. Gen. 3:7; cf. Gen. 17:1.

150. A.l.; cf. Gen. 10:25.

151. Ps. 51:7.

152. Gen. 12:12; Isa. 58:17, 59:15. This has its source in rabbinic passages. See B.T. Sanhedrin 180a, Gen. R. 31:3-5, Lam. R. 1:13. Cf. *M.T.* Hil. Teshuvah 3:2.

153. Amos 6:12.

154. Amos 2:6.

155. Amos 1:3; see Talmage, "Rationalist," p. 230. Cf. *M.T.* Hil. Teshuvah 3:13.

156. Twersky, "Aspects," p. 189.

157. Baer, I, 250f.

158. Amos 8:4; cf. Isa. 3:15, Ps. 9:13.

159. Amos 2:6.

160. Mic. 2:9.

161. Amos 5:12.

162. Jer. 5:5, cf. Jer. 5:4.

163. Isa. 5:12.

164. Isa. 3:23.

165. Ps. 49:12.

166. Jer. 4:30.

167. Baer, I, 250.

168. II Sam. 10:5.

169. I Sam. 7:17.

170. I Sam. 8:3.

171. A.l.

172. Jer. 10:7.

173. A.l.

174. I Sam. 8:15.

175. Jer. 22:15.

176. Ezek. 45:8.

177. Chron., int.; cf. passage from *Zohar* (III, 152a) cited in Scholem, pp. 63f.

178. Gen. 16:6.

179. Gen. 22:1.

180. Gen. 18:3, 7.

181. Gen. 16:5, 39:7.

182. Gen. 18:21.

183. Gen. 42:41. See also Gen. 18:5, 18:9.

184. Gen. 47:7.

185. See Toati.

186. Gen. 22:1.

187. See Heschel.

188. Altmann, pp. 13f.

189. *Kuzari,* II:36ff.

190. Bahya, I:10.

191. *Covenant,* p. 65.

192. Isa. 40:21.

193. *Covenant,* p. 37.

194. Introductory poem to Ps. Commentary.

195. A.l.

196. Ibn Ezra, int. to Torah.

197. A.l.

198. A.l.; cf. Ps. 8:3.

199. A.l.

200. Introductory poem to Ps. Commentary.

201. Isa. 43:7.

202. Isa. 40:26; cf. Isa. 5:12; Ps. 28:5, 104:1ff.

203. Isa. 40:26.

204. Ps. 84:6.

205. A.l.

206. *Ḥuqqah,* p. 1.

207. Jos. 1:8.

208. Ms. Bodl. Can. Or. 53, fol. 101r and ed. Soncino read "science."

209. A.l.

210. A.l.; cf. Isa. 28:29; Ps. 36:11; Prov. 1:20; Ms. Vat. Ebr. 89, fol. 6r.

211. In the comment on Isa. 55:1, some mss. (e.g., Ms. Bodl. Opp. Add. fol. 37, fol. 199v) place "science" first. Ms. Bodl. Or. 147, fol. 141v is more revealing, however. The first time the phrase appears, the scribe writes "science" first, strikes it out, and then writes "Torah and science." In the second appearance of the phrase, he simply writes "science and Torah." On the other hand, Ms. Bodl. Can. Or. 53, fol. 101r, omits the word "science" in the first appearance of the phrase. My translation follows the majority reading.

212. Jer. 4:22, 8:8f., 10:12f.; Ps. 25:14.

213. Ps. 25:14; cf. Isa. 5:12.

214. B.T. Qiddushin 40b.

215. Jos. int.

216. Ps. 119:152; cf. Ps. 119:160.

217. A.l.

218. A.l.

219. Gen. 1:6.

220. For a list of references to Maimonides, see Cohen, p. xxiii. See also Talmage, "Sources," pp. 460ff.; "Rationalist," *passim.*

221. B.T. Sanhedrin 63b.

222. Alfakhar 1, *Qove*z, III, 2d.

223. On the controversy over the writings of Maimonides, see Brüll, Sarachek, Silver; Baer, I, 289ff.; *NEJ*, XI, 747ff.

224. Alfakhar 2, *Qove*z, III, 2b.

225. Alfakhar 2, *Qove*z, III, 3b.

226. Alfakhar 2, *Qove*z, III, 3a.

227. Cf. Brüll, pp. 17f.

228. *Ha-ze'irim,* the Franciscans.

229. Kimhi 2, *Qove*z, III, 4c. On the question of the veracity of the charge that R. Solomon and his disciples were themselves the betrayers of the *Guide* to the Inquisition, see Talmage, "Rationalist," p. 177, n. 3, and most recently Shatzmiller, pp. 133f.

230. Kimhi 3, *Qove*z, III, 3d–4a.

231. Kimhi 3, *Qove*z, III, 4c.

232. Shatzmiller, p. 131, n. 24.

233. See the formulation of H. H. Ben Sasson, *NEJ,* XI, 749.

234. Kimhi 3, *Qove*z, III, 3d.

235. Graetz, III, 531.

236. *Qove*z, III, 1c. Radak was seventy-two at the time of his journey. He is generally assumed to have died three years later. In fact, however, we know nothing of his activities in Narbonne upon his return or of the actual length of his life.

237. See above, Chap. II.

238. I Kings 1:1.

239. Berman, p. 301; cf. *Iggeret,* pp. 36f., p. vii (English).

240. Ps. 102:24.

241. *Ibid.*

242. See above, n. 3.

243. See above, "Grammar and Masorah," in Chap. III.

244. See above, "Grammar and Masorah," in Chap. III.

245. Ibn Tibbon (1160–1230) was the translator of the *Guide for the Perplexed.* See *NEJ,* XV, 1130.

246. *Qove*z, III, 4a.

247. Abrahams, I, 63, 82.

248. Abrahams, I, 57f., 63.

249. See, for example, the discussion and the lengthy list of dedicatory statements brought by Reifmann, pp. 8–12.

250. A romance of Buddhist origin which underwent Jewish and Christian metamorphoses in medieval Europe. See *EJ*, II, 536ff.

251. *Yesodot*, text, p. 2.

252. See below.

253. A.l.

254. Jer. 48:1.

255. Ezek. 1:1; cf. Jer. 51:63.

256. B.T. Shabbat 156b *et passim*.

257. Nah. 2:13 *et passim*.

258. Presumably derived from the verb *'atah*, to come.

259. P.T. ʿEruvin V (22c). Cited at Jer. 19:2.

260. E.g., Jer. 26:10; Ezek. 8:3, 5, 9:2.

261. A.l.

262. Isa. 61:9.

263. See Baer, p. 484, n. 9; Talmage, "Rationalist," p. 177, n. 2.

264. Jos. 11:3; Jud. 20:1; I Sam. 11:14.

265. Cited from Hell, p. 22.

266. Abrahams, I, 65.

267. *Covenant*, p. 33.

268. *Ginze*, III, 168.

269. *Covenant*, p. 33.

270. Kimhi, *Qovez*, III, 3d.

271. Benjamin, pp. 2ff.

272. *Ginze*, III, 168, 173.

273. The Kimhis' Provençal surname was Petit.

274. Alfakhar 1, *Qovez*, III, 1c.

275. Alfakhar 1, *Qovez*, III, 1c–3b.

276. *Ibid*.

277. Alfakhar 1, *Qovez*, III, 2d–3b.

278. See above.

279. Alfakhar 1, *Qovez*, III, 3b.

280. *Mashal*, bearing also the connotation of "allegory."

281. A play on "Kimhi," presumably derived from *qemah* (wheat).

282. Alfakhar 1, *Qovez*, III, 2b–c.

283. Alfakhar 1, *Qovez*, III, 2c.

284. Alfakhar 1, *Qovez*, III, 2c.

285. Kimhi 2, *Qovez*, III, 4b.

286. Alfakhar 2, *Qovez*, III, 4a–b.

287. Kimhi 2, *Qovez*, III, 4b.

288. *Ginze*, IV, 3f.

289. *Ginze*, IV, 9.

290. *Ginze*, IV, 5f.

291. Alfakhar 3, *Qovez*, III, 4c–d.

292. Kimhi 3, *Qovez*, III, 3c.

293. Kimhi 3, *Qovez*, III, 3b–c.

294. Kimhi 3, *Qovez*, III, 3d.

295. Kimhi 3, *Qoveẓ*, III, 3d.
296. Kimhi 3, *Qoveẓ*, III, 3d.
297. Gen. 3:1.
298. Isa. 65:20.
299. Jos. 5:2, Ps. 136:13.
300. II Kings 6:6.
301. B.T. Giṭṭin 68a.
302. I Kings 6:7; cf. Amos 4:7.
303. Isa. 63:12; cf. Nah. 1:4, Ps. 24:2.
304. Amos 4:13.
305. A.l.
306. Jon. 2:1.
307. Gen. R. 5:5; *Pirqe*, chap. 10.
308. Alfakhar 1, *Qoveẓ*, III, 2a.
309. Jos. 6:5.
310. Jos. 5:2.
311. I Sam. 16:2.
312. II Kings 4:34.
313. *Guide*, I:42.
314. Alfakhar 1, *Qoveẓ*, III, 2b.
315. See the commentaries of Shem Tov Ibn Falaquera and Profiat Duran to the *Guide*, a.l.
316. I Kings 17:17.
317. I Kings 17:20.
318. I Kings 17:4. Cf. the similar attempt of Ibn Janah in his *Book of Roots*, s.v. ʿrb.
319. Lev. R. 26:7.
320. *M.T.* Hil. ʿAkum 6:1f.
321. E.g., Ms. Valladolid 355, fol. 76v (foliation reversed); Ms. Vat. Ebr. 73, fol. 67r; Ms. Bodl. Kennicott 5, fol. 58v; ed. Leiria, 1494.
322. E.g., Ms. Angelica Or. 72, fol. 60v; Ms. Parma 2550, no foliation; Ms. Vat. Ross. Ebr. 533, fol. 26vb. The essential difference lies in the inclusion or omission of the letter *yod* in *Va-'ani* (I do) or *Ve-'eni* (I do not) along with the appearance of the pronoun *mah*, the replacement of the word *bo* by the orthographically similar *ken*, etc. There are thus many variations on the two basic statements. Cf., e.g., Ms. Bodl. Huntington 300, fol. 65r: omission of *bo;* Ms. Bodl. Can. Or. 52, fol. 80r: *va-'ani ro'eh le-faresh hennah ma'aseh le-fi mah she-maẓati katuv ken;* Ms. Bodl. Or. 147, fol. 58r: omission of *nimẓa*.
323. A.l.
324. II Kings 2:11; cf. Mal. 3:11.
325. Cf. *Covenant*, p. 68, n. 83.
326. Ps. 78:39, 88:6, 88:11, 104:30.
327. Ps. 104:30.
328. I Sam. 2:6; Isa. 43:5, 58:14; Mal. 3:23; Joel 4:7; Ps. 106:4; Ps. 128:6.
329. Ezek. 43:20.

330. A.l.
331. Jer. 5:22; cf. Amos 9:6.
332. Ezek. 18:6.

Chapter II. NARBONA: EXILE

1. Ps. 102:8.
2. F. Braudel (*La Méditerranée et le Monde méditerranéen à l'époque de Philippe II*, Paris, 1949, II, 200) notes, "Pour Michelet, le Languedoc intérieur et 'pierreux' évoque la Palestine."
3. Rashi on Gen. 1:10; Radak on Ezek. 27:25.
4. Ps. 127:5.
5. A.l.
6. Mic. 7:8; Ms. Bodl. Huntington Don. 24, fol. 135r.
7. Ezek. 20:25; Ps. 126:6; Talmage, "Polemicist," p. 227.
8. Isa. 52:5, Ps. 22:19.
9. II Sam. 15:9, Ps. 18:19.
10. Gen. 15:11, Isa. 52:5; cf. Talmage, "Polemicist," pp. 227f. Significantly, under the Judeophile policies of Aimeri IV (1194–1239), Narbonnese Jewry enjoyed a fair respite from harassment. See Regné, *REJ,* LVIII (1909), 81ff.; cf. Twersky, "Aspects," p. 189.
11. Ps. 120:2.
12. Ps. 22:8, 14.
13. Ps. 102:9; cf. Ps. 44:15.
14. Isa. 52:14, cited from Ibn Ezra, a.l.; cf. Ps. 22:7.
15. Ps. 69:10f.
16. Ps. 42:4.
17. Ezek. 36:20.
18. Ps. 66:2.
19. Ps. 42:11.
20. Ps. 44:10.
21. Ps. 22:17.
22. E.g., Jos. 15:8, Jer. 4:13, Ezek. 16:40, 17:3.
23. Ezek. 5:5.
24. Gen. 14:18, Jos. 10:1.
25. Jer. 4:1, Ps. 87:3.
26. Ps. 48:3.
27. Ps. 116:9.
28. Jer. 2:7, 16:18.
29. Ps. 84:11.
30. Goitein, p. 345.
31. I Sam. 16:2.
32. A.l.
33. I Kings 9:28.
34. II Chron. 8:18.
35. *Covenant,* p. 65.
36. A.l.; cf. Jer. 9:23.

37. Ps. 127:5; cf. *Covenant,* p. 65; Naḥmanides, Lev. 26:16; Naḥmanides, *Letter upon Arrival in Jerusalem,* ed. A. Ya'ari, *Masse'ot 'Ereẓ Yisra'el* (Tel-Aviv: Gazit, 1945–46), p. 76.

38. Isa. 62:6.

39. Zech. 12:6; cf. Jer. 50:13.

40. Ps. 102:8.

41. Ps. 124:7.

42. Ps. 42:8, 69:2, 130:1.

43. Ps. 129:1.

44. Ps. 22:21.

45. Ezek. 19:13, Ps. 65:10, 126:4.

46. Isa. 57:15.

47. Ps. 102:13, 24.

48. Ezek. 37:11; cf. Ps. 106:4.

49. Ps. 74:20.

50. Prov. 15:30; Ms. Vat. Ebr. 89, fol. 46v.

51. Isa. 54:12.

52. Eliezer of Beaugency to Ezek. 1:1, pp. 1f.

53. Zech. 1:8, 6:1ff.

54. A.l.

55. E.g., I Sam. 22:29, Mic. 7:8, Ps. 18:8.

56. A.l.

57. II Kings 23:5; cf. Zeph. 1:4.

58. A.l., Ms. Bodl. Huntington Don. 24, fol. 160r.

59. Ps. 27:4.

60. Ps. 27:4; cf. Ps. 27:9, 12, 28:1, 36:12.

61. Ps. 56:14.

62. Ps. 118:1.

63. Ps. 63:2.

64. Ps. 119:46.

65. Twersky, *Sefer,* p. 11. *M.T.* Hil. Teshuvah 9:1f.; Twersky, *Sefer,* p. 11.

66. B.T. Bava Batra 21a.

67. Assaf, I, 11.

68. E.g., Ps. 21:1.

69. I Sam. 10:5.

70. Cf. Jos. 3:2.

71. Ps. 71:23.

72. Ps. 69:22.

73. See, e.g., *Roots, 'tr, sb'.*

74. *Roots, sb';* I. Davidson, *Thesaurus of Mediaeval Hebrew Poetry* (New York: J.T.S.A., 1924–33), I, 27b, no. 6047.

75. Jud. 9:13.

76. Isa. 28:8, Jer. 48:26.

77. Jer. 35:8.

78. Ms. Vat. Ebr. 320, fols. 23v–24v. See Appendix.

79. A.l.; cf. Jer. 11:7, Ezek. 7:7.

80. Ms. Vat. Ebr. 320, fol. 24v.

81. Ps. 5:4.

82. Ms. Vat. Ebr. 320, fol. 24r; cf. Ps. 92:3.

83. Ms. Vat. Ebr. 320, fol. 24v.

84. Ms. Vat. Ebr. 320, fol. 23v.

85. Ms. Vat. Ebr. 320, fol. 24r.

86. Cf. Zech. 9:11, Ps. 69:16.

87. Ms. Vat. Ebr. 320, fol. 23v.

88. I Kings 11:39.

89. Ps. 33:4, 37:24, 62:13, 94:12, 103:5; Prov. 3:11; Ms. Vat. Ebr. 89, fols. 11v–12r.

90. Ps. 107:17, II Chron. 6:31.

91. Isa. 40:28, Jer. 12:5, Ps. 92:6.

92. Isa. 65:13, Ezek. 16:59, Ps. 44:21, 23.

93. Ps. 92:7.

94. Ps. 92:9.

95. *Roots, qry.* Cf. *Guide,* III:17; *'Iggeret,* pp. 76f., p. xiv (English).

96. Ps. 107:1.

97. Ps. 8:3.

98. Talmage, "Polemicist," p. 194.

99. Ezek. 9:9.

100. Baer, I, 328f.

101. *Ibid.*

102. Ps. 22:16.

103. Isa. 61:1.

104. Baron, IX, 22f.

105. Ezek. 20:32.

106. *Covenant,* pp. 19f.

107. Ezek. 18:6; cf. *'Iggeret,* pp. 26ff. and n. 33, p. vi (English).

108. A.l.

109. Mic. 4:5.

110. Isa. 63:17, cf. Isa. 51:2, Ps. 77:12.

111. Ps. 92:16.

112. A.l.

113. A.l.

114. Ps. 119;10; cf. Isa. 63:17.

115. Ps. 89:39.

116. *Ibid.*

117. Ezek. 16:63.

Chapter III. THE WAY OF PESHAT

1. Finkelstein, p. xviii.

2. See above, "Family and Career," in Chap. I.

3. First published in Constantinople, 1525.

4. First published in Naples, 1479. An additional grammatical treatise,

the *Petaḥ Devarai*, was attributed to Kimhi by Abraham de Balmes in his *Miqneh Avraham* (Venice, 1523), chaps. *"ba-ḥaluqqat ha-pe'alim" "binyan hitpa'el"* but this was rejected by W. Bacher in "Un Abregé de Grammaire Hebraïque de Benjamin ben Juda de Rome et le Petaḥ Devarai," *REJ*, X(1885), 133f. On Kimhi as a grammarian, see Tauber; Chomsky; M. Steinschneider, in *Hebräische Bibliographie*, X, 110; Hirschfeld, pp. 83–86.

  5. *Roots*, epilogue, p. 420.
  6. *Mikhlol*, p. 1a.
  7. Geiger, p. 41.
  8. Graetz, III, 394f.
  9. Chomsky, pp. xxiiiif. See the critical notes to Luzzato's edition of the *Ma'aseh 'Efod* based on the *Magen David* (pp. 227–248) and to Chomsky.
  10. Constantinople, 1517.
  11. The chief critics were Joseph Ibn Caspi in his *Sharsherot Kesef,* Profiat Duran in the *Ma'aseh 'Efod*, and David Ibn Yahya in the *Leshon Limmudim.* The main criticisms concerned matters of arrangement connected with grammatical theory. Duran thus criticized Kimhi for placing the discussion of the pronouns in the section dealing with particles rather than in that dealing with the substantives (*Ma'aseh 'Efod*, p. 32). He further criticized Kimhi for listing *binyan nif'al* after *qal*, thereby implying that the former was the passive of the latter (*ibid.*, p. 91). Duran agreed with Ibn Janah that not the *nif'al* but the *quṭṭal* is the true passive of the *qal*, as is currently accepted (Chomsky, p. xvi).

The "defective order" of the work was stressed by David Ibn Yahya (*Leshon Limmudim*, p. 2a), and Solomon Ibn Melekh served as a witness to similar criticisms (*Mikhlol Yofi*, p. 2b). Although Ibn Melekh denied this charge (*ibid.*), his work lends it involuntary confirmation, for he rearranged the material in the *Mikhlol* in the order of a verse by verse grammatical and lexicographical commentary on the books of the Bible. This approach, of course, merely begged the question, since it was adequate only for one whose primary purpose was the study of the biblical text and not the study of grammar. The modern editor of the *Mikhlol*, William Chomsky, found he could achieve greater clarity by rearranging several sections and omitting much repetitious material. See his remarks, Chomsky, pp. xviiif.

  12. *NEJ*, X 1002f.
  13. Ibn Ezra, *Yesod*, p. 1.
  14. David Ibn Yahya, *Leshon*, p. 2a.
  15. Ibn Melekh, p. 2b.
  16. *Ibid.*
  17. See Baron, VI, 161.
  18. Chomsky, pp. 7ff.
  19. *M.T.*, int.
  20. Cf. *Kuzari*, II:68; Sarna, p. 329.
  21. Chomsky, pp. 7ff.
  22. *M.T.*, int.
  23. *M.T.*, int.

24. Chomsky, p. 8.

25. *Ma'amar Teḥiyat Ha-Metim,* ed. J. Finkel (New York, 1939–40), v. 9, p. 26; cf. the statement of Ibn Melekh concerning Radak's lexicological method that if he could "include all the aspects and nuances of a particular root in [one] general meaning, he sought [to do so] " *Mikhlol Yofi,* p. 2b.

26. *Miẓvot,* int.

27. Twersky, "Criticism," p. 173.

28. Jos. 8:32, II Chron. 34:22. The derivation is from the root *shnn.*

29. David Ibn Yahya, *Leshon,* p. 2a.

30. Twersky, "Criticism," pp. 170ff.

31. *Mikhlol Yofi,* p. 2b.

32. Hirsch, pp. 137ff.; Cohen, p. x; Newman, pp. 100, 479, 482, 539ff.

33. Geiger, p. 240. Finkelstein (pp. xciv–xcvi) deals with this question in detail. However, he believes on somewhat conjectural evidence that the Samuel commentary was written prior to that on Psalms.

34. Chron., int. See Bibliographic Note.

35. Jer. 17:12. See Bibliographic Note.

36. Jer., int.; Hos., int. See Bibliographic Note.

37. Isaiah before Jeremiah; see int. to Jer.

38. See Bibliographic Note.

39. See Bibliographic Note.

40. See Bibliographic Note.

41. See below, n. 534.

42. E.g. Rashi, see Lipschütz, pp. 64–78.

43. I Chron. 5:17.

44. II Chron. 18:19.

45. Algazi, p. 8.

46. Ibn Melekh, pp. 3b–c.

47. DeLattes, p. 43; *MJC,* II, 237.

48. Ibn Yahya, p. 225a.

49. Geiger, pp. 241f.

50. See Bibliographic Note. Cf. Sarna, p. 357 and especially Rabinowitz.

51. Ibn Yahya, p. 225a.

52. David Ibn Yahya, *Qav,* p. 219a.

53. Fols. 2v–3r. upper and lower margins.

54. Llamas, p. 28.

55. Cassuto, p. 129.

56. In addition to Cassuto's comments, the following striking parallels may be noted: Prov. 5:19 (fol. 19v) = *Roots, s.v. shgy;* and Prov. 5:23 (fol. 20r) = *Mikhlol* 25a (referred to as *ḥeleq ha-diqduq*). The expression *kafal ha-'inyan* is used several times, e.g., Prov. 9:8 (fol. 29v), Prov. 10:25 (fol. 32v), Prov. 11:6 (fol. 33v), Prov. 11:7 (fol. 33v). Kimhi's text is incomplete and goes only as far as Prov. 21:14 (fol. 62v). Thereafter, Jonah ben Abraham Gerondi's commentary replaces the missing portion.

57. Ms. Vat. Ebr. 89, fol. 2v.

58. Lipschütz, pp. 42–44.

59. See A. Freimann, "Manuscript Supercommentaries on Rashi's Commentary on the Pentateuch," in *Rashi Anniversary Volume* (New York, 1941), pp. 73-114.

60. Hos. 12:11.

61. I Sam. 28:3.

62. Jer. 16:19.

63. Baron, VI, 255-263.

64. Cohen, pp. xxxf.

65. E.g., Jos. 1:8, 2:1; Isa. 66:24.

66. E.g., Jos. 15:7, Isa. 7:3.

67. E.g., Amos 9:3, Mic. 2:4, Zech. 13:7.

68. Ezek. 27:6.

69. Jos., int.

70. See above, "Coincidence of Opposites."

71. Poznanski, pp. xixf., xxxvi, xlix, cxiv–cxxv, clxif; and in general Levy, *Contribution*.

72. Ps. 81:6.

73. Ps. 114:1.

74. B.T. Sanhedrin 60a; cf. Moshe Ibn Ezra and his citation of R. Hai Gaon, *Shirat,* pp. 58f.

75. II Kings 18:17.

76. Finkelstein, pp. lxxv–lxxix.

77. Baron, VIII, 386, n. 8.

78. Amos 6:8. In this Radak resembled the northern French *pashṭanim* of the school of Rashi; Rashi himself seems to have used a far greater range of *le'azim*. See above, n. 71.

79. Isa. 41:19.

80. Jer. 8:7.

81. Jer. 6:28, Zech. 6:1.

82. Isa. 44:12.

83. Cf. Radak and Ibn Ezra on Jon. 4:6.

84. Hos. 13:8.

85. Jer. 2:24.

86. Prov. 5:19; Ms. Vat. Ebr. 89, fol. 19v. Radak's citation is probably taken from Rashi; see Epstein, p. 216.

87. Sarna, pp. 322ff.

88. Cohen, p. xviiif.; cf. Barol, p. 25.

89. Abrahams, I, 59.

90. Hos. 4:13, Jon. 4:6.

91. Gen. 25:20, Joel 2:7, Ps. 45:9.

92. I Sam. 8:13.

93. I Kings 1:2.

94. In this case too, Arabic *sin* would require Hebrew *shin*. The true cognate would be *shaḥun.*

95. Assaf, I, 12; cf. Assaf, II, 29.

96. E.g., I Sam. 13:20.

97. I Sam. 13:18.
98. Jon. 1:6, Ps. 146:4.
99. E.g., Hos. 4:13, Nah. 3:17, II Chron. 2:9.
100. Gen. 43:11, Jer. 8:7.
101. B.T. Bava Batra 72a.
102. Darmesteter, p. 128.
103. B.T. Bava Batra 72a.
104. Ibn Janah, *'shr.*
105. *Roots, 'shr,* gives Italian *bosso;* *'Arukh,* I, 314f.
106. Isa. 41:19; cf. Jer. 8:7.
107. But see Jos. 1:1, Jer. 8:23.
108. Isa. 1:8.
109. *Ibid.*
110. Lev. R. 26:7.
111. I Sam. 28:13. According to the *'aggadah,* a spirit would ordinarily rise from Sheol in an inverted position. See Ginzberg, VI, 236, n. 75.
112. Jer., int.
113. E.g., Amos 7:5f.; Zech. 1:3, 4:4f., 8:5.
114. I Kings 11:26–40.
115. I Kings 11:26.
116. I Chron. 1:5; cf. 2:25, 3:1, 5:1.
117. Isa. 42:5.
118. Ps. 104:9.
119. B.T. Sanhedrin 26a.
120. See Baron, V, 282ff.
121. Ibn Ezra, int. to Torah.
122. See Ibn Ezra at Exod. 3:15, 20:1. Yet Joseph Kimhi, a model of verbal economy, allowed himself now and again in his grammatical writings to digress on a point which may be quite unrelated to grammar. See *Galui,* pp. 2, 134ff.
123. See above, "Obscurities and Discrepancies."
124. I Sam. 13:19.
125. I Sam. 14:3.
126. I Sam. 28:24; see above, "The Question of the Supernatural," in Chap. I.
127. II Sam. 21:1, Ezek. 18:6. See above, Chap. II and Chap. IV.
128. See Heinemann, pp. 154ff.
129. I Sam. 20:2.
130. II Sam. 12:20: cf. *M.T.* Hil. *'Evel* 1:1.
131. Jer. 16:2.
132. Gen. 31:30; cf. Gen. 35:2.
133. Gen. 22:13; cf. Gen. 7:7, 24:14, 28:16, 34:13, 38:2, 47:14; Jos. 9:7, I Kings 1:15, II Kings 22:8.
134. I Sam. 25:43, II Sam. 3:5.
135. I Kings 3:3.
136. B.T. Berakhot 4b, Pesaḥim 117a.

137. Int. to Psalms. On this passage, see Talmage, "Rationalist," pp. 185–193.

138. Cf., e.g., Ps. 104:9.

139. See Talmage, "Rationalist."

140. *Ibid.*, pp. 185–193.

141. *Ibid.*, pp. 193–201.

142. *Ibid.*, pp. 201–205.

143. *Galui,* pp. lf.; *Covenant,* pp. 13f.

144. In his *Improvement of the Moral Qualities;* Ibn Gabirol, pp. 35ff.

145. An early speculative work which gave rise to numerous commentaries and was widely studied in the Middle Ages; see *NEJ,* XVI, 782ff.; Talmage, "Sources," pp. 453ff.

146. Talmage, "Sources," pp. 460 *et seq.*

147. *Ibid.*, pp. 473f.

148. Gen. 1:1 (three times), 1:2, 1:3, 1:5 (twice), 1:6, 1:9, 2:4, 2:8 (twice).

149. Gen. 1:2, 1:10.

150. Gen. 1:1 (three times), 1:2, 1:3, 1:6, 1:9, 1:31.

151. Gen. 1:2 (four times).

152. Gen. 1:1, 1:6, 1:9, 1:16, 1:26.

153. Cf. Twersky, "Aspects," p. 185.

154. Finkelstein, p. xviii; cf. Cohen, p. xiii; Baron, VI, 280.

155. See above, "David Kimhi's Education," in Chap. I.

156. Cohen, pp. xxvf.

157. Posnanski, p. 10. On the above exegetes, see Smalley, pp. 149–155.

158. Rashbam, Gen. 37:2.

159. H. Cohen was of the opinion that the citations of Joseph Bekhor Shor and Samuel ben Meir (Gen. 45:24) and Joseph Kara (Gen. 19:31) found in Ms. München 48 were scribal additions. See Cohen, p. xx, n. 8; p. xxiii, n. 5. The remarks at Gen 19:31 are found also, however, in Ms. Paris Sorbonne 49, fol. 49r, and Ms. Alliance Israélite 157, fol. 116r, while the citation of Samuel ben Meir is found in Ms. Paris Ancien Fonds 75, fol. 75v. Even if these citations are genuine, however, they do not prove extensive knowledge of the northern French exegetes. See Cohen, p. xxxv.

160. See above, "David Kimhi's Education," in Chap. I.

161. Ezovi, p. 537.

162. Deut. 32:1; *Give ear O heavens . . . and let the earth hear.*

163. Isa. 1:2.

164. Jos. 4:11; cf. Gen 4:1.

165. Cf. II Chron. 5:9.

166. Gen. R. 63:6.

167. Gen. 25:22.

168. I Sam. 12:30, II Chron. 5:9.

169. Gen. 3:21, Jos. 7:5.

170. Jos. 5:14, Jud. 7:5, I Sam. 17:3, I Kings 1:1, 17:1.

171. I Kings 18:26.

172. Jos. 5:14.

173. See Rashi, Jud. 4:5.

174. B.T. Sanhedrin 101b.

175. I Kings 11:26.

176. Gen. 24:39. Many *midrashim* are based on a word's being spelt *plene,* or deficiently, i.e., with or without vowel letters. See Ginsburg, pp. 144ff.; I. J. Gelb, *A Study of Writing* (Chicago, 1952), pp. 166ff.

177. I Chron. 2:55.

178. Jos. 7:5.

179. Sifre, Devarim, 1:24.

180. Jos. 24:32, I Sam. 10:3, Isa. 54:15.

181. I Sam. 28:19.

182. E.g., I Sam. 28:7, 28:15.

183. Goldberg, p. xvii.

184. See Ginzberg, VI, 382, n. 5.

185. A.l.

186. B.T. Soṭah 10b.

187. At I Chron. 25:3.

188. I Chron. 25:1, midrash brought in Pseudo-Rashi.

189. See, e.g., Samuel ben Meir at Gen. 1:1; Joseph Bekhor Shor at Exod. 23:19.

190. II Chron. 6:1.

191. B.T. Pesaḥim 56a; i.e., that he declared a leap year (one with thirteen months) so that Nisan, the month of Passover, became second Adar. According to this stratagem, the "second month," Iyyar, would now be considered Nisan. However, according to halakhah, the intercalation would have to be declared before Nisan commenced, as Radak goes on to state. Cf. Maimonides, *M.T.* Hil. Bi'at Miqdash 4:17.

192. B.T. Sanhedrin 12a, b: "R. Judah observed: It once happened that Hezekiah king of Judah declared a leap year because of uncleanness, and then prayed for mercy . . . R. Simeon said: [He did so] because only an Adar can be intercalated and he intercalated a Nisan in Nisan. R. Simeon b. Judah said on behalf of R. Simeon, that it was because he persuaded Israel to celebrate a Second Passover [unduly]." (Sonc., Sanhedrin, pp. 54f.)

193. A.l.; Ms. Escorial, G-II-6, fol. 78r.

194. Gen. 38:8; cf. Gen. R. 85:5.

195. Gen. 38:24; cf. Gen. R. 85:10, Tanḥuma, Buber, I, 187.

196. Gen. 32:33; cf. *M.T.* Hil. Melakhim 9:1; *ET,* VI, 1ff.

197. Ibn Ezra, int. to Torah.

198. Cited in *'Eshkol,* II, 47; translation from Baron, VI, 176.

199. *'Eshkol, ibid.*

200. Baron, VI, 177f.

201. Abrahams, I, 155f.; cf. II Kings 17:9.

202. Midrash Tehillim 91:1, pp. 395f.

203. Midrash Tehillim 91:8, pp. 400f.

204. Midrash Tehillim 91:3-5, pp. 297f.

205. Ps. 91:6.

206. B.T. Shevu'ot 15b; Midrash Tehillim 91:1, p. 396.

207. Ps. 91:16.

208. *Guide,* III:51.

209. I Sam. 28:13.

210. It is noteworthy that Radak modifies the midrash cited by Rashi (B.T. Ḥagigah 4b). Instead of Samuel's raising up Moses in his own defense, he calls on him to intercede for Israel. (Cf. Lev. R. 26:7.)

211. Williams, p. 237 with references; cf. Williams, pp. 235ff., 388ff.; Merchavia, pp. 93-127, 128-152.

212. Ms. Parma 2749, fol. 215v. Ramban, I, 308; Rankin, p. 188; Shem Tov Ibn Shaprut, " 'Even Boḥan," Ms. Brit. Lib. Add. 26964, fols. 162v, 167v. Cf. the opening statement of the Jewish disputant in the chapter on *'aggadot:* "All *'aggadot* are to be taken as allegories—not literally—for they have several senses" (fol. 162r).

213. Baron, VI, 171. Baron refers to material stemming from the Book of Jubilees or closely related to it, but see Belkin.

214. Millás-Vallicrosa, pp. 8f.; Rosenthal, *Ḥazir.*

215. B.T. Yoma 39b, cited in *PL,* 157:573.

216. Lukyn-Williams, pp. 233-40; Merchavia pp. 114, 117; *PL,* 157:573, 596f.

217. Baron, VI, 172.

218. Stein, "Disputations," p. 8.

219. Ms. Parma 2749, fols. 215r-225r.

220. Abraham Ibn Ezra, int. to Torah, in Friedlander, Heb. appendix, p. 1.

221. *Covenant,* p. 47.

222. Millás-Vallicrosa, p. 32.

223. *Covenant,* pp. 22f., 46f.

224. Stein, p. 51.

225. Ps. 119:129.

226. Ps. 119:152.

227. Ps. 132:12; cf. Gen 22:1, Ps. 119:160.

228. Ms. Bodl. Huntington Don. 24, fol. 177v.

229. Ps. 19:10.

230. Stein, "Disputations," p. 11.

231. See above, "David Kimhi's Education," in Chap. I.

232. *Galui,* p. 2.

233. *Mikhlol,* p. 1a. On lexical works and poetry, see Morag, p. 578; Sarna, pp. 330f.

234. *Mikhlol Yofi,* Vienna, 1818.

235. Song of Songs, int.; int. to Torah, end.

236. *Yom* (day) is masculine.

237. Isa. 56:2.

238. Isa. 44:4.

239. Ezek. 16:4.

240. In *Kol Kitve D. Frischman* (Warsaw, 1938), II, 107-114.

241. See above "Grammar and Masorah."

242. Lev. R. 1:3; Ruth R. 2:1.

243. See Heinemann, pp. 28, 166f., 169; and see above, "Obscurities and Discrepancies."

244. Chron., int.

245. *Ibid.*

246. See Kirchheim.

247. See above, "Joseph and Moses Kimhi," in Chap. I.

248. Baron VI, 254f.

249. Ibn Ezra, *Moznayim,* p. 1a.

250. Ibn Ezra, *Yesod,* p. 1.

251. Ibn Ezra on Exod. 25:31.

252. Simon, p. 193.

253. Ibn Daud, *'Emunah Ramah,* Hebrew p. 80 from Baron, VI, 254. Cf. *'Iggeret,* pp. 38ff., p. viii (English); *M.T.* Hil. Sefer Torah 7:8; Profiat Duran, *Kelimat ha-Goyim,* ed. Z. A. Posnanski, *Ha-Zofeh,* IV (1915), 122f.; Duran, p. 4. Cf., however, the remarks of Isaac Pulgar in *'Ezer ha-Dat,* ed. G. S. Belasco (London, 1906), p. 86, where he attacks the Kabbalah on the basis of the fact that discrepancies in biblical manuscripts render it untenable. On the accusation of tampering, see Samau'al al-Maghribi, pp. 53ff.

254. Ibn Ezra, *Yesod,* pp. 1ff.

255. *Covenant,* pp. 58ff. and n. 64.

256. *Covenant,* p. 54. Cf. pp. 28ff., 49ff., 64.

257. Ps. 110, end.

258. *PL,* 24:56.

259. A.l.

260. A.l.; cf. Vulgate, a.l.

261. *Qui mittendus est (shaliah).*

262. *Dileh (shello).*

263. Based on *shilyatah* (afterbirth), Deut. 28:57.

264. Gen. 49:10; *Roots, shyl;* but see the version recorded by Martini, pp. 316f.

265. B.T. Shevu'ot 35b.

266. Baron, V, 121.

267. Ibn Ezra, a.l.

268. Cf. *Covenant,* p. 63.

269. Ibn Ezra, *Moznayim,* p. 19a.

270. Gen. 18:13.

271. *Covenant,* p. 63.

272. On this problem, see Simon, pp. 210f.

273. B.T. Shevu'ot 35b.

274. Gen. 19:18.

275. Ps. 110, end.

276. Following the reading of many mss., e.g., Ms. Escorial G-I-5, fol. 65r; Ms. Bodl. Mich. 381, fol. 119r; Ms. Bodl. Can. Or. 68, fol. 109r; Ms. Bodl. Opp. 757 (*Teshuvot la-nozerim*), fol. 66r; Ms. Madrid Bibl. Nac. 5457, no foliation; Ms. Vat. Urb. 16, fol. 295v.

277. Ps. 110, end.

278. On the spread of Oriental mss. in France, see Aptowitzer, p. 92, n. 2.

279. Abulafia, int., beg. (no pagination).

280. Barol, pp. 12ff.

281. *'Eṭ Sofer*, p. 1a.

282. *M.T.* Hil. Sefer Torah, 8:4.

283. Goshen-Gottstein, pp. 39f.

284. Isa. 44:4; Ms. Brit. Lib. Add. Or. 27046, fol. 30r.

285. Cf. Simon, p. 194, n. 11a.

286. Isa. 43:14.

287. B.T. Megillah 29a.

288. For further references, see *Minḥat Shai,* a.l.

289. I.e., Do not read *x* but *y*.

290. See *Minḥat Shai* and Ibn Ezra, a.l.

291. Isa. 43:14.

292. E.g., Jer. 15:14; Simon, pp. 219. Radak was confident of the antiquity of the masoretic vowel points in that they were "given to Moses from Sinai" (*Mikhlol,* p. 73a; see Cohen, pp. xxviiif.) He spoke too of those who "instituted the vowel points" (*Mikhlol,* p. 55a). Yet it is possible that Radak's attitude was similar to that of a contemporary: "It is true that the vowel points were revealed at Sinai but they were forgotten until Ezra came and they redis-covered them but they could not be written down for they were considered to be in the same category as the oral law" (Nutt, p. 12). See Cohen, p. xxviiif. Other masoretic apparatus is considered dispensable, however, and Radak finds no practical justification on the level of *peshaṭ* for such phenom-ena as the *puncta extraordinaria,* the *litterae majusculae, minusculae* and *suspensae.* For these, "there was no reason except that which is found in the *derash*" (Gen. 18:9; see Simon, p. 224, n. 120). The accents, which indicate punctuation and verse division as well as syllable stress, are not, however, considered binding: "The sense of Scripture does not always follow the accents" (Hos. 12:12). In this Radak follows Saadia, his father, and his brother against Ibn Ezra. See Cohen, pp. xxixf., Simon, pp. 224f.

293. Isa. 38:19.

294. Isa. 58:3.

295. Hos. 12:1. For further references, see Simon, p. 195.

296. Ibn Ezra, *Yesod,* p. 1.

297. Cohen, pp. xxviif., n. 2; Simon, p. 195.

298. E.g., Jer. 24:9; Simon, p. 195.

299. Cohen, p. xxvii.

300. E.g., Gen. 25:1, Jos. 21:7, Jud. 6:19, Isa. 43:14, Zech. 6:11, I Chron. 2:55; *Roots, dḥh, rqḥ, shkh.*

301. *Mikhlol,* pp. 46b, 164a, 164b; *Roots, qshb.*

302. Ps. 109:10, although this may have been derived from Jacob ben Eleazar. See Finkelstein, pp. xxviif.

303. At I Chron. 6:43f.

304. Jos. 21:7.

305. I Kings 1:18. Simon observes that this observation is an incipient application of *lectio difficilior;* Simon, p. 222.

306. Ps. 17:5.

307. See also *Roots, ngs, ngsh.*

308. See above.

309. Simon, p. 196.

310. Chron., int.; cf. II Sam. 15:21, I Kings 17:14.

311. Although, in some instances, he related to only one: Gen. 24:33, Ps. 10:10; cf. Ps. 30:4.

312. Cf. Jos. 6:7; I Sam. 4:13; II Kings 16:6; Ps. 17:11, 24:4, 24:6.

313. See above, "Biblical Stylistics."

314. Jos. 24:3, Hag. 1:8, Zech. 11:2, Ps. 6:4.

315. II Kings 6:25.

316. II Kings 7:12.

317. A.l.

318. See Bibliographic Note.

319. Pp. 1a–1b.

320. Pp. 2b–30a.

321. Pp. 30a–32b.

322. *Mikhlol,* 194b.

323. Heinemann, p. 97.

324. Ibn Ezra, int. to Torah.

325. Bacher, *Ibn Esra,* p. 3.

326. Bacher, *Ibn Esra,* p. 41.

327. Ginsberg, p. 277.

328. *Roots, shbʻ;* Simon, p. 231, n. 156.

329. A.l.

330. A.l.

331. A.l.; cf. Ezek. 9:8.

332. Brown, p. 37.

333. A.l.

334. E.g., I Chron. 4:33.

335. II Kings 6:4.

336. Ezek. 22:18.

337. Jos. 7:7.

338. Jos. 10:24.

339. See Hirschfeld, pp. 76f.

340. Ezek. 8:3, Hos. 5:11, Amos 6:10, 9:30; *Mikhlol,* pp. 51a–b; *Riqmah,* p. 263.

341. Ps. 142:5; Bacher, *ʻErke,* p. 19; *Ibn Esra,* p. 143.

342. Hos. 8:2; Bacher, *ʻErke,* p. 114. Ibn Janah uses the concept *muqdam u-meʻuḥar* as well, *Riqmah,* p. 354.

343. Hos. 14:3; *Mikhlol,* p. 90a; Bacher, *Ibn Esra,* p. 141; *Riqmah,* p. 352.

344. Hos. 5:11, Ps. 142:5.

345. A.l.

346. Isa. 47:3.
347. Jos. 14:11.
348. Isa. 44:4.
349. E.g., Hag. 2:15.
350. A.l.
351. E.g., Isa. 44:26.
352. Isa. 51:11.
353. Isa. 58:4.
354. It was an established exegetical principle that components of a verse might have a dual function. Bacher, *Ibn Esra*, p. 139.
355. Cf. Ibn Janah, p. 85.
356. Cf. Ibn Janah, p. 83.
357. A.l.
358. See below.
359. Jos. 1:1; cf. Ezek. 16:22.
360. Nah. 3:19; cf. *Roots, ḥlh.*
361. A.l.; cf. *Roots, 'nh.*
362. Jer. 8:23.
363. Sifre, 'Eqev, p. 41 cited a.l.
364. A.l.
365. A.l.
366. Num. R. 67:1.
367. Jos. 2:4.
368. Jer. 7:20.
369. A.l.; cf. Nah. 3:7.
370. See Rashi to Ezek. 14:1.
371. Ezek. 14:1.
372. Isa. 60:9.
373. E.g., Isa. 51:12.
374. Isa. 60:8.
375. Hos. 4:5. The term *'edah* is used at Ezek. 22:4. The concept of *kenasah* is not applied to Israel uniquely. See Jer. 50:11, Ezek. 16:44 and Ben Yehudah, V, 2448. Radak treats changes of person in the same fashion as in his interpretation of Joshua 15:4: *"This shall be your south border.* Scripture should have said *their border* since the entire passage is a narrative. Perhaps we are to understand it as follows: This will be their border as it is written in the Torah, *this will be your south border"* (Numbers 34:3). Cf. Isa. 42:40, Amos 9:1, Mal. 2:15.
376. Heinemann, p. 97.
377. *Ibid.*
378. Menahem ben Simeon to Ezek. 7:6.
379. A.l.
380. A.l.; cf. Ibn Ezra a.l.
381. Jer. 7:4.
382. *Shirat,* pp. 158–208.
383. *Shirat,* p. 22.

384. Gen. 16:8ff.
385. Gen. 16:9.
386. Cited in Rashi a.l. in the name of *Seder 'Olam.*
387. A.l.
388. B.T. Berakhot 31b.
389. I Sam. 1:11.
390. Midrash Samuel, p. 49.
391. A.l. See Finkelstein, pp. xxivf.
392. Gen. R. 68:6.
393. A.l.
394. Gen. 28:10.
395. Jer. 8:13.
396. Heinemann, p. 118.
397. A.l.
398. *Ibid.*
399. Jer. 38:4. *'Et* generally appears before a direct object.
400. Gen. 25:16.
401. Isa. 56:4.
402. Jer. 15:18.
403. Isa. 64:4.
404. Hos. 3:1, 3:33.
405. Mic. 1:10, 1:12, 2:4.
406. Gen. 23:1, Amos 5:5, Mic. 1:10, Zeph. 2:4.
407. Jer. 15:18.
408. Jer. 4:19.
409. A.l.; cf. Jer. 6:1; Mic. 1:10f., 1:13f.
410. Jer. 51:27.
411. Cf. Gen. 49:11; Isa. 60:7,; Jer. 2:32, 4:23, 20:6, 38:9, 44:22; Hos. 2:1; Zeph. 1:3; Hag. 2:6.
412. Isa. 59:16.
413. II Sam. 2:1.
414. Amos 4:4.
415. Ibn Ezra, int. to Exod. 20; Simon, pp. 203f.
416. Gen. 24:39; cf. Gen. 18:13, 20:1, 21:1, 32:10, 41:17; Jer. 8:10. Simon (p. 205) has observed that Radak is more systematic than Ibn Ezra in this connection.
417. Eissfeldt, pp. 158f.; Soloweitschik, pp. 31ff.
418. Rashi, Gen. 1:1.
419. Sarna, pp. 344ff.; Soloweitschik, pp. 41ff.; Ginsberg, p. 277.
420. Chron., int.
421. I Chron. 5:6.
422. I Chron. 4:9; cf. Gen. 4:2.
423. I Chron. 1:41.
424. I Chron. 4:24; cf. I Chron. 2:7, 6:13, 6:18, 12:3.
425. I Chron. 6:54.
426. Simon, p. 207.

427. I Sam. 9:1; I Chron. 6:5, 6:18, 6:39, 7:12, 8:33f., 9:2; II Chron. 11:18, 13:2.

428. I Chron. 6:13.

429. Ps. 34:1; cf. Ibn Ezra a.l.

430. I Chron. 13:6.

431. II Chron. 13:2.

432. Ps. 34:1.

433. Jos. 15:17; cf. Gen. 36:12, I Chron. 2:18.

434. At I Chron. 3:19.

435. At Hag. 1:1, 1:12, 1:14, 2:23.

436. I Chron. 3:19; cf. I Chron. 7:17, 23:8. The principle is talmudic in origin. See B.T. Yevamot 62b.

437. Vulgate, Pseudo-Rashi, a.l.

438. I Chron. 6:13.

439. I Chron. 2:7.

440. I Chron. 8:33.

441. E.g., I Sam. 9:1, I Chron. 3:1, 3:17.

442. I Chron. 2:55; cf. Gen. 4:18, 14:17, 30:21; I Chron. 4:18, 4:22, 6:39.

443. Gen. R. 25:2.

444. Gen. 5:29; cf. I Chron. 4:9.

445. Jos. 5:9.

446. M. Simon, pp. 107f., 224; cf. Blumenkranz, pp. 275ff.

447. *Nizzahon,* 70, 112.

448. *Covenant,* p. 67, n. 82.

449. Isa. 44:2; cf. Gen. 32:29, 35:11.

450. Ps. 105:6; cf. Ps. 20:2.

451. Ezek. 20:5; cf. Isa. 63:16, Ezek. 37:25, Hos. 7:9.

452. Mic. 1:14; cf. Amos 7:9, Mic. 1:5, Nah. 2:3, Ps. 24:6.

453. Simon, pp. 207f.

454. See above, "Grammar and Masorah."

455. Cf. Gen. 5:4; Simon, p. 209.

456. The common substitution of *nun* for *mem* is noted without explanation. See I Chron. 6:16.

457. Following Ms. Esc. G-II-6, fols. 41v-42r.

458. I Chron. 1:7.

459. Gen. 10:4.

460. Jer. 25:1, Ezek. 1:1.

461. Cf. Menahem ben Simeon to Ezek. 1:1.

462. I Chron. 18:4, 19:18; II Chron. 3:4, 16:1.

463. At I Chron. 23:27.

464. At Num. 4:3 and *passim.*

465. I Chron. 23:27.

466. II Chron. 8:18.

467. II Chron. 13:1.

468. At II Chron. 8:2.

469. I Kings 9:11.
470. I Kings 9:11, II Chron. 8:2.
471. At I Chron. 5:11 and Deut. 3:13.
472. I Chron. 5:11.
473. See above, "Grammar and Masorah."
474. I Chron. 10:10.
475. I Chron. 7:18.
476. I Chron. 22:8.
477. I Chron. 29:2.
478. I Chron. 10:14.
479. Joseph Kara, a.l.
480. I Sam. 9:9.
481. B.T. Bava Batra 15a.
482. Chron., int.
483. Gen. 10:6.
484. Psalms, int.
485. Ps. 90:1.
486. Gen. 12:6.
487. Jos. 15:63.
488. At Jud. 18:1.
489. Gen. 36:31.
490. Gen. 14:14, Jos. 11:21. Cf. Jud. 13:25.
491. Gen. 14:14.
492. Jos. 5:1 (*ha-kotev*); I Sam. 4:1 (*ha-sofer*); Jer. 51:64 (*mi she-kotev ha-sefer*).
493. Chaps. 17ff.
494. Rashi at Jud. 17:1.
495. Jud. 18:1.
496. *Pirqe,* chap. 47; cf. Mal. 2:5, I Chron 9:20.
497. Isa. 6:1.
498. Bacher, "Einleitung," p. 371.
499. Ibn Ezra, int. to Torah.
500. J. Heinemann, p. 27.
501. *Ibid.*
502. II Sam. 23:8; B.T. Berakhot 18b, Mo'ed Qaṭan 16b.
503. II Sam. 23:20, B.T. Berakhot 18b.
504. II Sam. 23:20; cf. II Sam. 23:16.
505. B.T. Sanhedrin 38b (in ms.); cf. *Iggeret,* pp. 46f., p. ix (English).
506. Amos 2:6; Berkowitz, p. 31.
507. Ps. 87, end.
508. A.l., Ms. Brit. Lib. Add. Or. 27046, fol. 137r. See Jerome, commentary to Ezek. a.l., *PL,* 25:430.
509. At Isa. 7:14. Blumenkranz, p. 238.
510. Isa. 7:14.
511. Ibn Ezra, int. to Torah.
512. Mal. 3:22; Ms. Bodl. Huntington Don. 24, fol. 177v.

513. Ps. 119:129.

514. *Covenant,* pp. 44f.

515. See as well *Guide,* II:29f.

516. Ibn Ezra, int. to Torah.

517. *Guide,* int.

518. *Guide,* II:30, 46; III:1ff.

519. *Qovez,* III, 1c.

520. Samuel Ibn Tibbon, p. 132.

521. See Talmage, "Rationalist," p. 206.

522. Samuel Ibn Tibbon, p. 132.

523. See Vajda.

524. See above, "Radak's Role in the Maimonidean Controversy," in Chap. I.

525. *Ibid.*

526. First Letter of Alfakhar, *Qovez,* III, 1c.

527. *Qinyan,* play on *qayin* (Cain).

528. *Hevel,* Hebrew for Abel.

529. On the allegorical commentaries in detail, see Talmage, "Rationalist," pp. 205ff.

530. *Guide,* III:2.

531. *Guide,* III:int.

532. *Guide,* II:10.

533. Ms. Brit. Lib. Add. 27179, fols. 63r, v. Cf. Hopper, pp. 42f., 84f., 112f., 117.

534. Gen. 2:8, 2:9, 2:13, 2:17, 3:1, 3:15, 3:22; Ezek. 1:3, 1:9, 1:10, 1:12, 1:14, 1:15.

535. Gen. 3:1.

536. Ezek., int.

537. B.T. Ḥagigah 13b.

538. Ezek., int.

539. Ms. Vat. Ebr. 89, fol. 2r.

540. *Ibid.*

541. Prov. 5:3; Ms. Vat. Ebr. 89, fol. 17v.

542. Prov. 1:2; Ms. Vat. Ebr. 89, fol. 3r; cf. 1:18, fol. 5v; 1:29, fol. 7r.

543. Prov. 11:29; Ms. Vat. Ebr. 89, fol. 36r; cf. Prov. 17:12, fol. 51r, but see Prov. 19:18, fol. 56v.

544. Radak understood the verb *tishgeh* as "err" so that the passage would read *in loving her constantly, you shall err.* For Ibn Janah, the verb has a positive connotation: *"you shall rejoice* or *be constantly occupied* [in love of her (wisdom)]." See Derenbourg, pp. 172f. Ibn Janah, *Roots, shgh.* Cf. Radak, *Roots, shgh:* "Rabbi Jonah explained this verse altogether differently since he feels the verse talks of wisdom. The fact is that the verse speaks of one's wife [as is seen from the context]. Even though it *may* speak parabolically of wisdom, the letter (*melizah*) speaks of one's wife. The intent of the speaker is thus two-fold and so it should be interpreted [as we have said]."

545. Prov. 5:19; Ms. Vat. Ebr. 89, fol. 19v.

546. *Ḥuqqah* to Prov. 9:1 (p. 12), 11:29 (pp. 16f.).

547. *Galui,* pp. 1f.

548. Ps. 119, int.

549. Prov. 1:7, 4:7, 8:22, Ms. Vat. Ebr. 89, fols. 3v, 15v, 28r.

550. Ps. 132:2.

551. Midrash Tehillim 90, p. 396.

552. Gen. R. 69:7.

553. *Sefer Yeẓirah,* 4:3.

554. *Guide,* III:54.

555. Jer. 9:23; cf. Hab. 2:14.

556. On the difference between *peshaṭ* and *mashma'* in Rashi, see Lip-schütz, pp. 164ff.

557. See above, "Allegorical Interpretation."

558. Tanḥuma, Vayiqra 6.

559. Zech. 3:2.

560. Chron., int.

561. See above, "*Peshaṭ* and *Derash.*"

562. *Ibid.*

563. *Ibid.*

564. Jud. 11:31. Cf. Gen. 20:3, Jos. 4:11, Jud. 12:8, II Chron. 5:9. Cf. Ibn Ezra, int. to Exod. 20; Menahem ben Simeon, Jer. 30:5.

565. See above, "*Peshaṭ* and *Derash.*"

566. Jud. 16:21, I Chron. 1:36.

567. Ps. 22:30.

568. B.T. Berakhot 62b.

569. I Kings 1:1; see *Pirqe,* chap. 43.

570. According to the *'aggadah,* it was Passover, and the Hallel, a group of psalms of praise, was read.

571. Jud. 6:11,; *Yalquṭ,* II:62,; Midrash ha-Gadol, Genesis, cols. 222f.

572. Midrash Tehillim 3, p. 37.

573. II Sam. 19:21; Midrash Tehillim 3, p. 37.

574. B.T. Sanhedrin 107a.

575. II Sam. 3:3.

576. Jud. 11:31.

577. B.T. Megillah 13b, Qiddushin 38a.

578. See *Seder 'Olam,* p. 42, n. 11; Ginzberg, VI, 167, n. 966.

579. Jos. 3:2.

580. E.g., Gen. 1:14, 4:2ff.; Isa. 57:19; Jer. 7:31; I Chron. 4:21.

581. Tanḥuma, *Shelaḥ,* 1.

582. Ruth R. 2:1.

583. A.l., B.T. Berakhot 34b.

584. B.T. Bava Batra 8a, translation based on Sonc., Bava Batra, p. 36.

585. Gen. R. 76:17.

586. Gen. 32:16; cf. Gen. 6:2, I Chron. 8:33.

587. II Chron. 32:33; B.T. Bava Qama 16b.

588. Baron, VI, 280.

589. A.l., Gen. R. 91:9.

590. A.l., Tanḥuma, Mi-qez, 8.
591. A.l.; Gen. R. 75:5; cf. Gen. 3:8, Zech. 3:3, II Chron. 3:10.
592. I.e., dividing a word into "components."
593. A.l., B.T. Berakhot 59b.
594. See above.
595. II Chron. 3:10; cf. *Roots, z'z'*; see B.T. Bava Batra 99a, Rashi, a.l. *Arukh*, VII, 32. The etymology *keruv—ke-ravya* is rejected at *Roots, krb*.
596. Hos. 15:19.
597. Gen. 25:22; see above, *"Peshat* and *Derash."*
598. Mal. 2:5, I Chron. 9:20; Ginzberg, VI, 316f.
599. Jud. 18:1.
600. Gen. 2:8, Jos. 13:3, Ps. 92:1.
601. Ps. 33:15; cf. Isa. 58:13.
602. Gen. 39:9.
603. Gen. 4:2.
604. I Sam. 6:4.
605. B.T. Bava Mezi'a 87a.
606. Gen. 25:19.
607. B.T. Ḥullin 91a.
608. Gen. 28:13.
609. Gen. R. 64:4.
610. Gen. 26:5; cf. *M.T.* Hil. 'Akum 1:3 and Rabad a.l.
611. *Qovez*, III, 3d.
612. See especially Gen. 5:3, I Sam. 28:24.
613. *Guide*, II:30.
614. See, e.g., *Guide*, I:7.
615. See, e.g., *Guide*, III:29.
616. See Gen. R. 1:4.
617. Isa. 22:11.
618. Gen. R. 2:2.
619. Gen. 1:2.
620. Gen. 2:9.
621. Gen. 3:1.
622. Gen. 2:9 (*Guide*, II:29).
623. Gen. 1:14 (*Guide*, II:30).
624. Gen. 18:1 (*Guide*, II:6, 24). Cf. Talmage, "Sources," p. 472.
625. See above.
626. See, e.g., Jer. 49:38.
627. See the general commentary to Ezek. 1, *passim*.
628. I Kings 22:20.

Chapter IV. "LET COME THE MORN"

1. A.l.
2. Prov. 1:26, 11:21; Ms. Vat. Ebr. 89, fols. 6v, 35r.
3. Gen. 3:14, Ps. 13:2.

4. Gen. 32:26.

5. Gen. 37:2.

6. Jud. 13:14.

7. A.l.; cf. II Sam. 13:15; Jer. 18:17; Hab. 3:6; Zech. 5:6; Mal. 2:3, 2:9.

8. *Covenant,* p. 65.

9. See below.

10. Ezek. 18:6.

11. A.l. Ms. Brit. Lib. Add. 27046, fol. 33v,; Ms. Bodl. Opp. Add. fol. 37, fols. 193r, v; Ms. Bodl. Or. 147, fols. 129r, v.

12. A.l.; Ms. Vat. Urb. Ebr. 13, fol. 254v; Ms. Vat. Urb. Ebr. 14, fol. 104r.

13. A.l., Ms. Brit. Lib. Add. 27046, fol. 160v.

14. Zech. 9:9.

15. Zech. 9:9.

16. Ps. 87, end.

17. Ps. 2, end.

18. Ps. 21, end.

19. Ps. 87, end.

20. Ezek. 16:53; Ms. Brit. Lib. Add. 27046, fol. 110v.

21. Isa. 52:12.

22. Jer. 23:3.

23. Ezek. 40:2, 44:17, 44:27, 45:13, 46:1.

24. Hos. 2:2.

25. A.l.

26. Jer. 3:8.

27. Amos 5:2.

28. A.l.

29. Ezek. 47:23.

30. Isa. 66:20f.

31. Isa. 66:20.

32. See *NEJ,* VI, 576f.

33. *Roots, shgh.*

34. Jer. 3:18.

35. Isa. 27:12, 41:25.

36. A.l.

37. Zech. 11:7; cf. Isa. 2:9, 4:1f., 24:13; Zech. 2:14; Ps. 137:7; Talmage, "Polemicist," p. 222, n. 38.

38. E.g., Zech. 10:12.

39. Zeph. 2:9, Zech. 5:2.

40. Isa. 4:1f., 43:5; Ezek. 25:4.

41. Jer. 31:3; cf. Jer. 30:2.

42. Mic. 4:11.

43. A.l.

44. Hab. 3:13.

45. Jer. 23:19; cf. Gen. 48:22, 49:26; Amos 9:7; Obad. 1; Mic. 7:8.

46. *Covenant,* p. 44.

47. I Sam. 15:29.

48. Jer. 31:30; Ms. Bodl. Or. 143, fol. 78v. Cf. Mal. 3:22; Ms. Bodl. Huntington Don. 24, fol. 177v.

49. Mal. 3:6, II Chron. 16:14.

50. Ps. 118:22; cf. Gen. 49:24, I Chron. 16:16.

51. Isa. 27:12.

52. Nah. 1:2.

53. A.l.

54. A.l.; cf. Ezek. 37:25, Amos 7:9, Isa. 63:16.

55. *Qovez*, III, 3d. Cf. the words of his father, *Covenant*, p. 24, pp. 32ff.

56. *Covenant*, p. 24.

57. Ps. 15:3.

58. See above, Chap. II.

59. Zech. 9:7.

60. II Sam. 13:2.

61. *Covenant*, pp. 24f.

62. Ps. 110, end.

63. A.l.

64. Isa. 2:19.

65. Isa. 2:21.

66. A.l.

67. Ps. 24:2.

68. Isa. 26:2, Ezek. 18:6.

69. Isa. 2:19, 21.

70. A.l.

71. Millás-Vallicrosa, p. 15.

72. Cf. Millás-Vallicrosa, pp. 15f.

73. See above, "External Form and Characteristics," in Chap. III.

74. I Sam. 21:7.

75. Jos. 5:2.

76. *Dialogus*, chap. 12; *PL*, 157:659.

77. Millás-Vallicrosa, p. 16.

78. Jos. 5:2.

79. Millás-Vallicrosa, p. 16.

80. Ezek. 16:4; cf. Gen. 34:25.

81. Millás-Vallicrosa, p. 17.

82. *PL*, 157:571f.

83. Merchavia, pp. 112f.

84. *PL*, 157:570; Merchavia, pp. 111f.

85. B.T. Sanhedrin 27b.

86. *PL*, 157:571f.

87. *PL*, 157:573.

88. A.l.

89. Isa. 65:1.

90. Prov. 11:21; Ms. Vat. Ebr. 89, fol. 35r.

91. II Kings 5:27.

92. II Sam. 12:11.

93. II Sam. 21:1.

94. I Sam. 1:11.

95. See above.

96. E.g., I Sam. 28:23, Hag. 2:15.

97. Ezek. 18:6.

98. Isa. 56:1; Ms. Bodl. Can. Or. 53, fol. 109r. Isa. 59:16, 63:11; Ps. 85:10.

99. Isa. 61:8, 63:7; Ps. 108:5. At Isa. 59:16, Radak treats at length the rabbinic passages which discuss whether redemption will come about through repentance or not. His solution is that it will come of its own accord but when it does, most people will repent. Cf. Ezek. 36:22.

100. A.l.

101. Ps. 103:8.

102. Ps. 103:10.

103. Ezek. 20:32.

104. Ezek. 18:6.

105. A.l.

106. Gen. 15:10.

107. Joel 4:19; cf. Jer. 48:47, Ps. 108:1.

108. Obad. 20; Ms. Bodl. Opp. Add. fol. 37, fol. 358v.

109. Obad. 20; Ms. Bodl. Can. Or. 58, fol. 126v.

110. Isa. 63:1, Jer. 49:7.

111. Isa. 27:1, 66:19.

112. Isa. 34:1.

113. A.l.

114. Isa. 34:1; Isa. 66:17; Ms. Brit. Lib. Add. 27046, fol. 44r; Ms. Bodl. Or. 147, fols. 172r, v; Joel 4:19.

115. Zech. 6:3; Ms. Brit. Lib. Add. 27046, fol. 170v.

116. Isa. 52:11.

117. A.l.; Ms. Bodl. Or. 147, fols. 172r, v; Ms. Brit. Lib. Add. 27046, fol. 44r.

118. Isa. 34:5.

119. Isa. 2:13, 14:1, 40:6; Amos. 9:12; Mic. 7:14; Ps. 29:1.

120. A.l.; cf. Isa. 54:17.

121. Zech. 2:1ff.

122. Ezek. 35:4.

123. Obad. 1.

124. Isa. 24:22; Jer. 48:47.

125. Amos 9:12; cf. Jer. 49:8.

126. Obad. 10; cf. Ibn Ezra, a.l.

127. Joel 4:21; cf. Ps. 22:30.

128. Isa. 44:5, Ps. 125:3.

129. Isa. 24:13.

130. Obad. 2.

131. Isa. 24:5, cf. Isa. 54:1.

132. Joel 4:19; Ms. Brit. Lib. Add. 27046, fol. 151v. Cf. Isa. 25:1, 43:1; Obad. 1, 11.

133. At Deut. 23:21.

134. See *Covenant,* p. 35, n. 19.

135. *Covenant,* pp. 33ff.

136. A.l.

137. Ps. 15:5.

138. Jer. 49:12; cf. Amos. 9:12.

139. Gen. 25:23; cf. Hos. 12:3.

140. Jer. 48:47; cf. Isa. 59:17.

141. Isa. 24:22.

142. Isa. 24:22.

143. Isa. 42:6.

144. A.l.

145. Zech. 9:1.

146. Isa. 42:6.

147. Zech. 9:1.

148. Isa. 26:2.

149. Mic. 7:20.

150. Gen. 10:19.

151. Gen. 26:23, 32:3, 35:1; cf. Gen. 48:22, Ps. 111:6.

152. Rashi at Gen. 1:1.

153. Gen. 36:20.

154. Isa. 52:1; Ms. Brit. Lib. Add. 27046, fol. 35v.

155. A.l.

156. A.l.; Ms. Brit. Lib. Add. 27046, fol. 42v.

157. Isa. 62:5.

158. A.l.

159. Ezek. 11:18; Ms. Bodl. Can. Or. 58, fol. 5r; Ms. Brit. Lib. Add. 27046, fol. 105v.

160. Ps. 125:3, Ps. 145, int.

161. Joel 4:17.

162. Ps. 145, int.

163. Ps. 108:5.

164. Ps. 126:6.

165. Isa. 54:5.

166. Mal. 3:6.

167. Isa. 60:18.

168. Isa. 59:17.

169. Jer. 30:21.

170. Isa. 54:7.

171. A.l.; cf. Ps. 72:16.

172. Ezek. 47:17.

173. Ezek. 40:2.

174. Ps. 48:14.

175. Isa. 54:12.

176. Isa. 61:9.
177. Zech. 4:6.
178. Joel 4:18.
179. Ezek. 47:12.
180. Isa. 65:17.
181. See above.
182. Isa. 65:17, 65:22.
183. Isa. 65:20; cf. Ezek. 37:14, Ps. 92:15.
184. Isa. 65:19.
185. Jer. 31:30.
186. Ezek. 43:10, Ps. 125:3.
187. Ezek. 16:60.
188. A.l.
189. Mal. 3:1.
190. Mal. 3:1.
191. Ps. 90:12.
192. Isa. 59:16.
193. Ps. 39:13; cf. Ps. 119:19.
194. A.l.
195. *Ibid.*
196. Cf. Finkelstein, p. lvii; Gen. R. 16:5.
197. Philosophical commentary on Gen. 2:15.
198. Isa. 40:21; Ms. Bodl. Can. Or. 53, fols. 73r, v.
199. Ps. 103:14.
200. Ps. 103:14; cf. Ps. 139:14, Philosophical commentary on Ezek., int.
201. Ps. 19:12.
202. Ps. 91:16; cf. Ps. 25:5.
203. *Ibid.*
204. Gen. 5:24; cf. Gen. 49:12.
205. Gen. R. 15:6.
206. Gen. 2:9. Cf. *Guide,* II:30.
207. See above.
208. Ps. 1:5.
209. Ps. 17:15; cf. Ps. 25:5, 30:10.
210. Ps. 36:9f.
211. Ps. 26:8.
212. Ps. 28:2.
213. Ps. 27:4.
214. Ps. 138:2.
215. Ps. 43:3.
216. A.l., cf. Ps. 11:4.
217. A.l.
218. Ps. 132:2.
219. A.l.
220. See above. Cf. Ps. 27:4, 27:9, 27:12, 28:1, 36:12.
221. Ps. 36:12; cf. Ps. 115:11.

222. A.l.
223. See above.
224. A.l.
225. A.l.
226. *Guide*, III:17, 18, 51.
227. A.l.
228. Gen. 6:5, 11.
229. *Guide*, II:36.
230. Ezek. 34:31; Philosophical commentary on Ezek., end.
231. Ps. 36:7.
232. Provided that they have a certain natural disposition for study; see, e.g., the introduction to the philosophical commentary on Ezekiel 1 and cf. *Guide*, I:34. At Prov. 8:36 (Ms. Vat. Ebr. 89, fol. 28v), everyone is declared capable of acquiring wisdom but here practical wisdom is meant.
233. Jon. 4:10.
234. Isa. 45:20, Ps. 115:4.
235. Cf. *Covenant*, pp. 64f.
236. Ps. 87:4.
237. Jon. 4:10.
238. Isa. 43:7.
239. Jer. 31:33.
240. A.l.
241. Jer. 9:23.

Index of Biblical Citations

Index of Persons and Topics